The Quest
Moral Foundations

The Quest for Moral Foundations

AN INTRODUCTION TO ETHICS

Montague Brown

GEORGETOWN UNIVERSITY PRESS / WASHINGTON, D.C.

Georgetown University Press, Washington, D.C.   20007
© 1996 by Georgetown University Press. All rights reserved.
Printed in the United States of America.
10 9 8 7 6 5 4 3 2 1   1996
THIS VOLUME IS PRINTED ON ACID-FREE OFFSET BOOKPAPER.

Library of Congress Cataloging-in-Publication Data

Brown, Montague,   1952
    The quest for moral foundations :   an introduction to ethics /
Montague Brown.
        p.   cm.
    1. Ethics.   I. Title.
    BJ1012.B737   1996
    170—dc20
    ISBN 0-87840-602-6 (cloth :   alk. paper)
                                                                95-42088

to my wife
first partner in the quest

Contents

Preface   xi

1

Anything Goes: Relativism   1

RELIGION AND ETHICS 2
CULTURAL RELATIVISM 4
HISTORICAL RELATIVISM 5
IMPLICATIONS OF GROUPS 7
SUBJECTIVE RELATIVISM 9
THEORETICAL VS. MORAL RELATIVISM 10
MORAL RESPONSIBILITY 21

2

Do What You Feel: Emotivism   23

EMOTIVISM ACCORDING TO HUME 24
LATER DEVELOPMENT OF EMOTIVISM 31
SUMMARY 33

3

Me First: Egoism and the Social Contract   35

SOCIAL CONTRACT THEORY 37
SOCIAL CONTRACT MORALITY SINCE HOBBES 43
CONCLUSIONS 48

4

All's Well That Ends Well: Utilitarianism   50

PLEASURE, PAIN, AND MORALITY 50
UTILITARIANISM OF J. S. MILL 56
RULE UTILITARIANISM 60

SCIENTIFIC APPROACH   62
FOUNDATION FOR MORAL JUDGMENT   64
CONCLUSIONS ABOUT PLEASURE / PAIN THEORIES   65

5

Duty Calls: Kant's Formalism   **68**

KANT'S REEVALUATION OF REASON   68
DETERMINISM OR FREEDOM   81
PRACTICAL REASON   84

6

Do Good and Avoid Evil: Natural Law   **87**

COMPARISON WITH OTHER THEORIES   89
MORAL RESPONSIBILITY   96
RELATIONSHIPS AMONG TRADITIONS   100
SYNTHESIS OF CICERO   106
FREEDOM AND NATURAL LAW   108

7

Retrospective and Reevaluation   **115**

UTILITARIAN THEORY   115
SOCIAL CONTRACT THEORY   119
EGOISM   120
EMOTIVISM   120
RELATIVISM   121
NATURAL LAW AND PLURALISM   123
HISTORICISM   127
CONCLUSIONS   133

8

Ethics and Religion Revisited   **134**

ETHICS DERIVED FROM RELIGION   134
RELIGION AS AN ETHICAL OBLIGATION   135
MORAL IMPORTANCE OF RELIGION   140

9

Epilogue: To Care or Not to Care   **142**

Notes   147

NOTES FOR CHAPTER 1   147

NOTES FOR CHAPTER 2   149

NOTES FOR CHAPTER 3   150

NOTES FOR CHAPTER 4   151

NOTES FOR CHAPTER 5   152

NOTES FOR CHAPTER 6   154

NOTES FOR CHAPTER 7   159

NOTES FOR CHAPTER 8   161

NOTES FOR CHAPTER 9   163

Index   165

Preface

It is curious how rapidly, in contemporary moral discourse, passionate certitude and radical doubt follow each other in and out of favor. At one moment people are arguing for their moral convictions with gusto, apparently free from any doubt about the moral absolutes which justify them. Next moment, in order to discount a contrary conviction, they solemnly profess a deep skepticism about the existence of any absolute moral norms at all. Having begun to doubt, they may even hedge about their own convictions: "Of course, I could be wrong; some cultures think differently; anyway, everyone has a right to his or her own opinion." How is it that outrage at some unprovoked murder, ethnic cleansing, child abuse, rape, or dishonest practice in business or government can coexist with such doubts and disclaimers? Justification for such outrage is considered so obvious as to be beyond debate. Whence, then, comes the skepticism?

That both outrage and disclaimers should be part and parcel of our everyday talk about ethical matters presents us with a problem, for it cannot be that there both are and are not adequate foundations for correct moral judgment. If there are not, then why all the dedicated debate? How could anyone be wrong? If there are, then which foundations are the true ones? Who is to say what is right and what is wrong? Where lies the proper authority (literally, source or origin) for moral condemnation or approval?

One popular candidate today is religion. Many think that moral absolutes are just a matter of religious conviction. A strong stand on the absolute value of human life or an insistence on high ideals of honor and honesty concerning sexual mores and the family are thought to be consequences of religious commitment. This dependence of moral absolutes on religion is espoused by many believers (in favor of moral absolutes) and by many unbelievers as well (against moral absolutes). It is odd how both sides adopt the same position but for opposite intents. The believers claim that the only way to be good is to accept and practice the true faith. The unbelievers glory in their own disbelief and are glad to be well-rid of traditional morality.

Since God's word is thought to be eternal and unchanging, the thesis that ethics depends on revelation might appear to support the idea of moral absolutes; however, such a thesis actually contributes to the skepticism and relativism so much in evidence today. One cannot deny the fact that we live in a pluralistic world with no consensus on religious belief. If moral norms are derived from religion but there is no universal religion, it would be the pinnacle of arrogance or the nadir of ignorance to claim that there are universal moral norms by which all human beings are bound.

Indeed, the claim that ethics depends on religion invites the twin dangers of religious fanaticism (in which the person of another faith or without faith is considered morally benighted), and relativism (in which all ethical objectivity is denied). In both cases authority is usurped by power. For the believer, the power resides in religious authority, wherever that may be found. For the unbeliever, the power resides in the individual's arbitrary will. In both cases, reason and personal responsibility are renounced. But if moral actions operate outside the constraints of reason and personal responsibility, ethical obligation is at an end.

Besides a religiously diverse world, two other general factors have contributed to the ascendancy of moral relativism in our day. As children of the modern age, most of us have been nurtured under the twin banners of science and democracy, accepting them as essential characteristics of enlightened living. And, of course, there are good reasons for our allegiance to them: each has advanced human well-being, science in the realm of knowledge of the world and our consequent ability to control our environment (often to the real betterment of the human condition) and democracy in the realm of self-government and freedom. So great is the authority of these two principles of the modern age that we are likely to take them as first principles, as indisputable axioms from which all conclusions about things human can be deduced. But if science and democracy are accepted as axioms for ethical thought, then a general skepticism about the real existence of any absolute moral norms is bound to follow. Here, then, are two well-respected authorities which seem to deny that there is any universal moral authority.

Consider first how accepting science as axiomatic leads to moral relativism. The explanations offered by science for why we act in the ways we do and why we think some acts are right and others wrong have nothing to do with rational free choice and responsibility. Science explains what used to be thought of as real moral obligations in terms of sociological, psychological, biological, chemical, or physical factors. Since these factors explain why people consider some acts right and others wrong, and since these factors differ for each individual (one's upbringing is not identical to any one else's; one's genetic make-up and the configuration of one's atoms are unique), ideas of right and wrong are naturally bound to differ.

Consider also the democratic axiom. It is a fact that people disagree about whether certain choices and actions are right or wrong. If one accepts as axiomatic the idea that everyone has an equal right to hold and express (ultimately by vote) his or her own opinion, then it is an easy transition to the idea that each opinion is just as good as any other. Political suffrage tends to lead to ethical suffrage—that is, to moral relativism.

Thus, these three things—the assumed dependence of ethics on religion, the ideal of a purely scientific explanation of the world, and the political standard of democracy—have contributed to the current drift toward relativism and away from moral absolutism (by which I mean simply that there are moral norms which do not admit of exceptions). What this book hopes to show is that relativism can make no coherent claim on our allegiance and that, of all the attempts to explain morality, only a position which holds that there are absolute moral norms can make such a claim.

The method and structure of the book are systematic; that is, the book proceeds according to the demands of logical argument, not historical sequence. Nevertheless, the positions of some individual philosophers, past and present, will be discussed in order to elucidate the various options for explaining moral obligation. The argument begins with a critique of the present malaise of moral relativism and proceeds to examine alternative accounts of morality, searching for the real foundations of moral responsibility.

Any account of moral obligation is only as good as its foundations. If the foundations are weak, the edifice crumbles. If the first principles of an ethical theory are incoherent or somehow incompatible with the freedom which makes responsibility possible, then all conclusions based on such principles are open to question. On the other hand, if there are any moral conclusions which are certain (such as, it is wrong to kill a five-year-old child for fun), there must be equally certain principles, which are coherent and do not preclude freedom, on which these conclusions are based. Uncovering these principles is the project of this book.

One might ask, at this point, why anyone should be concerned with a systematic search for rationally coherent foundations. Why bring reason into the picture? In contemporary culture, the idea that morality is based on feelings enjoys wide credence. If feelings are the source of morality, it would be a waste of time to pursue rational foundations for moral responsibility. There are really two questions here: (1) Why use reason at all? and (2) Why pursue the rather esoteric route of examining and formulating rigorous philosophical arguments?

The answer to the first question is that reason is the only tool we have for adjudicating in some public way among various ethical positions. Feelings are personal; one does not expect that everyone will feel the same way about the same things. But people do disagree, even about whether or not there are any absolute moral norms. All we have (short of mere power) to determine who is right and who is wrong is reason—the faculty for understanding what is common and universal as opposed to what is mere particularity.

As to the second question, the examination of philosophers is important for a couple of reasons. First of all, their philosophical works have deeply influenced contemporary thought, and so to understand their positions is to better understand our own. Secondly, these philosophers have made the disciplined effort to present coherent and complete explanations of morality according to the first principles they have chosen as their starting points. Hence, much of the work of understanding the implications of holding certain first principles has already been done, and done well. We need not reinvent the wheel. It only makes sense to build upon the work of others where that work is relevant to one's project.

This book does not presuppose the reader's acquaintance with the works of any of the philosophers discussed nor with the technical terminology of philosophical ethics. However, while every effort has been made to make the text accessible to the nonprofessional, the difficult problems to be faced in defining moral responsibility have not been skirted. Thus, a serious concern for the subject matter on the part of the reader is presupposed. This is a book for ethical amateurs, for those whose love for what is true and good has led them to the question (the first step in the quest) of how best to live.

I owe a debt of thanks to Johann Moser and Robert Anderson for reading an earlier draft of this work and making many valuable suggestions for improvement.

The Quest for
Moral Foundations

1

Anything Goes: Relativism

There are two good reasons for beginning a book on the foundations of responsibility with a discussion of moral relativism. In the first place and most radically, if the arguments for moral relativism are correct, then there simply are no foundations for moral responsibility, and we must give up our quest before it begins. It would be absurd to search for something that does not exist. In the second place, although I think that the arguments for relativism all fail in the end, the attempt to understand these arguments and the conditions which have prompted them is worth undertaking. For there is at least an initial, and not superficial, plausibility in some of them which has led a great many fine minds to embrace relativism. These minds have profoundly influenced and continue to influence the world in which we live. As we have grown up surrounded by these ideas, it is well to be conscious of them, both to understand their plausibility and to recognize their shortcomings.

Essential to relativism is the claim that there are no absolutes. There can, however, be different degrees of relativism. Moral values may be said to be relative to different things—to feelings, to situations, to cultures, to religions, to history, etc. Among the many possible meanings of relativism, two in particular require our attention: cultural relativism and subjective relativism. While both deny moral absolutes, morality is relative to some group in cultural relativism, while it is relative to the individual in subjective relativism. The former carries with it a degree of universality corresponding to the size of the group; the latter, which is obviously the more radical stance, carries no universality and presents the greatest challenge to real ethical responsibility. Let us consider these two positions in turn.

Cultural relativism claims that morality is based on values shared within a particular group. This group may be defined in terms of religion, custom, or mutual agreement. What is permissible and what is impermissible are determined by the members of the group. Since there are different religions, different customs, and different political units, there may very well be different moralities. If there are, who is to judge between them? If it is true that cultures disagree about morality and that human beings are bound by their cultures, then moral relativism is not only plausible but necessarily true.

1

RELIGION AND ETHICS

Before getting into specific arguments for cultural relativism, let us consider the relation between religion, which has traditionally been the defining mark of a culture, and ethics. The idea that moral responsibility depends on religion is very popular at the moment. When moral issues come up in public discourse, one constantly hears it said that religion must be kept out of politics. The obvious implication is that morality is a religious matter and therefore not to be legislated.

This connection between religion and morality is a natural enough one to make. For one thing, most religions have an ethical component. For another, if one believes in a religion of creation, it makes perfect sense to say that God, who made everything, also made moral obligation.

Religion as Basis for Ethics

However, while the connection between religion and morality may be a natural one to make, the claim that morality is *merely* a matter of religious conviction seems to make no sense at all. It seems perfectly absurd to say that the willful killing of an innocent five-year-old child is not wrong for an atheist, who does not believe in the Old Testament with its ten commandments.

Not only is the claim that ethics is merely a matter of religion absurd in itself, but even the Scriptures themselves deny such a claim. For example, in the Old Testament book of Amos, God punishes the pagans because they do inhumane actions such as betraying their allies, attacking their neighbors without a just cause, and killing women and children in war. They are accounted as without excuse, even though they do not have revelation.[1] St. Paul, in his letter to the Romans, insists that the pagans have access to moral norms even though they are without the law. "When Gentiles who have not the law do by nature what the law requires, they are a law unto themselves, even though they do not have the law. They show that what the law requires is written on their hearts, while their conscience also bears witness and their conflicting thoughts accuse or perhaps excuse them. . . ."[2] And it has been the constant teaching of the Roman Catholic Church that moral obligation is based on the natural law immediately available to every human being through reason and conscience.[3]

How, then, did we arrive at the point where so many people, religious and nonreligious, think that morality is a matter of faith? Part of it has to do with secular trends accompanying the rise of the scientific method, which I shall discuss later, but part of it also has to do with trends which developed within religion itself. Radical fundamentalism has always been an option in the revealed religions. If God is creator, then everything depends on God. Some have interpreted this as meaning that there is really nothing in the created world which has any order and integrity of its own, and that natural reason is hopelessly inadequate to know what is true and good. Thus Tertullian, an early Christian apologetic, asked what Athens (philosophy) has to do with Jerusalem (revelation).[4] So also, there was a movement in tenth-century Muslim thought which claimed that God is the sole cause at work in the universe.[5] In the late Middle Ages and Renaissance, this attitude grew particularly strong and was applied to moral as well as speculative topics. William of Ockham, a fourteenth-century theologian, held that all morality is based on the arbitrary will of the creator. He went so far as to say that God could make it good for us to hate God.[6] The reformers followed this line of thinking, stressing the depravity of the human being and the transcendent power of God. In this way, what has come to be known as "the divine command theory" was in place at the birth of the modern era.

Divine Command Theory

Held by most Protestant thinkers and some Catholics as well, this theory of the foundations of responsibility was also adopted by the growing secular community of scientists and philosophers of the Renaissance and Enlightenment. After all, if the Christians themselves (who are the ones declaring that there are absolute moral norms) say that morality is what God declares it to be, why should the scientists and philosophers disagree? Since morality is simply what God arbitrarily wills it to be, and since (according to these thinkers) we can know nothing about God through natural reason, it is a logical step to the conclusion that we can know nothing about morality by natural reason. On this line of thinking, moral judgments are scientifically and philosophically meaningless.

Now the logical consequence of such a line of reasoning would clearly have been for such thinkers to cease making judgments about good and evil. But that such a consequence did not follow is equally clear. In fact, one of the arguments against religion which the secular community adopted for their purposes was the argument from evil in the world.[7] Any God who would create a world with so much evil in it is himself evil and therefore should not be worshipped but rejected in scorn. Now the so-called "problem of evil" is a difficult one and more appropriate for a book on natural theology than one on ethics. What is appropriate here is to make clear what such criticism of God implies: to reject God and religion on moral grounds is obviously incompatible with the idea that morality derives merely from religion.

CULTURAL RELATIVISM

Turning now to the arguments for cultural relativism, it is no good denying the fact that there are different cultures and that sometimes these cultures disagree about what is morally permissible. If these disagreements are superficial, then they need not be taken very seriously. For example, the fact that different cultures have different ways of showing honor to parents or of punishing theft does not prove that they disagree about the importance of honoring parents and not stealing. Whether there are disagreements about the deeper moral principles is a subject of some debate. There are certainly those who argue that cultures do disagree in fundamental ways, and that ethical norms are culturally determined. Ruth Benedict presents a classical formulation of such a position.

> Normality, in short, within a very wide range, is culturally defined. . . . It is a point that has been made more often in relation to ethics than in relation to psychiatry. We do not any longer make the mistake of deriving the morality of our locality and decade directly from the inevitable constitution of human nature. We do not elevate it to the dignity of a first principle. We recognize that morality differs in every society, and is a convenient term for socially approved habits.[8]

On the other hand, there are also those who argue that cultures actually agree about the basics of morality. For example, Edward Westermarck, himself a relativist (but for different reasons), argues that relativism cannot be based on cultural differences since it turns out that cultures ultimately agree.[9] In his anthropological work, he found that no culture permitted murder or rape among its members, and that all recommended charity and concern for the common good.

The strongest counterexample to Westermarck's thesis might be taken from differences in religious practices. We know that some religious practices (those of the Aztecs, many of the tribes around ancient Israel, and the Carthaginians of Roman times, for example) included sacrificing human beings, in some cases the children of the faithful themselves, while other religions (Judaism and Christianity, for example) have always abhorred such activities. To this, Westermarck would respond that both kinds of religious practice are ultimately used for the same good purposes—to honor the deity and to foster the well-being of the community—and so the cultures really agree about the most important things. While this may be true, it is clear that there is a fundamental disagreement about the means which may be taken to achieve true worship and the common good. As killing (especially one's own children) is not a superficial issue, it seems we are faced with a fundamental moral difference.

The question is: Does such a fundamental moral disagreement support the claim of cultural relativism that there are no moral absolutes? Westermarck denies (and I think rightly) that this is so. Why should we assume that all moral teachings and practices are equally correct? Just as 7 is an incorrect answer to the question of what is the sum of 4 + 4, so it is perfectly possible that sacrificing human life is an incorrect answer to the religious question of what is owed to God and the social question of how to preserve and foster the community. The simple fact that different answers are given to a particular question does not imply that no answer is better than another.

HISTORICAL RELATIVISM

Besides cultural and religious differences, there are numerous other ways in which people can be grouped and hence morality relativized, some of which bear mentioning. Chief among these ways is historicism, or grouping by time. On this view, human beings are subject not just to cultural conditions, but to the historical period in which they live. While this may look a lot like cultural relativism, it differs in that the primary feature is time, not environment. Although the two overlap, they are not identical; one could belong to western culture, but differ from others in that culture because one lived at a different time. Conversely, there can be many cultures at one time.

The idea that relativism could be a function of time goes back to the German philosopher Hegel. In his theory of absolute idealism, Hegel explained all reality as moments in the unfolding of Absolute Spirit. This unfolding occurs in time, and its progress is inevitable. Thus, all times leading up to the present had to come to be and pass away in order that this moment could come. Those who live in different epochs are bound by their moment in this grand unfolding. They are no more able to know what is absolutely true and good than they are able to exist at all times.

> To comprehend what is, this is the task of philosophy, because what is, is reason. Whatever happens, every individual is a child of his time; so philosophy too is its own time apprehended in thoughts. It is just as absurd to fancy that a philosophy can transcend its contemporary world as it is to fancy that an individual can overleap his own age, jump over Rhodes. If his theory really goes beyond the world as it is and builds an ideal one as it ought to be, that world exists indeed, but only in his opinions, an unsubstantial element where anything you please may, in fancy, be built.[10]

According to Hegel, all historical ideas of how the world ought to be (i.e., all theories of moral obligation) are only opinions; there is no absolute standard of morality applicable to people over time.

Since Hegel, this idea that all truth is historically conditioned has become something of a canon. Darwin's theory of evolution plays out this theme in biology. Nietzsche, following Hegel and Darwin, declares that there are no moral absolutes, that human nature is growing inevitably into a new phase, transcending good and evil.[11] Contemporary thinkers such as Alasdair MacIntyre and Richard Rorty show the influence of Hegel in their thinking. MacIntyre claims that one is bound by one's tradition and that ultimately there is no standard by which one tradition could be judged to be more rational or better than another.[12] Richard Rorty is even more radical in his account of the inevitable limitations of human insight into absolute norms. Historicism (the claim that all philosophical or moral statements are conditioned by the historical context in which they are made) is a constant theme in his book *Philosophy and the Mirror of Nature*. In the Introduction he writes: "The moral of this book is also historicist, and the three parts into which it is divided are intended to put the notions of 'mind,' of 'knowledge,' and of 'philosophy,' respectively, into historical perspective."[13] And in the last chapter he commends those philosophers who honor Hegel's claim that everything is historically conditioned.

> These writers have kept alive the suggestion that, even when we have justified true belief about everything we want to know, we may have no more than conformity to the norms of the day. They have kept alive the historicist sense that this century's "superstition" was the last century's triumph of reason, as well as the relativistic sense that the latest vocabulary, borrowed from the latest scientific achievement, may not express privileged representations of essences, but be just another of the potential infinity of vocabularies in which the world can be described.[14]

In short, no claim of reason is absolute; all are conditioned by time.

Besides culture and time, there are many other criteria which can be invoked to show that ideas or moral norms are merely relative to some group. One could apply economic status, as did Marx, claiming that morality is a function of the means of production: economic power dictates morality. On bourgeois morality, Marx and Engels write: "The selfish misconception that induces you to transform into eternal laws of nature and of reason, the social forms springing from your present mode of production and form of property—historical relations that rise and disappear in the progress of production—this misconception you share with every ruling class that has preceded you."[15] Or one could apply the conditions of gender: the kind of morality one holds is a function of whether one is male or female. Thus Carol Gilligan argues that as the psychology of women differs from that of men, so does their conception of morality. "The psychology of women that has consistently been described as distinctive in its greater orientation toward relationships and interdependence implies a more contextual mode of judgment and a different moral understanding."[16] The arguments for relativism are as many as the ways human beings can be distinguished into groups.

IMPLICATIONS OF GROUPS

Now there is no doubt that culture and religion influence us, or that we are affected by our historical context, or even that our economic status and gender are factors in how we judge what is good or bad. In general, environment and upbringing are certainly important in one's moral formation. How one is raised in the family, the religious and secular education one receives, the kind of social and political structures of one's culture—all of these factors clearly influence one's idea of right and wrong. As children grow to maturity, they learn by imitating the authorities which surround them; unconsciously, they absorb the customs and assumptions of their culture. This point is indisputable. Traditional moral teachers such as Plato and Aristotle would hardly disagree. In fact, Aristotle goes so far as to say that one's upbringing is the single most important element of one's moral formation.[17]

Whatever the plausibility of distinguishing people into groups according to various environmental factors, there is no logical implication from the fact that groups disagree to the judgment that no position is more right or wrong than any other. But not only is there no logical implication from disagreement to relativism; any claim of relativism carries with it its own refutation. The obvious response to any claim that morality is merely a function of some time or group is to say that the claim itself is just a product of a particular time or group and that anyone not of that time or group need not (indeed cannot) accept the claim.

But there are two more serious problems with the claim that morality is merely a function of one's position within a group or historical context: (1) How is one to adjudicate between groups? (the question of standards for judgment) and more radically (2) How is one to judge at all? (the question of freedom to judge).

Standards for Judgment

Consider, as to the first question, the claim that gender determines morality. While it may be admitted that there are psychological differences between men and women, to make these decisive in moral matters would obviously destroy the possibility of a justifiable settlement of disagreements between male and female. If men and women think differently in any kind of essential way, then reason cannot help in settling disputes. One of the plausible supports of feminism is that women have sometimes been unjustly treated by men. But if there is no standard of justice which transcends male and female and to which each has access, why should men rectify the so-called "injustice"? In short, if there is no common reason but only male reason and female reason, then there is no reason for men to be fair to women or vice versa. And if reason fails as an arbitrator, then we are back to power—might makes right. To make power the only standard is certainly amoral (by definition) and immoral by even the feminist's own claim to have been oppressed by the power of patriarchy. In general, to claim that morality is determined by membership within a group is to cut off access of that group to either an understanding of justice itself or any legitimate expectation that another group should accord it justice.[18]

Freedom to Judge

Consider the second problem, the problem of freedom. Even if it could be proven that cultures or groups disagree about fundamental moral obligations (perhaps true in a few cases), and even if this implied (which it does not) that there are no ultimate standards by which one could judge between groups, moral relativism would follow from cultural or group differences only if human beings were completely determined by their culture or group—in other words, only if they were not free.

However, while there is no doubt that all human beings are influenced by the various groups to which they belong, there is also no reason to believe that they are completely determined by family background, culture, religion, historical epoch, etc. In the first place, as we already mentioned, there is no reason to accept the claim that we are so determined, for (according to the relativist's own line of reasoning) such a claim itself must be relative to cultural, religious, historical, economical, or sexual conditions. To the person claiming that all is relative to some condition (any of the ones we have discussed), the obvious response is that the person making the claim only makes it because of the same conditioning power and that, therefore, the claim carries no absolute status and so can be legitimately ignored.

In addition to the self-refuting character of any claim that ethics is only a function of some kind of relativizing influence, there are experiential reasons to believe that we are not so determined. As children grow to maturity their reasoning abilities develop, and with this development comes the ability to make independent judgments. No child is a clone of his or her parents, nor a mere mirror of environmental factors. Doing what Mummy and Daddy think is right is not always the pattern of behavior (mild understatement). Children show some independence of thought and judgment at a remarkably early age. Not to deny environmental factors, there is an element in each human being which is unique and irreducible to the sum of environmental influences. Some measure of freedom (increasingly evident as reason develops) is as certain as the influences of upbringing.

More to the point than the observation of growing freedom in a child's development are the logical implications of any choice. The very possibility of criticizing one's own culture or adopting aspects of other cultures would be ruled out if we were culturally determined. Most radically, if human beings are not free to choose, any moral judgment at all becomes absurd—even that torturing and killing innocent people for fun is bad or that protecting the innocent is good. If the murderer, the rapist, and the defender of the innocent act merely as products of their culture, then no blame or praise can reasonably be attached to their actions.

SUBJECTIVE RELATIVISM

Given that there is some measure of individual freedom (a prerequisite for any possible responsibility), the cultural relativist is left with a crucial question: Why should the individual within the culture adhere to the morality of that culture's religion or custom? If ethics is merely a matter of religious faith or custom or some other particular context, and an individual has somehow not received faith or adopted the custom, what reason would he or she have to conform? There are many possible answers to this question—feelings, self-interest, consequences, duty, and knowledge of basic human goods. These answers form the subject matter for the following chapters. But one possible response is that there simply is no reason.

This view is subjective relativism and it is the rejection, not only of absolute moral norms, but of any degree of universal obligation at all. To any criticism of wrongdoing, the subjective relativist replies: "I and my situation are different from all other persons and situations, and therefore what obligation might attach to another in another situation is irrelevant." It would not matter whether the obligation came from moral absolutes, from religion, or from cultural custom. The subjectivist would reject any moral obligation, which position is either moral nihilism (the denial of any moral standards) or—ultimately the same thing—an acceptance of determinism (the denial of free choice).

THEORETICAL VS. MORAL RELATIVISM

Before looking into arguments which seem to support subjective relativism, let us discuss the meaningfulness of the very idea of such a radical relativism. To avoid confusion, it is necessary to distinguish theoretical relativism from moral relativism. Theoretical relativism holds that no statement about reality is really true or false. Moral relativism holds that no choice about what is to be done is really good or evil. Although it is moral relativism with which we are directly concerned here, it is important to discuss theoretical relativism and its roots first, for if no statement can be said to be true or false, then statements about what ought or ought not to be done are, like all other statements, neither true nor false, but simply meaningless.

One can begin with the simple observation that there can be no justification for theoretical relativism (understood as the denial of the meaningfulness of any distinction between truth and falsity). For justification is only possible if a conclusion can be deduced from something known with certainty; but that anything can be known with certainty is precisely what theoretical relativism denies. But more than unjustifiable, theoretical relativism is self-refuting: if it is true that there is no such thing as truth, then (since a purportedly true statement has been made) it is false that there is no such thing as truth. The one thing that the claim "there is no such thing as truth" cannot be is true. Like all contradictions, theoretical relativism leads to absurdity, the destruction of all meaning. Thus, one need not be overthrown at the very outset of the pursuit of speculative truth or moral wisdom by any claims of the theoretical relativist. This is not, of course, to have proven what the truth is or just how much can be known with certainty, but it does show that the claim that there is no such thing as truth is nonsense.

There is a similar foundational problem with radical moral relativism; it, too, is unjustifiable and finally self-refuting. As theoretical reason judges what is true and false, practical reason (thinking about choices and actions) judges what is good and bad. For example, it is good to protect innocent human life and bad to destroy it; it is bad to betray a friend; it is good to respect and tolerate others. To ask, as we are doing, whether or not there are moral absolutes (that is, to ask whether or not moral relativism is acceptable) is not absurd. What would be absurd, however, would be to judge that ethical relativism is better than some other ethical theory. Relativism expressed as a moral judgment would look something like this: "It is better to be a relativist than an absolutist," or "It is good that there are no moral absolutes." While such judgments might arise out of a fear of oppression by absolutists or in the spirit of tolerance and respect for others, they are internally incoherent. The one thing that simply cannot be meaningfully said about moral relativism is that it is good and should be embraced. It is impossible that the conviction "there is no such thing as good or evil" could itself be good. In short, moral relativism cannot be considered better than any other position since it denies that the word "better" has any definitive meaning. Thus, if one holds that oppression is bad and that tolerance is better than intolerance and favoritism, then one has, in fact, rejected moral relativism.

Barriers to Absolute Norms

However, while one might be forced to agree that moral relativism cannot be coherently recommended as good or better than some other theory of ethics, one might still think that there are features of the world and our experience which rule out the possibility of knowing what is good and evil. If there are, in fact, such insurmountable barriers, then whether or not we wish moral relativism to be true, we are stuck with it.

Let us turn now to an examination of a couple of these barriers which appear to rule out absolute moral norms—science and freedom. The modern world is characterized by the rise of the empirical sciences with their demand for strict adherence to the method of hypothesis and verification through sense experience (experiment). Since good and evil, right and wrong, justice and injustice do not appear to be empirically verifiable, science declares them unreal. To the extent that we think of ourselves as children of the enlightened ages, we shall follow science's lead here and deny that there are any absolute moral norms. In addition to failing the test of scientific verification, moral absolutism appears to threaten our freedom. There is the fear that the existence of absolute moral norms, obligatory for all, would diminish or destroy the individual's freedom of choice. Since freedom is a central tenet of democracy, this desire to protect freedom lies deep within our political ideals as well our individual desires. Let us consider, in turn, these two apparent barriers to affirming absolute moral standards.

Consider, first, the authority of science and its rejection of moral absolutes. If scientific method is accepted as paradigmatic for human thinking and knowing, then certain conclusions about morality are inevitable. Scientific method is that procedure whereby hypotheses are made and verifications for these hypotheses are sought in sense experience. In the modern age, Francis Bacon introduced this method as the sole method suited to the human mind.[19] The method was further systematized in the Enlightenment and can be found presented with its implications for religion and ethics in the thought of David Hume. While we shall wait until the next chapter to develop Hume's position, one implication of such a theory is already obvious: to insist on scientific method as the sole method by which knowledge can be justified is to assume that all that is real is material.[20] For if every legitimate hypothesis must be verifiable by some possible sense experience, then only hypotheses concerned with the objects of sense experience—that is, material things—are legitimate. In short, adherence to scientific method is adherence to materialism.

Materialism of Science

If all that can be known to be real is material, then such traditional moral norms as justice and kindness cannot be known to be real. For no one who holds that there are absolute moral norms thinks that a moral norm is a material thing. Justice is not subject to quantitative analysis. It makes no sense to ask how big justice is, or what color it is, or where it is, or how fast it is moving. These are scientific questions applicable to material things but not to immaterial things (if there are any). If the scientist believes that only scientific method puts one in touch with reality, then he or she will conclude that questions about moral absolutes are meaningless.

The question is: Is the assumption of materialism justifiable? First of all, it is clear that materialism cannot be justified according to the strictures of scientific method itself, for it is not a fact verified by experience. If one's hypothesis is that a cubic centimeter of lead weighs more than the same volume of cheese, one can verify this hypothesis by weighing each. If one's hypothesis is that black paint absorbs more light than white paint, one can verify this by setting up the appropriate experiment. But what experiment could test the hypothesis that everything that is real is material? Lead and cheese can be measured out and weighed; two like surfaces can be painted, one black and the other white, and the temperature of each can be measured after equal exposure to the sun. However, there are no particular things which can stand for "all" in an experiment designed to verify the hypothesis "all that is real is material." Nor is this hypothesis a general claim about a certain kind of thing, as is the claim that the law of gravity applies to all matter; rather, it is an absolute claim which transcends all possible experience. As such, it is not verifiable according to any particular method, even the scientific method.

Perhaps the only reason why the proposition "all that is real is material" cannot be proven is because, like other first principles such as the law of noncontradiction (something cannot be and not be at the same time and in the same respect), it is self-evident. If this is so, there is no need to justify it. However, far from this being the case, the proposition is self-refuting: If materialism is true, then it is false. If all that is real is material (the basis for materialism), then the idea "all that is real is material" is not real, and the basis for materialism vanishes. The scientific method lays down, as its cardinal rule for confirming that something is real, the requirement that it be subject, at least in principle, to sense experience. Granted that the proposition "all that is real is material" can be verified as black ink patterns on this page, or, when read aloud, as vibrations in the air and one's eardrums; neither verification touches what is essential to the proposition. The proposition is an idea; its essence is meaning, not matter. Thus, if it is assumed that all that is real is material, then the statement "all that is real is material" is by assumption not real.

The fundamental problem with materialism is that it cannot account for meaningful thought. Considering thought as mere "agitation of the brain,"[21] science can, and does, make progress in discovering and understanding neurological and chemical functions; but in terms of the meaning or truth of thought, science has nothing to say. If one insists upon materialism, then thought as truth-bearing is impossible, including the assumed true proposition that "all that is real is material." If, on the other hand, meaning is real (and it is assumed to be real by one who insists that materialism is the case), then materialism is false. This, of course, is not to say that matter is unreal, only to point out that it is incoherent to hold that *only* matter is real.

On pain of contradiction, the scientist must allow that there is at least one thing that is not merely material—the scientist's own thought. If immaterial things are not to be ruled out simply because they are not material, then the argument against absolute moral norms such as justice and kindness based on their nonverifiability by scientific method (their not being material) fails.

Historical Materialism

This presupposition of materialism is not an invention of the scientific mentality of the modern world. It has a long heritage going back to the beginnings of western philosophy. And the curious thing about the origin of materialism is its relationship to religion and ethics: not, as one might think, that materialism led to a certain ethical and religious position but, on the contrary, that a certain ethical and religious position led to materialism.

A characteristic common to most of the pre-Socratic philosophers was an interest in explaining what was fundamental in the makeup of things.[22] Thus, for example, Thales said it was water; Anaximenes thought it was air; Heraclitus held that it was fire; and Empedocles said it was earth, air, fire, and water. Democritus, sounding very modern in his analysis, said that what is really real is the atom. The theory of atomism was later taken up and expanded by Epicurus in the third century B.C. and presented in systematic form by Lucretius in the Roman era (first century B.C.).

Atomist Tradition   The atomist tradition differs from the other pre-Socratic philosophical theories about reality in its insistence that *all* that is real is matter in the form of atoms. The others recognized the existence of other kinds of causes, irreducible to matter. Thales, for example, besides saying that all things are made of water, also said that all things are full of gods.[23] Heraclitus talked of the *logos* (roughly definable as reason or order) as a principle in addition to his material principle. In addition to earth, air, fire, and water, Empedocles recognized love and strife as ultimate causes. And Anaxagoras, who had said that what is really real is the mixture of tiny seeds in everything, also said that the first principle in reality is intelligence. In short, each of these thinkers, while attempting to give a scientific account of things in terms of their material makeup, also recognized the need for some other kind of explanation to fully explain reality. What was unique about the atomists was their lack of any explanation other than the material one. Addressing the question of how the atoms get in motion and produce the various things which we immediately recognize around us, such as trees, dogs, rocks, and people, the answer they gave was chance—which is the same as to say that there is no explanation.

Why would they profess such a system which rules out any ultimate explanation of order? This is a very good question, for the human mind— even (and perhaps most especially) the scientific human mind—when presented with the world of experience, tries to explain it, and every explanation is a formulation of order. The answer to this question brings us back to religion by a different route, and eventually to the very foundations of ethics.

By their own admission, the overall purpose of the philosophy of Epicurus and Lucretius is therapeutic.[24] People are afraid and need to be consoled. The greatest fear we have, according to Epicurus and Lucretius, is the fear of death, and the reason we fear death is because we fear the punishment that we are told we must face for the wrongs we have committed in this life. Religion, then, with its doctrine of divine rewards and punishments, is the cause of our worst fear.

This is where materialism comes in. If we are nothing more than atoms, then at death we shall be annihilated. If we are to be annihilated, then we need not fear ultimate judgment and the punishment it would bring. The gods, if they exist (a materialist has no reason to believe immaterial things exist), cannot punish what does not exist. Materialism in the form of atomism frees us from the superstition which people call religion and from that worst of all enemies—the fear of death. Thus, behind this supposedly disinterested scientific theory of atomism lies an antireligious crusade.

Antireligious Attitude Part of the motivation behind this antireligious attitude is understandable and even morally commendable. In the first place, to offer consolation and comfort is a very noble purpose in itself; it is good to help one's fellow human beings. To this extent the philosophy of Epicurus and Lucretius is grounded in traditional, normative ethics; we ought always to relieve the fears of our fellows if possible. In the second place, the gods of Greek religion were often portrayed as being highly arbitrary in their commands and actions. Lucretius mentions the command of Artemis that Iphegenia must be sacrificed before the goddess will allow the Greek fleet to sail for Troy.[25] Any divinity who would issue such a command and see it carried out should be rejected. To worship immoral deities is certainly immoral.

However, while the refusal to praise and serve immoral deities is certainly legitimate and even commendable, the desire to comfort human beings by denying any kind of judgment after death (thereby removing from them the ultimate responsibility for their evil deeds) is another matter altogether and far from being ethically justifiable. To remove such ultimate responsibility is to make human choices trivial. What is more, to deny the existence of ultimate rewards and punishments is to turn a blind eye to truth and justice. If such blindness is involuntary, then, of course, it is not blameworthy; but since what atomism denies in terms of truth and goodness is so basic and obvious, it seems that the blindness is chosen; if so, it is immoral.

Immortality The position of atomism clearly violates the truth, for to be a thinker and a knower is to be in some way immaterial and hence immortal. To know is to grasp what is universal, that is, what transcends time and space. Even the scientific atomist, when declaring that only atoms are real, is making a statement which claims universality through space and time—that is, a statement which goes beyond the mere materiality of atoms in motion. Thus, the very truth claim of the atomist is something that cannot be explained by his system. Since there is an aspect of being human which is immaterial (we know but do not sense ideas), it is untrue to say that the material dispersal of the atoms of our bodies must be the end of us. Immortality is not just a doctrine of religion; it is also a philosophical doctrine which can be known from the evidence of what it is to be a thinking and knowing being. To knowingly reject what is obvious in order to do away with anxiety is to treat truth as if it is merely of incidental interest to the human being, to be accepted or rejected depending on some prior and more important aim. But truth is fundamental to human well-being—indeed, the quest for truth is the driving force behind science.

Reward and Punishment   Besides disregarding the truth of immortality, the claim that there should not be ultimate rewards for good actions or punishments for bad actions indicates a disregard for justice. To recognize the real difference between good and evil actions in the world (which even Epicurus and Lucretius do in their contention that it would be better to relieve anxiety than to promote it) seems to call more for the affirmation of ultimate rewards and punishments rather than for their denial. Consider a person who has led an upright life, always telling the truth and sacrificing for the well-being of others, yet who has been deceived and cheated by others. What is more, this person has lost his family at an early age and dies a painful death, having long suffered physical anguish. Does it not seem unjust that no reward be granted such a person for a life of goodness? Or consider, on the other hand, someone who has spent a life of lying and cheating, raping at will, and even murdering, and yet lives a full life in good health, with great material success, and even enjoys a good reputation. Is it fair that such a person should escape punishment? Given what we know about the inequitable happenings of this world, it would seem unjust if there were no life after death in which such inequities could be corrected. Whether or not the argument proves that there is life after death, the judgment that there *should not* be life after death with rewards and punishments because it causes us to be afraid is a judgment that justice ultimately does not matter. Such a judgment is obviously immoral.

If we have done wrong, we ought to be afraid. We ought to change our ways, not comfort ourselves with the idea that we need not worry since, as merely a chance configuration of atoms, we shall completely cease to be when this configuration of atoms breaks up. In addition, it would seem to be highly immoral to give people false comfort. If there are good reasons, metaphysical as well as moral, for believing that there is life after death, to tell people that they need not worry nor prepare themselves for death by leading the best possible lives is false comfort. It is, in fact, an act of inhumanity in the greatest degree.

Were materialism a self-evident and sufficient explanation of all reality, then, indeed, one would be forced (on pain of contradiction) to embrace it. But materialism, which rules out ethical obligation, is not a matter of scientific fact but is presupposed without proof. And this presupposition is based on the desire that there *should not* be any ultimate rewards and punishments for good or evil actions: this desire is profoundly immoral.

Lack of Moral Responsibility   Such misguided antireligious (and ultimately antiethical) purposes are the foundations of the philosophy of Epicurus and Lucretius. One finds similar foundations implied in the thinking of the other materialists we mentioned. Francis Bacon, self-proclaimed "trumpeter of a new age," constantly insists that his new method is the only way to rid the world of superstition. For him, all metaphysics and absolutist ethics are to be buried along with the religious tradition (Roman Catholicism) by which they were adopted and nurtured.[26] The position of David Hume seems to be much the same. In his *Dialogues Concerning Natural Religion*, Hume says that the worst of all the miseries of humanity is subjection to superstition—that is, to religion.[27] And in his *Enquiry Concerning the Human Understanding* Hume devotes a whole chapter to the philosophy of Epicurus, quite clearly commending this philosophy with its presuppositions based on the intention of ridding the world of superstition.[28] As for the pre-Socratic Democritus, very little of his work has come down to us, and most of what has is concerned with his physical principles as recounted by Aristotle. However, Montaigne, the renowned skeptic of the early Renaissance, does commend Democritus, saying that he prefers Democritus to Heraclitus because, while the latter is doubtful about the human ability to be good, Democritus just laughs at humanity.[29]

This attitude of disdain for human capacities, which is typical of the skeptic, is itself a sign of an absolute renunciation of moral responsibility. It is not as if these thinkers, upon recognizing the great moral failures of humankind (which are all too obvious), go on to suggest a plan for rectifying the human condition. Instead, they proclaim the absolute corruption and hopeless condition of humanity. And, according to Montaigne's report, Democritus goes so far as to laugh at this, not even grieving for this sorry state of affairs. Surely, such an attitude is rather odd. If one can recognize that humankind is in a sorry state, morally speaking, then surely one knows what a better state would be. Only by knowing a standard of goodness could one conceivably judge that anyone has fallen below that standard. This judgment made, the project should become one of rectifying the failures, not of despairing of all hope—or worse, making fun of the human attempt to know the truth and do what is good.

Desire for Freedom

Having seen that science cannot justify moral relativism, let us turn to the other plausible reason for espousing moral relativism—the desire for freedom. When faced with the proposition that there are absolute moral norms which one is required to follow, one's initial reaction might very well be rebellion. How can such absolutes be compatible with the freedom of the individual? Since freedom is something that we treasure, it is plausible and perhaps even morally commendable to reject moral absolutes in the name of freedom. For if freedom is a prerequisite for responsible action and moral absolutes mean that we do not have freedom, then moral absolutes would appear to rule out responsible action (that is, morality itself). Some such argument lies behind the thought of Nietzsche and Sartre.[30] They both choose to protect freedom, rejecting what they think are its enemies—a provident God and absolute standards of morality. As others before them, they hold that God and morality are a package deal, that normative ethics has its seat in the myths of religion. Therefore, it is not surprising to find them rejecting both in the name of freedom. If human freedom is incompatible with divine providence and hence also with morality (on this view, God's arbitrary imposition of moral laws), then it is plausible to choose freedom, for without freedom all choices and actions would be meaningless; one would cease to be human.

But freedom is *not* incompatible with either providence or normative ethics. Since this is not a book on metaphysics or the philosophy of God, a detailed treatment of the problem of freedom and providence would be out of place.[31] However, the relationship between freedom and morality is very much to the point.

To show that freedom and normative ethics based on moral absolutes are not incompatible, one must begin by distinguishing two different meanings of freedom, each of which has direct bearing on our ability to act.[32] First of all, there is the freedom to do as one pleases. This is a freedom from outside interference or coercion. Let us call this kind of freedom social/political freedom. Such freedom is one of the great standards of our democracy, which is founded on the sanctity of life, liberty, and the pursuit of happiness. Of course, there are some restrictions on behavior, for one is not free to steal or murder; but these restrictions could be reconciled with social/political freedom by appeal to one's having freely entered into a mutual agreement with others to restrict one's freedom if they will restrict theirs. So long as one's neighbor is not harmed, one should be free to pursue any course of action.[33] This freedom is, indeed, at odds with the existence of absolute moral norms. If one has responsibilities, then there are restrictions on the freedom to do as one pleases.

However, there is another and more fundamental meaning of freedom—the freedom to choose. This is not freedom from external constraint but an internal principle of the rational will. Unlike the other animals—who seem to be guided (one might even say determined) by instinct, environment, and immediate pleasure and pain—human beings also have the ability to act by reasoned choice, which is the heart of ethical responsibility. What is meant by this kind of freedom can be grasped quite easily by considering that one does not hold animals ultimately responsible for their behavior the way one does adult human beings. Since animals do not have the capacity to deliberate according to principles of reason and thus have no real choice in how they act, we do not apply the categories of good or bad, right or wrong, just or unjust, to their behavior. One might, sometimes, wish it were true that human beings were like the animals just so that one might share their lack of responsibility and freedom from judgment. But this is the road to the intellectual despair of skepticism and determinism, and I do not think that anyone truthfully wishes to follow it.[34]

Let us call this second kind of freedom moral freedom. It is the freedom to make oneself into the kind of person one recognizes as good (or bad). It is the freedom to choose whom one will love, the freedom to bind oneself to particular purposes and actions. In contrast to social/political freedom, which is a freedom *from* responsibility, moral freedom is the freedom *for* responsibility. While it is clear that both kinds of freedom are attractive, without the second kind of freedom—freedom of choice—there can be no meaningful choices at all. Even social/political freedom is just a charade if there is no freedom of choice, for it would not be "I" who chooses to do whatever I please, but the determinations of environmental conditions ultimately reducible to the matter/energy matrix of the physical world. Freedom of choice is real only if it is not reducible to matter; thus, just like our thinking and knowing (to which it is essentially related), our freedom to choose indicates that there is something real that is not material.

So far from freedom of choice being an argument for relativism, if relativism is the case, there is no real freedom of choice. Freedom of choice depends upon knowledge, and if moral relativism is the case, then there is no knowledge of good and bad, of right and wrong. To be unable to deliberate and choose according to knowledge of the comparative goodness of each option (which action requires knowledge of some absolute standard) is to be determined; one's "choices" then are ultimately dictated by instinct, environmental conditioning, or immediate reaction to pleasure and pain—the motivations of animals. Since relativism denies the possibility of choosing according to knowledge of right and wrong, it implies that one's choices are determined. While it is true that moral relativism frees one from the responsibility for one's actions, it only does so by denying that any actions are really one's own—that is, by denying that one has freedom of choice.

So it is that, although relativism seems to hold out the promise of freedom and normative ethics to deny such freedom, the opposite turns out to be the case. For the deepest meaning of freedom is moral freedom, the freedom of choice. Without freedom of choice, which depends on the ability to know that some intentions and actions are really better than others, all one's choices are ultimately meaningless, mere reactions rather than self-initiated actions. Freedom is indeed fundamental to being human, but freedom is incompatible with subjective relativism, with the rejection of absolute moral norms which could serve as the guides for deliberate choice.

Evaluation of Moral Relativism

In our consideration of relativism, we have found that neither cultural relativism nor subjective relativism is warranted. Moral relativism is not established by the argument that ethics is derived from culture or religion since, even if one accepts the connection between cultural or religious differences and moral differences (which one is not logically required to do), there is still the question of why the individual within a culture or religious group should follow the moral teachings of that culture or religion. More radically, since we do not think that someone, merely by denying affiliation with any religion or culture, is thereby justified in torturing, raping, or killing innocent people, it is clear that we do not really believe that the foundations for moral responsibility are in religion or culture. Therefore, the existence of different religions or cultures and the fact that some people do not profess affiliation with any religion or culture at all do not prove that there are no absolute moral norms.

Pushing relativism to its logical extreme of subjective relativism, we found that, in addition to being an impossible position to recommend (since calling it good contradicts relativism's denial of good and evil), neither the attempt to place scientific method at the center of all intelligibility nor an appeal to freedom can justify subjective relativism. Science does not rule out the possibility of there being absolute moral norms. For while it is proper for science to use the scientific method of hypothesis and verification in its own sphere, it is impossible to extend this method to all aspects of thought and reality. The attempt to do so destroys the very validity of science itself: to insist that all that is real is material is to insist that the statement "all that is real is material" is not real. Meaning is not a materially verifiable thing; if it is therefore unreal, then so is the whole project of scientific knowledge itself. Nor is subjective relativism justified because it guarantees freedom. While a certain meaning of freedom (that of license) denies responsibility and to this extent leaves one free to do as one pleases, the deepest sense of freedom (freedom to choose one's actions) is impossible unless there are standards that are absolute—that is, grounded in reason, not impulse.

MORAL RESPONSIBILITY

Having looked at the general arguments in favor of relativism and found them wanting, it is time to turn to some systematic treatments of the foundations of moral responsibility. Five fundamental options for the basis of morality can be fairly easily distinguished and have been so distinguished over the years: feeling (emotivism), self-interest (egoism), consequences (utilitarianism), duty (formalism), and the self-evident knowledge of basic human goods and the requirement to honor and not violate them (natural law). This order reflects closeness of kinship with relativism—emotivism being closest and natural law farthest away. The order also reflects a kind of ranking of plausibility to the modern mind. Something of all these ways of thinking about ethics exists in our minds, with the easiest to grasp and to follow (emotivism) lying near the surface, and the more complicated, subtle, and ultimately more plausible option requiring some deeper reflection to bring to light.

As children of the modern age, we have all grown up under the authority of science and hence under the shadow of doubt about the existence of moral absolutes. It takes some time to get clear about the limits of science in answering questions about what one ought and ought not to do. The first three theories—emotivism, egoism, and utilitarianism—all accept (at least in their original forms) the assumption that the scientific method is the only way to know reality. They all deny that reason can tell us what is good and evil. However, while they all accept this common assumption, they disagree about its implications for ethics. The last two, Kant's formalism and the ethics of natural law, take as fundamental to ethics the principle that reason can know what is good or evil as well as understand the world scientifically.

Since we spent some time discussing the thought of Epicurus, we might note that the foundations for all three of the first ethical positions can be found in his work. First of all, Epicurus is clear in placing pleasure as his first principle and feeling as the motivation which moves the will. In this he expresses admirably the principles of emotivism. "Wherefore we call pleasure the alpha and omega of a blessed life. Pleasure is our first and kindred good. It is the starting point of every choice and of every aversion, and to it we come back, inasmuch as we make feeling the rule by which to judge every good thing."[35] Secondly, Epicurus is clear that any notion of right and wrong is merely conventional, an agreement designed to further one's self-interest. In this he neatly presents the principles of egoism or social contract theory. "Natural justice is a symbol or expression of expediency, to prevent one man from harming or being harmed by another. . . . There never was an absolute justice, but only an agreement made in reciprocal intercourse in whatever localities now and again from time to time, providing against the infliction or suffering of harm."[36] Finally, Epicurus says that what count in evaluating an action are its consequences, and laws are to be judged good or bad according as they bring the best consequences for the society. In this he presents the principle of utilitarianism. "Injustice is not itself an evil, but only in its consequence. . . . Where without any change in circumstances the conventional laws, when judged by their consequences, were seen not to correspond with the notion of justice, such laws were not really just . . ."[37]

That Epicurus should foreshadow three such prominent contemporary ethical positions is not, perhaps, that surprising. For if, prompted by the idea that universal moral norms are relative to an unjustifiable belief in religion, one rejects such norms, a vacuum is created in one's ability to explain choices and actions. Like all vacuums, this one will be filled if there is any alternative explanation, and there is—the mechanics of pleasure and pain moving the human will. With pleasure and pain as first principles, one or another of these three theories seems inevitable. While Epicurus was content to rest with a general pleasure-and-pain theory of ethics, philosophers of the modern age, driven by the demands of coherency and consistency, have distinguished the three theories of emotivism, egoism, and utilitarianism.

2

Do What You Feel: Emotivism

Perhaps the most popular candidate for moral authority today is emotion. What we need in moral decision-making is not a lot of fancy reasoning but a return to nature, getting in touch with one's feelings. Would we just do this, all sorts of personal problems would be corrected and interpersonal relations straightened out. This is the Romantic ideal; our problem is that we have lost touch with our basic instincts, at the heart of which is a deep affection for humanity. The problem with outright relativism is that it cannot explain why we really do feel that lying, rape, torture, and killing are wrong, and we really do feel that all people, if only they were in touch with their feelings, would feel the same way. The universality so necessary to even talk about right and wrong is supplied not by reason, but by a universal feeling, an instinct of kindliness, a moral sense.

There is something to be said for this position. That morality involves feelings and emotions is indisputable. In whatever way one might wish to explain approval or disapproval, these responses are normally accompanied by some feeling or emotion. And quite often the feeling or emotion seems to carry the conviction of an infallible moral judgment. Thus, on hearing of a brutal and senseless murder, one's stomach turns, and one squirms in anguish and despair at man's inhumanity to man. Or hearing of some heroic deed of self-sacrifice, one's heart skips a beat and one is filled with a feeling of joy and hope. That such emotional responses exist and are normal is not to be doubted. Whether they indicate either that morality is ultimately a matter of emotion or that emotion ought to be our moral guide is the matter before us in this chapter.

Emotivism (this idea that feeling or emotion is the source of moral judgments) is not a new theory. We mentioned that Epicurus espoused such a position in ancient Greece. In the Enlightenment, David Hume was the chief exponent of such a theory.[1] While the facts that we do react emotionally to actions and that sometimes emotions move us to act provide a general plausibility for the position, Hume thought that he had a philosophical argument which made emotivism not only plausible or likely, but certainly the case. Let us take a look at his line of reasoning.

EMOTIVISM ACCORDING TO HUME

Hume agreed with Epicurus and Lucretius that the worst thing for human beings was their domination by superstition—that is, religion. In this he was following in the footsteps of such Renaissance figures as Francis Bacon and Thomas Hobbes. Hume had also inherited an empiricist theory of knowledge from these same sources and from the more recent work of John Locke and Bishop Berkeley. Empiricism is the theory which holds that all knowledge begins in the senses and that any legitimate idea must be traceable to an original sense impression of which it is the copy. It is essentially the same theory as the materialism we discussed in Chapter One. Hume's empirical presuppositions meant that he could not count traditional moral norms such as justice and honesty (which Plato, Aristotle, and their followers held to be known by reason) to be real, since they could not be verified by sense experience. Nor was the other traditional source of ethics—religion—a serious contender for the job of grounding morality, since the idea of an immaterial cause of all things cannot be traced back to a sense impression. When Hume went to explain the origin of morality, he was forced (by his presuppositions and consistency) to try to account for it in terms compatible with the empirical or scientific method.

Origin of Morality

The initial problem Hume addresses in his analysis of the origin of morality is whether or not morality originates in reason. According to traditional morality, reason should guide us in our actions, controlling and directing the passions. Against this traditional view, Hume argues that reason cannot influence the will and that, therefore, the origin of morality must be in the passions. His argument is as follows. Reason is capable of two operations. It can deal with "relations of ideas," and it can deal with "matters of fact."[2] By "relations of ideas" Hume means such disciplines as logic and mathematics. According to Hume, these disciplines have nothing to do with objective reality but are mere inventions of the mind. By "matters of fact" Hume is referring to what can be known through experience of really existing things, whether through the hard sciences or just in everyday experience. He has in mind, here, the general idea of scientific method which he inherited from Bacon: one seeks through sense experience to verify hypotheses about the world. Since this method alone yields information about objective reality, *all* disciplines which make judgments about reality must use scientific method; that is, they all must verify their conclusions by sense experience.

What happens when one tries to apply these two operations of reason to morality? One finds that they do not apply. First of all, one immediately recognizes that morality is not just a matter of relations of ideas. For one thing, morality is about actions we do in the real world, not just about how ideas are logically related to each other. To make this point clear, Hume presents two situations which differ morally but not in terms of the relations of ideas. He chooses the act of parricide (the murder of parent by child) and asks the reader to compare it, from a moral standpoint, to the case of an oak tree sapling which kills its parent tree by overshadowing it. Although the logical relation of ideas is precisely the same in each case (child : parent : : young tree : parent tree), the reader morally condemns the human but not the vegetative killer. This indicates that morality is not to be found in the act of reason which relates ideas. Of course, Hume recognizes that the human child has a will and the oak sapling does not, but this does not indicate some difference in their logical relation; rather, this is some difference in the facts.

But are these facts themselves the origin of morality? Is morality based on matters of fact? The matters of fact, here, would be simply the observable specifics of the situation: the fact that John is the son of Peter, the fact that John and Peter are in the same place at the same time, the fact that John has a knife and is not paralyzed, the fact that Peter is not invulnerable, and the fact of John killing Peter. But these facts do not explain the immorality of the act, for in themselves they are morally neutral. When one searches for the moral characteristics of the act, one finds that there is no objective thing called "vice" or "wrong" or "evil" which can be verified by scientific method. Hence, such terms are without referent and therefore meaningless when applied to the activity in question.

What one really means by "vice" or "wrong" or "evil" is the feeling one experiences in the face of certain actions. Morality is something intuitive and innate, not the fruit of rational deliberation, whether relating ideas or verifying facts. Let me quote Hume himself here.

> Take any action allow'd to be vicious: Willful murder for instance. Examine it in all lights, and see if you can find that matter of fact, or real existence, which you call *vice.* In which-ever way you take it, you find only certain passions, motives, volitions and thoughts. There is no other matter of fact in the case. The vice entirely escapes you, as long as you consider the object. You never can find it, till you turn your reflexion into your own breast, and find a sentiment of disapprobation, which arises in you, towards the action. Here is a matter of fact: but 'tis the object of feeling, not of reason. It lies in yourself, not in the object. So that when you pronounce any action or character to be vicious, you

mean nothing, but that from the constitution of your nature you have a feeling or sentiment of blame from the contemplation of it.[3]

Ultimately, judgments about right and wrong issue not from reason, but from feeling. As for reason, it can neither know right from wrong nor move the will to choose. It is from emotion or passion that both moral judgment and moral action originate.

Human Behavior

Having determined that morality must have its seat in the passions, Hume turns to an explanation of human behavior. Since people are generally nice to each other (at the very least, everyone shows some kindness at one time or another), it must be that we have a passion which moves us to be kind to others, a benevolent impulse toward our fellow human beings. We know that reason cannot guide the passions, curbing our selfishness and reminding us of our obligation to others. Therefore, it simply must be the case that we are naturally inclined to be kind to each other.

> It is sufficient for our present purpose, if it be allowed, what surely, without the greatest absurdity cannot be disputed, that there is some benevolence, however small, infused into our bosom; some spark of friendship for humankind; some particle of the dove kneaded into our frame, along with the elements of the wolf and the serpent Let these generous sentiments be supposed ever so weak; let them be insufficient to move even a hand or finger of the body, they must still direct the determinations of the mind, and where everything else is equal, produce a cool preference of what is useful and serviceable to mankind, above what is pernicious and dangerous.[4]

It is here that Hume's theory begins to reveal the weakness of its foundations. It may or may not be a fact that we have a benevolent impulse. Hobbes, whom we shall discuss in the next chapter, vehemently denies that we do. But even if we allow that we have such an impulse on the basis that we sometimes are kind to each other, it is difficult to understand how it could predominate among our passions, or why we should try to make it predominate. Why *must* the very weak benevolent impulse prevail over the raging passions of greed, lust, anger, and the other selfish desires? It is like putting a dozen 250-pound wild fighters in the ring against one 98-pound weakling without a referee who favors the weakling and betting that the 98-pound weakling will win the fight For remember, according to Hume there is no power above the passions that can influence the will; the practical reason of the natural law tradition has been denounced as illusory. It is the legion of selfish passions against one weak feeling of benevolence. The outcome of the fight can hardly be in doubt. Hume might point out that the fight must, in fact, not be so one-sided since we are not always cheating and killing our fellow human beings, but Hume does not offer us a plausible explanation of why this is so.

No Moral Obligation from Facts

Perhaps, then, one might interpret Hume's position as saying that we *should* promote the benevolent passion and restrain the aggressive passions. But this will not do on Hume's own terms, and Hume himself has seen this. From facts alone no conclusions of obligation can be drawn. The fact that we have a benevolent sentiment in no way implies that we ought to follow it. This is a very important point that Hume is making. So let me quote Hume himself, and take a little time to discuss what exactly is being said.

> In every system of morality, which I have hitherto met with, I have always remark'd, that the author proceeds for some time in the ordinary way of reasoning [theoretical reasoning], and establishes the being of God, or makes observations concerning human affairs; when all of a sudden I am surpriz'd to find, that instead of the usual copulations of proposition, *is*, and *is not*, I meet with no proposition that is not connected with an *ought*, or an *ought not*. This change is imperceptible; but is, however, of the last consequence. For as this *ought*, or *ought not*, expresses some new relation or affirmation, 'tis necessary that it shou'd be observ'd and explain'd; and at the same time that a reason should be given, for what seems altogether inconceivable, how this new relation can be a deduction from others, which are entirely different from it.[5]

The point Hume is making is based on a simple rule of logic. If an argument is to be valid, there cannot be something in the conclusion which is not already in the premises. A logical argument proceeds from premises (propositions which are "put first") to a conclusion which is supposed to be implied by the premises. If one agrees to the truth of the premises and the form of the argument is logically valid, one must agree to the conclusion. Here is a simple example.

PREMISE 1: All dogs are mortal.
PREMISE 2: Fido is a dog.
CONCLUSION: Therefore, Fido is mortal.

If one accepts the truth of the first two premises, then one must logically accept the conclusion, on pain of being incoherent in one's thinking (simultaneously accepting and not accepting the same thing as true). But now consider the same argument with the invalid move to which Hume is objecting.

PREMISE 1:   All dogs are mortal.
PREMISE 2:   Fido is a dog.
CONCLUSION: Therefore, Fido can fly.

There is very obviously something in the conclusion which was not in the premises. That Fido is a dog and that he is mortal in no way imply that he can fly. There is no reason why one should accept the conclusion just because one has accepted the premises.

Consider now an argument more precisely like what Hume has in mind, where from premises which merely give the facts (*is* or *is not* statements) a conclusion is drawn of obligation (*ought* or *ought not* statement).

PREMISE 1:   Someone is being mugged.
PREMISE 2:   If I call the police, the person will be saved.
CONCLUSION: Therefore, I ought to call the police.

To agree to the truth of the first two premises in no way requires that one accept the conclusion, for there is something in the conclusion—namely, the imperative expressed in the word "ought"—that appears nowhere in the premises, which are both indicative statements of facts ("is" statements). From facts alone, no conclusion of obligation can be drawn. Hume is consistent enough to see that, if he begins by limiting the role of reason to making statements about what *is* the case in terms of relations of ideas and matters of fact, then he has no business making any statements about what *ought* to be the case.

It is here that Hume's theory of emotivism reveals itself as finally meaningless, morally speaking. For while it attempts to describe the mechanism of our actions, it has absolutely nothing to say about what we ought to do. And if morality is not about what we ought to do, then it provides no criterion for distinguishing right from wrong, nor any principle by which we may guide our actions.

Relativism and Determinism

Ultimately, Hume's theory leads back to relativism and determinism. Since morality is but a matter of passion and not reason, there can be no universal obligation (or in fact, any obligation at all—for all obligation is universal). In the end, one does what one does. If selfish passions predominate, well then they do. If the benevolent impulse predominates, well then it does. There is simply no more to be said. We are back to mere relativism. No choice or action is right or wrong; none is better or worse.

In addition, since our choices are not made by reason, they are not freely made. If Hume's analysis is correct, our actions are determined by our passions. If all that is real are the physical facts of our animal nature, then just like the animals, we are determined. What will be will be, regardless of what we appear to think or wish.

Role of Reason in Morality

However, although Hume does not account reason to be the foundation of morality, he does grant it a secondary role. Reason cannot say what is good or evil, right or wrong, but it can say whether or not one is correct about the facts of the situation and what the probability is that one's desire can be fulfilled by the particular means under consideration. Thus, reason has an ancillary, calculative role in morality. The activities which reason can perform in morality are, in fact, precisely the same ones it performs anywhere else: reason deals with matters of fact and relations of ideas. It can neither make value judgments nor move the will to action; its true role is descriptive (matters of fact) and calculative (relations of ideas), not prescriptive. Hume puts it this way.

> '[T]is only in two senses, that any affection can be call'd unreasonable. First, When a passion, such as hope or fear, grief or joy, despair or security, is founded on the supposition of the existence of objects, which really do not exist. Secondly, When in exerting any passion in action, we chuse means insufficient for the design's end, and deceive ourselves in our judgment of causes and effects.[6]

Only if one has the facts wrong or has chosen insufficient means to achieve what one's passions desire can one's act be called unreasonable.

Thus, it is not in itself unreasonable to want to murder someone. Motives of the will come merely from emotions as they respond to prospects for pleasure and pain. Reason might counsel against murder, but only on such grounds as "this is not the person you want to murder" (fact) or "the pleasure you hope to achieve through the murder cannot be achieved by carrying out the murder" (insufficient means to achieve the desired end). Hume is very serious about denying reason any fundamental role in morality. Consider the following statement

> 'Tis not contrary to reason to prefer the destruction of the whole world to the scratching of my finger. 'Tis not contrary to reason for me to chuse my total ruin, to prevent the least uneasiness of an *Indian* or person wholly unknown to me. 'Tis as little contrary to reason to prefer even my own acknowledg'd lesser good to my greater, and have a more ardent affection for the former than the latter.[7]

If read with any kind of commonsensical[8] understanding of morality, these statements are horrifying and the last completely absurd. Given the choice of having one's finger scratched by a thorn or having the world destroyed, Hume says that it would not be unreasonable for one to choose the destruction of the world. Nor would it be unreasonable for one to prefer (that is, think of as better) what one knows to be worse. If any statements about morality are irrational, these are. But Hume's point here is that, since reason can only deal with relations of ideas and matters of fact, it simply *cannot* deal with questions of value. He is perfectly consistent with his principles—and perfectly absurd, morally speaking.

To be fair to Hume, he is not saying that he is in favor of one destroying the world rather than scratching one's finger, or that one ought to choose what one knows to be worse. Such questions of obligation are simply meaningless to Hume. Perhaps he would say that our emotions *are* upset by such prospects and that our benevolent impulse *will* prevent us from doing such horrendous deeds. But it would not be wrong to do them, for the word "wrong" has no universal meaning; it merely designates what some particular person happens to feel.

We need not repeat how weak Hume's theory of the benevolent impulse is, except to note, once more, that it seems unlikely that timid benevolence will defeat fierce self-interest in a free-for-all. And even if it did in some cases (perhaps for David Hume), one could not say that someone would be wrong for not following his or her benevolent impulse. For if reason is denied its fundamental role of knowing right from wrong, then one is not free to choose but rather is under the domination of passions. If one destroys the world to avoid scratching one's finger, well then one does. There is no more to be said about it in terms of praise or blame; in fact, there is no such thing as moral judgment at all.

The bottom line is that it is one's emotional reaction to the possibility of pleasure and pain which determines one's will. "'Tis obvious, that when we have the prospect of pain and pleasure from any object, we feel a consequent emotion of aversion or propensity, and are carry'd to avoid or embrace what will give us this uneasiness or satisfaction."[9] While Hume is not, perhaps, far wrong in his analysis of our reaction to pleasure and pain, he cannot by this analysis alone account for the fact that we do think that certain actions are wrong and deserving of punishment. Having denied our ability to know right from wrong, Hume has destroyed the heart of morality. For, if no one can know what is right or wrong, there is no point in recommending that certain actions be done and others avoided. For Hume, reason is but a technical tool of the passions to help the passions achieve what they desire. "Reason is, and ought only to be the slave of the passions, and can never pretend to any other office than to serve and obey them."[10] Aside from the fact that Hume has no business, according to his very principles, using the word "ought" here, this is a good summation of his position.

LATER DEVELOPMENT OF EMOTIVISM

There have been a number of philosophers who have argued the case for emotivism since Hume's time, and Hume has also had substantial influence on thinkers of other ethical persuasions. However, most who accept his emotivist foundations reject the idea of a universal benevolence.

The twentieth-century philosopher A. J. Ayer is perhaps the most radically consistent of these followers. In his writings, he openly refers to Hume's division of propositions into "relations of ideas" and "matters of fact." The former make no claims about external reality but "simply record our determinations to use symbols in a certain fashion."[11] Since we make up the rules, these kinds of propositions have absolute certainty; however, they do not refer to anything in the real world. If we wish to speak about the real world, we must use propositions dealing with matters of fact. Matters of fact are the results of applying the scientific method; their meaningfulness requires verification by sense experience, and their degree of certainty (they are never absolutely certain) is relative to the number and consistency of verified instances. "Propositions concerning empirical matters of fact . . . I hold to be hypotheses, which can be probable but never certain. And in giving an account of the method of their validation [what he calls 'a modified verification principle'] I claim also to have explained the nature of truth."[12] Thus, like his master Hume, Ayer restricts reason to relations of ideas and matters of fact; what will not fit into these two categories is not an operation of reason.

Applying these principles to ethical judgments such as "stealing is wrong" or "cheating is unjust," Ayer says that the words "wrong" and "unjust" are meaningless. What is meaningful in any statement about a state of affairs (and moral statements are about states of affairs) is contained in the empirically verifiable aspects of that statement. Thus, an empirical description of the act of stealing or cheating is the true content of the quoted judgments. Since "wrong" and "unjust" are not material things subject to sense experience, they are not real. These ethical symbols are therefore, strictly speaking, meaningless. What, then, is their function in the propositions? It is merely emotive: they serve to express or stir up emotion. The conclusion that Ayer draws from all of this is that ethical judgments have no validity—a conclusion of radical relativism.

> We can now see why it is impossible to find a criterion for determining the validity of ethical judgments. It is not because they have an "absolute" validity which is mysteriously independent of ordinary sense-experience, but because they have no objective validity whatsoever. If a sentence makes no statement at all, there is obviously no sense in asking whether what it says is true or false. And we have seen that sentences which simply express moral judgements do not say anything. They are pure expressions of feeling and as such do not come under the category of truth and falsehood. They are unverifiable for the same reason as a cry of pain or a word of command is unverifiable—because they do not express genuine propositions.[13]

Neither a judgment of good or evil (right or wrong) nor a moral imperative such as "Do not kill innocent people" has any meaning whatsoever. Thus, whatever the function of moral language, it is not rational.

As we already mentioned, the main difference between Hume's position and that of his followers is that the followers tend to recognize the inconsistency of Hume's introduction of a universal benevolent impulse which must guide us to do what is serviceable to mankind. Barring this universal passion, emotivism reverts to relativism. Edward Westermarck, the anthropologist we mentioned in connection with relativism in Chapter One, draws this conclusion with consummate consistency. Having concluded from his anthropological research that all cultures do, in fact, share the same fundamental values (such as life, friendship, truthtelling, and generosity), he tries to explain why it is, then, that people are not universally kind to one another. His conclusion is that the range and strength of the "altruistic sentiment" (notice the similarity to Hume's moral sense or benevolent impulse) vary. Some feel kindness just toward those closest to them; some extend this kindness further afield. Some feel this kindness intensely, others only mildly. Putting all these points together, Westermarck concludes that it is the fact that actions are based ultimately on emotions that accounts for moral relativism.

This is just what may be expected if moral opinions are based on emotions. The moral emotions depend upon cognitions [presumably of some particular matters of fact], but the same cognitions may give rise to emotions that differ, in quality or intensity, in different persons or in the same person on different occasions, and then there is nothing that could make the emotions uniform.[14]

Indeed, if emotions are the basis of our morals, then even the statement that one often hears—"everyone has his or her own individual morality"—cannot be true. Not only do emotions differ among people, but they vary over time within the same person. As a statement of fact, this seems to be true. Contrary to Hume's conclusion, there is no guarantee that different people will react emotionally in the same way to the same situation, nor even that one's own emotional reaction will always be the same in similar situations. We are back at subjective relativism, where there are no better or worse choices or actions. On these terms, moral responsibility is, as Ayer said, a meaningless concept.

SUMMARY

In closing this chapter, let us sum up the argument of emotivism as presented by Hume and his followers. Reason only deals with relations of ideas and matters of fact. Since morality falls under neither operation of reason, morality is not a matter of reason. The only other possible motive of the will is passion. Therefore, it must be that the passions dictate our actions. This conclusion might seem to imply moral anarchy since our emotions are notoriously changeable. However, the fact that we are not always flying off the handle following all sorts of violent passions indicates the existence within us of a universal peaceful passion—the moral sense. What had been thought by traditional moralists to be the guiding hand of reason is really only the presence of a universal benevolence for humankind. In short, Hume attempts to account for our normally civilized behavior by the hypothesis of a universal passion of love for mankind.

Whether or not Hume got the facts right about our passions, it remains that there is ultimately nothing in Hume or in any other emotivist which can serve as a foundation for moral responsibility. For even if there is, in fact, a benevolent impulse in us all, the question remains: Why should we follow it and not another impulse—say that of greed or lust or the desire to dominate? Since Hume denies any absolute standards of morality, he has no way of justifying the obviously true judgment that killing innocent five-year-old children is worse than devoting one's life to caring for orphans, or even the judgment that it is better to choose what one considers to be better rather than what one thinks is worse. In the end, Hume fails to provide any foundation for morality. Passions alone, without any higher guide, cannot tell us what we ought to do. If we are searching for the foundations of moral responsibility, we shall not find them here. To embrace emotivism is to embrace relativism. Westermarck draws out the implications of saying that morality is based on emotions when he concludes that, since the range and strength of the altruistic sentiment (the same as Hume's benevolent impulse) varies among people and even within the same person at different times, there is nothing which can provide any moral consistency or certainty.

3

Me First:
Egoism and the Social Contract

Since the emotivist attempt to provide a universal basis for morality in feeling fails to deliver, must we conclude that morality is not a matter of the passions? Or might it not simply be that Hume focuses on the wrong passion—that he gets his facts wrong? Perhaps Hume's fault is that he looks to an ideal that cannot be substantiated by the facts. What is needed is a more realistic appraisal of human nature, which recognizes human beings for the selfish animals they really are. Armed with the right passion and a systematic use of reason as a mechanism for calculating means-to-end relations, might it not be possible to arrive at some universal moral rules? Is it not true that it is ultimately in one's self-interest to treat others fairly? This approach to morality is known as egoism or, in its political extrapolation, the social contract theory.

As we begin our discussion, it might be well to comment briefly on why this approach to ethics can be called both egoism and the social contract theory. One might think that the two ideas conflict, for while egoism is mere self-interest, the social contract theory implies laws for the common good which one must obey whether one wants to or not. This conflict, however, is not real, at least not according to those who hold such a theory. Egoism and the social contract are really on the same side of the benevolence/self-interest face-off. In fact, the social contract is considered by its adherents to be just the necessary consequence of consistent self-interest. The only reason why one joins a group under law is to better one's position. It is not through an understanding that one should be fair to others that one agrees to live by laws. It is not because one thinks that everyone deserves to be treated with equal respect that one is willing to restrain one's egotistical passions. On the contrary, according to the theory, no person cares at all about anyone else. Each is willing to abide under law simply because it is in his or her best interest to do so.

There is a certain plausibility in this theory. The facts that people are selfish and that sometimes they cooperate with others only out of self-interest are certainly as credible as Hume's claim that people help each other out of a benevolent impulse, and egoism does not carry any overtones of such moral ideals as kindness and nobility of spirit. In short, the strength of this position is in its realism; its foundation is the universal fact of selfishness. In addition to its realism, egoism is commended by its simplicity and consistency; it explains all behavior, both what appears selfish and what appears kind in terms of self-interest. Hume needs at least two principles to explain human behavior—selfishness and benevolence—and founders on the problem of explaining why one or the other does or should triumph. Egoism avoids this problem by stating that all actions are based on self-interest, hence simplifying and unifying explanation while at the same time not expecting human beings to act in any way differently from the other animals. That people are sometimes selfish is beyond question. That they are always selfish or that they somehow ought to be selfish is the matter for our discussion in this chapter.

The social contract theory is not something which developed in the modern era but has been around for as long as there have been ethical theories. It is perhaps most forcibly presented in Plato's *Republic*, where it is championed by Thrasymachus (and rejected by Socrates). The following quotation is a summary of the basic principles of social contract theory.

> They say that to do wrong is naturally good, to be wronged is bad, but the suffering of injury so far exceeds in badness the good of inflicting it that when men have done wrong to each other and suffered it, and have had a taste of both, those who are unable to avoid the latter and practice the former decide that it is profitable to come to an agreement with each other neither to inflict injury nor to suffer it. As a result they begin to make laws and convenants, and the law's command they call lawful and just. This, they say, is the origin and essence of justice; it stands between the best and the worst, the best being to do wrong without paying the penalty and the worst to be wronged without the power of revenge. The just then is a mean between two extremes; it is welcomed and honored because of men's lack of power to do wrong. The man who has that power, the real man, would not make a compact with anyone not to inflict injury or suffer it. For him that would be madness. This then, Socrates, is, according to their argument, the nature and origin of justice.[1]

The ideal is to have everything one's own way, to be able to reap pleasure whenever, wherever, and from whomever one wants. Since one lacks the ability to dominate everyone else, one is willing to compromise in order to protect oneself from being subject to pain inflicted by others. Thus, out of self-interest one enters into an agreement to live with others under certain rules and regulations.

SOCIAL CONTRACT THEORY

In the modern era, Thomas Hobbes is a pure exponent of this egoism/social contract theory. Given the other options which the history of philosophy offers, how and why did Hobbes settle on this? As one begins reading Hobbes's *Leviathan*, one is immediately struck by the fact that Hobbes is operating under the same scientific presuppositions as Hume. Indeed, Hobbes declares that all explanation follows from the laws of matter in motion; for all thought arises from the senses, and the senses are activated by the motions of external objects.[2] The immediate influence here is Galileo, whom Hobbes actually met. As a strict materialist, Hobbes refuses to let other factors influence his interpretation of nature, and this includes human nature in all its dimensions—ethical and political, as well as physical and biological.

As for the similarities between Hume and Hobbes, these are not hard to explain. Both were fellow countrymen and philosophical descendants of Francis Bacon,[3] who declared that the only method suitable for human knowing is the scientific method of hypothesis and verification through experimentation. Bacon also rejected the idea that there could be anything real about material things except for their matter and their motion.[4] Any explanation in terms of the intrinsic uniqueness of things (irreducible to their matter) or in terms of their purpose in the larger context of the universe were rejected as unscientific, as fictitious. Since such explanations (what Aristotle called formal and final causes, respectively) cannot be verified in terms of sense experience, Bacon concluded that they were illusory. Beyond this, the explanation in terms of purpose was rejected on the grounds of being pernicious superstition, implying as it does some ultimate purpose of things—i.e., God.

In addition to the Baconian influence, both Hobbes and Hume (along with Bacon) were caught up in the anti-Roman Catholic and hence anti-Aristotelian mindset of the Reformation. Since Thomas Aquinas and other eminent Catholic theologians made extensive use of the philosophy of Aristotle, a rejection of Catholic theology tended to include the rejection of Aristotelian philosophy. Allowing the pagan Aristotle to influence the purity of Scripture study was viewed by the reformers as one of the most serious errors of Roman Catholicism. Hobbes counts as one of the four causes of spiritual darkness "mixing with the Scripture divers reliques of the Religion, and much of the vain and erroneous Philosophy of the Greeks, especially of Aristotle."[5]

Given these similar backgrounds, it is not surprising to find Hobbes in agreement with Hume on the fundamentals of moral explanation.[6] For example, although Hobbes does not present the same kind of argument as Hume for morality being a matter of the passions, he certainly agrees that the passions move the will to act. Hobbes is also in agreement with Hume as to the role of reason in morality. Reason cannot say what is universally right or wrong, just or unjust; rather, it can only say how to get what one wants. For Hobbes, reason is a technique for fulfilling self-interest and decidedly *not* a judge declaring that one ought to be fair to others because they have as much intrinsic worth as oneself.

The great difference between Hume and Hobbes is, of course, that Hobbes has no use for any universal moral sense or benevolent impulse. First of all, he does not think that human beings are naturally endowed with such a passion. On the contrary, people do not by nature like each other. "Men have no pleasure, (but on the contrary a great deale of griefe) in keeping company, where there is no power to over-awe them all."[7] Hobbes considers the natural state of humanity to be a war of everyone against everyone. In such a state of nature, far from benevolence ruling, the cardinal virtues are "Force and Fraud."[8] Secondly, Hobbes thinks he knows the mechanism behind the origin of law: the passion of fear on the part of every person leads to the formation through a social contract of a power of protection to alleviate this fear. Power is the underlying principle for Hobbes, whether it be understood as the power of matter in motion (which is its root sense), or as the power of the passion of fear over the other passions, or as coercive political power to keep people in line.

Origin of Society and Morality

Let us look in more detail at the origin of society and morality according to Hobbes. Hobbes begins with what he takes to be the obvious facts of bare human existence. First of all, human beings are innately selfish. This he finds true to his experience. (Of course, from experience alone, Hume could make an argument to the contrary; people are, in fact, sometimes kind to one another without any obvious reference in their motives to self-interest.) This innate selfishness is also compatible with his mechanistic account of all human actions in terms of physical reactions to pleasure and pain. Secondly, human beings are roughly equal, not in moral worth (for such an evaluative term is incompatible with mechanistic explanation), but in power, whether the power be bodily strength or cunning. This being so, while each person would like to have everything his or her own way, no one is able to do so consistently enough to avoid the pain of being harmed by others. Therefore, since everyone wants to come out ahead in terms of more pleasure and less pain, some kind of compromise is in order. Reason, in its calculating function of tabulating the facts and judging whether the means chosen will lead to the desired end (precisely the same two functions which Hume allows reason) leads one, in the name of self-interest, to the decision that it is best to compromise. For life in the state of nature is not very appealing—"continuall feare, and danger of violent death; and the life of man, solitary, poore, nasty, brutish, and short . . ."[9]

To account for the transition from a state of nature to life in a commonwealth, Hobbes has recourse to his laws of nature. Hobbes defines natural law in the following way. "A LAW OF NATURE, (Lex Naturalis,) is a Precept, or generall Rule, found out by Reason, by which a man is forbidden to do, that, which is destructive of his life, or taketh away the means of preserving the same; and to omit, that, by which he thinketh it may best be preserved."[10] Two things should be noted here. First, Hobbes' natural laws refer only to the nature of being an animal, for Hobbes did not admit any essential difference between human beings and animals. Such differences would be matters of intrinsic form and purpose, which he rejected as unscientific. Second, this natural law and those that follow are not human constructions; they do not depend on an agreement among a group gathered by compromise for mutual protection.

The question remains, how does concern for one's life lead to willingness to abide by laws which restrict one's ability to do all that is possible to increase pleasure and decrease pain? The first principle of Hobbes' thought is self-interest; this is the basis for the fundamental right of everyone to do what is necessary to preserve his or her life. Since an argument can be made that all acts of domination—killing, stealing, even adultery as a show of power—are acts that serve to preserve one's life, there are no acts that could be called naturally wrong. Everything belongs to oneself by right of power, and of course to everyone else by right of power, as well. Thus, Hobbes says that in a state of nature, "every man has a Right to every thing; even to one anothers body."[11]

Peace and Defense

It is because such a state of affairs is one of continual violence and anxiety (and hence does not bring what one really wants—a life of pleasure and freedom from pain) that one is obliged, out of self-interest, to try to find a way out of this state of nature. Thus, the first law of nature is: "*That every man, ought to endeavor Peace, asfarre as he has hope of obtaining it; and when he cannot obtain it, that he may seek, and use, all helps, and advantages of Warre.*"[12] For one's own sake, one ought to seek peace, for only with peace comes freedom from pain and from the fear of aggression. However, if peace is unavailable, one ought (again, for one's own sake) to defend oneself by any means. This obligation to preserve oneself is the most fundamental of the natural laws. From it Hobbes deduces all the rest, imitating the model of geometry by deducing conclusions from axioms.[13] Hobbes goes on to speak of nineteen natural laws, getting quite specific by the end. For our purposes, it will be enough to examine his first three, which are the most general.

The second natural law, which Hobbes says is derived from the first, is as follows: *"That a man be willing, when others are so too, as farre-forth, as for Peace, and defence of himselfe he shall think necessary, to lay down this right to all things; and be contented with so much liberty against other men, as he would allow other men against himselfe."*[14] Keeping both parts of the first law in mind, Hobbes says that one ought to enter into mutual agreement with others to lay down arms, but only if there is some guarantee that one will not suffer harm from such an action. It would be against the first natural law to lay down one's defenses based merely on another's promise to do the same. Thus, unilateral disarmament is anathema to Hobbes. Only if there is a coercive power in place which can guarantee that others will not take advantage of one's move toward peace may one make such a move. Trust is not only foolish, but unlawful. The logistics here are somewhat difficult to grasp, but what Hobbes has in mind in this second law is that, at the moment the mutual disarmament is effected, there must be set up a sovereign power to guarantee that no one will break the truce.

Although, prior to there being a coercive power in place, it would be unlawful to trust others to disarm and also unlawful to keep one's promises if one had need to break them, once such a power is in place, one is obliged to trust in this sovereign power and to keep one's agreements. Thus, Hobbes' third natural law is: *"That men performe their Covenants made."*[15] It is at this point that the word "justice" becomes meaningful. Justice is the fulfilling of contracts, injustice the breaking of them.

The order of priority in Hobbes' theory is: power, law, justice. The first principle is power; before there can be any law or justice, there must be power. Only when the fear of being attacked is removed by the presence of an ordering coercive power is one permitted to enter into any agreements limiting one's freedom to do as one pleases. From power are derived the laws. The sovereign power, which comes into being through the primary act of compromise and is thus accounted the common will, establishes the order and laws by which people are to live. These laws declare what is just, and one is obliged to obey them. In short, might makes right.

Nothing has really changed in the transformation from the state of nature to the commonwealth. In the state of nature might makes right because whoever has the ability to act is legitimated precisely by the ability to accomplish the action, and there is no constraint on such activity by any extrinsic power. Under a social contract might still makes right, only in this case the might is that of the sovereign power, be it the king, parliament, or the people. That things have not really changed is a compliment to Hobbes' consistency. He has stuck to his first principle of analyzing all reality in terms of the power of matter in motion. Power dictates what will be, whether it is the power of atoms from the environment determining sensations, or the power of passions moving the will, or the power of a coercive power overriding individual passions with its fearful ability to punish.

As a thoroughgoing materialism, Hobbes' theory is also a thoroughgoing determinism. If all sensations depend on the motion of atoms impinging on sense organs, and thoughts and choices depend on sensations, and political life depends on thoughts and choices, then the structure of society is determined ultimately by the movement of atoms in the environment.

Moral Responsibility

This, it must be admitted, is a tidy package. The only problem with it is that it fails to offer any explanation of moral responsibility. Hobbes does say that in a commonwealth one is obliged to keep one's contracts, to do what the sovereign power says. But what can this mean? It cannot mean that there is a universal obligation to keep promises. This would be incompatible with Hobbes' foundation of self-interest, for if one is to keep contracts even when they do not bring pleasure and freedom from pain, then one is operating under a directive different from that of mere self-interest. Hobbes, of course, understands that such a view would be incompatible with his principles. Therefore, he says that it is in one's self-interest not to break contracts, for to do so is to place oneself in a state of nature outside the protection of the sovereign power.[16] The law about keeping covenants is not a universal obligation, only a counsel of prudential self-interest.

Thus, while Hobbes may appear to have presented an explanation of how self-interest gives rise to the great boon of stable political life, he has failed to give adequate justification for his conclusion. According to Hobbes' first principles of power and self-interest, there is no reason why one should not break the social contract or disobey the dictates of the sovereign. For if one succeeds in deceiving or (better yet) overthrowing the sovereign, then it cannot be said that one has done wrong. In the first place, one has acted to promote one's own self-interest In the second place, if one succeeds in overthrowing the sovereign, then (according to Hobbes' scheme) what one says is just *is* just, for the power has shifted and now is in one's own hands.

Even if one fails to gain power, the statement that the attempt should not have been made is meaningless. This brings us to the heart of Hobbes' failure to offer a plausible ethical code. Even the very first and most fundamental of the natural laws (which justifies breaking the third) is inconsistent with Hobbes' first principles. Here the voice of David Hume can be heard, reminding us that one cannot get obligation from facts. The fact that one *does*, very often or even always, act in such a way as to protect one's self-interest (especially one's life) in no way leads to the conclusion that one *ought* to act in such a way. Were Hobbes consistent, he would not have any moral laws at all. From the mechanics of matter in motion, no conclusions about how one ought to act—not even the very obvious and apparently noncontroversial one of acting in self-interest—can be derived. All Hobbes can consistently present are descriptions of certain patterns of behavior.

In the end, like emotivism, Hobbes' theory of morality, if consistently followed, leads to relativism. This relativism might not seem as complete as that which is implied by emotivism, since right and wrong depend not on what any individual feels, but on the will of the sovereign power. In a democracy, where the sovereign power is the people, "justice" as the will of the sovereign is based on a universality coextensive with majority opinion. Thus one might call Hobbes's theory a kind of cultural relativism based on political power. One implication of this theory is that, if justice is what the sovereign says it is (i.e., limited to the range of political sovereignty), then there cannot be justice among sovereign nations. According to the social contract theory, nations are, in fact, in a state of war where force and fraud are the cardinal virtues. If there were a universal coercive power, say a United Nations with the ability to make its decrees stick by use of force, then there could be a world-state and worldwide laws. But even here, the universality of moral principle would be based merely on power. If the power shifted, then the notion of right or wrong might shift Or if those continuing in power changed their minds about what is just and unjust, then the notions of justice and injustice would change.

Without absolute moral principles which do not originate in power, any moral universality cannot justify itself and logically reverts to subjective relativism. If justice is based ultimately on power, and power is finally passion traceable back to matter in motion, then the foundations of social contract morality are just as particular and variable as those of emotivism.

SOCIAL CONTRACT MORALITY SINCE HOBBES

Social contract views of morality since the time of Hobbes have tried to deal with the arbitrariness of "might-makes-right" morality. John Locke and the American founding fathers, Madison and Jefferson, mixed a good deal of the ancient and medieval notions of ethical responsibility and absolute moral norms into their social contract views. Most obviously, they made equality— as an ideal of justice and not simply a statement of fact—foundational to their theories. Thus one finds in Locke's account of the state of nature two obligations: to preserve oneself and to preserve the rest of humanity.

> The *state of nature* has a law of nature to govern it, which obliges every one: and reason, which is that law, teaches all mankind, who will but consult it, that being all *equal and independent*, no one ought to harm another in his life, health, liberty, or possessions: for men being all the workmanship of one omnipotent, and infinitely wise maker; all the servants of one sovereign master, sent into the world by his order, and about his business; they are his property, whose workmanship they are, made to last during his, not one another's pleasure: and being furnished with like faculties, sharing all in one community of nature, there cannot be supposed any such *subordination* among us, that may authorize us to destroy one another, as if we were made for one another's uses, as the inferior ranks of creatures are for our's.[17]

While it is a little unclear whether Locke considers this obligation to be known merely through natural reason, or whether it requires some kind of revelation that God is creator (Locke's empiricism would not allow him to prove the existence of an immaterial creator) is an open question. What is clear is that Locke wishes to extend obligation beyond mere self-preservation, as it is found in Hobbes, to the preservation of others. The "life, liberty, and pursuit of happiness" of the Declaration of Independence are obvious echoes of this text. And Madison makes it clear in *The Federalist Papers* that the justice foundational to his political theory is not derived from power. "Justice is the end of government. It is the end of civil society. It ever has been, and ever will be pursued, until it be obtained, or until liberty be lost in the pursuit."[18] Liberty is the servant of justice, not justice a way to maximize liberty.

Rawls' Theory of Morality

A particularly innovative version of the social contract theory is offered by the contemporary philosopher John Rawls. Rawls' theory seems to get away from the might-makes-right basis and achieve some kind of real universality.

For Rawls, morality is not based on the dictates of some external coercive power; rather, justice can be known by each individual regardless of who has the power. Such a theory seems to square with our notion that right and wrong are not merely relative to place and time but are, in some rudimentary way at least, the same for all human beings. Thus, Rawls' philosophy seems to offer plausible foundations for ethical responsibility.

Although Rawls takes as his point of departure the philosophy of John Locke more than that of Hobbes,[19] his system can be fairly compared to Hobbes', for Rawls' professed fundamental principles are identical to those of Hobbes. In the thought of Rawls as well as Hobbes, the passion of self-interest is the rock on which a system of justice is to be grounded, and the only legitimate role for reason is to know the facts and to make means-to-ends calculations. Rawls does, however, arrive at conclusions considerably different from those of Hobbes. Hence, it is necessary to discover just where and why they diverge.

Before showing differences, let us establish the agreement between the two philosophers in terms of their shared foundation of self-interest and their definition of reason. In sketching out his general theory, Rawls states that his principles of justice are derived from rational self-interest. "They [the principles of justice] are the principles that free and rational persons concerned to further their own interests would accept in an initial position of equality as defining the fundamental terms of their association."[20] The basics of the Hobbesian starting point are here: equality (which does not mean for either philosopher equality of intrinsic worth, but merely a factual equality in basic circumstances and abilities) and the concern of people to promote their own self-interest.

Rawls' use of the word "rational" might lead one to believe that he is presenting an idea of self-interest fundamentally different from the "state-of-war" scenario which Hobbes gives us. And indeed, Rawls' position is different, but its difference has nothing to do with his notion of rationality. He is emphatically *not* bringing back the traditional notion of practical reason which is able to tell us what is right or wrong based on an understanding of moral absolutes. Rather, Rawls sticks close to the definition of reason as presented by Hume (and shared by Hobbes). "The concept of rationality must be interpreted as far as possible in the narrow sense, standard in economic theory, of taking the most effective means to given ends. I shall modify this concept to some extent . . , but one must try to avoid introducing into it any controversial ethical elements."[21] In other words, rationality as understood by Rawls is merely a calculative technique for maximizing pleasure and minimizing pain—precisely the same as it is for Hume and Hobbes.

Original Position and the Veil of Ignorance

Let us follow Rawls as he moves from these principles common to Hobbes and him to his "principles of justice," considering how his major steps compare to Hobbes'. To begin with, Rawls presents a parallel to Hobbes' state of nature in his "original position of equality."[22] Unlike Hobbes, however, Rawls does not think of this state as having actually existed historically prior to the foundation of a commonwealth. And while people in Hobbes' state of nature actually find themselves driven by fear and self-interest to develop rules for justice based on a sovereign power, Rawls' original position is not an actual fact at any time, past or present, but is a "hypothetical situation" which one adopts by putting on "the veil of ignorance."[23]

This veil of ignorance plays the same role as Hobbes' three natural laws. As Hobbes' natural laws provide for the transition from the self-interest of "the state of nature" to "justice" as the will of the sovereign, so Rawls' veil of ignorance provides for the transition from "the original position" of rational self-interest to the "principles of justice." To put on the veil of ignorance means that one pretends not to know one's actual position in society, whether one is rich or poor, young or old, healthy or sick, black or white, male or female, etc. Self-interest, operating behind this veil of ignorance, leads to the formulation of Rawls' two principles of justice. Let us briefly discuss these principles and how they are the conclusions of applying self-interest behind the veil of ignorance.

Principles of Justice

The first principle of justice is the principle of equal liberty. "Each person is to have an equal right to the most extensive basic liberty compatible with a similar liberty for others."[24] What is the basis for such a principle? It is not and cannot be the idea that everyone *should be* treated equally well, for that would be presenting a "controversial ethical idea" from traditional morality and would be incompatible with Rawls' foundation in self-interest. Rather, the reason why everyone would agree to this principle is because, behind the veil of ignorance, no one knows what position he or she holds in society. Therefore, one chooses the principle of equal liberty *not* because one thinks that all people are as deserving as oneself, but because one does not want to be shortchanged. This first principle is prior to the second and must always be considered the ideal.

The second principle of justice concerns distribution of wealth and power, taking into account the fact that some inequalities in these areas are inevitable and can actually lead to improved conditions for all. For example, the profits of a large textile company are bound to be better if the company attracts a qualified executive by giving him more money and power than the average worker. While such practice does not honor the perfect law of equality, it is acceptable because everyone in the company benefits, even the lowest paid workers. Again, one need only apply the veil of ignorance to understand the general point. Since one does not know one's position in society, one would choose that economic system which would benefit more people, for then the odds would be in favor of oneself achieving a higher level of wealth and power.

However, this principle which allows for inequalities is secondary to the first and so must never be allowed to override the ideal of equal liberty. No one must be completely excluded from the chance of upward mobility. Thus, there is also a kind of affirmative action component to this second principle, that is, inequality working the other way, in favor of the less qualified. "Social and economic inequalities are to be arranged so that they are both (a) to the greatest benefit of the least advantaged and (b) attached to offices and positions open to all under conditions of fair equality of opportunity."[25] Again, it is not because one thinks that others should be benefited or allowed upward mobility that one chooses this second principle as basic to the idea of justice. It is just that, behind the veil of ignorance, one does not know whether or not oneself is the least advantaged or denied equal opportunity. Self-interest is the motivation for choosing this second principle as well as the first.

Motivation for Justice

Thus, while for Hobbes justice is what the sovereign power (which frees one from pain and fear) says it is, for Rawls it is what one would choose in the hypothetical state of not knowing where one stood in society. Now it is hard to disagree with the conclusions of Rawls. One would not want to say that it is unjust for there to be equal liberty, for the least advantaged to be helped, or for those who have been systematically excluded to be given access to better jobs. However, there is the problem of foundations. In the end, one can ask Rawls the same question one asked Hobbes: why should anyone follow these laws, or any laws? To this question Rawls could answer: because it is in one's self-interest if one is behind the veil of ignorance. But it is precisely one's status behind this veil of ignorance that is in question. Since Rawls admits that the veil of ignorance is a hypothetical state, why would one, out of self-interest, choose to put on this veil? One could, perhaps, answer that it would be advantageous, if one were poor and excluded, to agree to these rules. But what of those who actually do have all the advantages of money and power and prestige and health and nondiscrimination? It certainly does not seem to be to their advantage to put on the veil. Perhaps, one might argue, their fortunes could fail, and they could end up at the bottom needing help. This, of course, is possible, but unlikely when one looks at how money makes money and how the very rich go bankrupt without any appreciable change in their living habits.

Perhaps one senses that this discussion is off track, that the point is not whether or not people *would* put on this veil of ignorance but that they *should*. But, alas, there is no way to come to this conclusion from the principles which Rawls supplies. Like Hume and Hobbes, Rawls is operating in the world of scientific method, this time in the form of economic theory applied to the formation of society. In other words, Rawls only allows reason to establish the facts and determine means to ends. And, as Hume reminds us, there is no getting obligation from facts alone. Whether or not it would be in one's self-interest to put on the veil of ignorance, it could never (given the parameters of Rawls' argument) be the case that one should enter it.

If it cannot be the case that one should enter the veil of ignorance (for obligation belongs to the realm of practical reason which Rawls, along with Hume and Hobbes, has rejected), then there must be some mechanism which explains the fact that some of us (Rawls, for example) are willing to enter such a hypothetical state. And indeed, there is such a feature in Rawls' thought. When discussing the original position, Rawls mentions a feature of our emotional nature that might move one to put on the veil. He assumes that human beings are "capable . . . of a sense of justice."[26] This must be taken precisely here. Rawls is speaking of a *sense* of justice, not a knowledge of justice.[27] Knowledge of justice, such as it can be attained, follows from the decision to apply self-interest behind the veil of ignorance. The "rational" in rational self-interest refers merely to the calculation of how best to get what one wants. The willingness to apply this rationality behind the veil of ignorance is not itself a function of one's being rational; therefore, it must be explained by some other feature of our nature. Perhaps human beings are so constituted that they have a sense, or passion, or feeling of justice that makes them willing to put aside their immediate self-interest to enter this hypothetical state in which they will be able to understand the principles of justice. What else is this but Hume's benevolent impulse in a new guise? It is a natural sentiment of kindness toward mankind that makes one willing to put aside the knowledge of one's advantages in order to decide on rules of justice that are fair for all.

The fundamental problem here is that this admission of a natural benevolence in the human constitution contradicts Rawls' first principle, which holds that human beings are motivated solely by rational self-interest. Selfishness seemed the perfect rock upon which to found morality, for it is an obvious feature of our experience and one which could not be suspected as being an importation of some "controversial ethical claim." Unfortunately, the introduction of benevolence as an additional first principle turns this rock to mud. No longer does self-interest stand alone as the origin of actions; now there is also benevolence. As passions, the two are opposites. A system of morality which claims them both as foundational has a contradiction for a foundation, and a contradiction is nothing. If one says that the first principle of morality is self-interest *and* non-self-interest (that is, benevolence), then one has said nothing at all; the affirmation and negation of the very same thing cancel each other out. Of course, one could simply allow that there are two first principles of morality, but then one needs some kind of way to explain the proper balance between them. It cannot be that we understand that we *should* favor benevolence and therefore that we *should* be willing to enter the veil of ignorance. Such a conclusion would be based on a supposedly illusory practical reason which is incompatible with a properly scientific approach to things. Hence, it must be that people *will* follow benevolence and that they *will* enter the veil of ignorance. But clearly this is not so. Rawls' explanation furnishes neither a moral directive nor an adequate account of the facts.

CONCLUSIONS

In the end, the social contract theory fails to erect a consistent and coherent social ethics on the foundation of self-interest. Hobbes' theory fails because there is no way to show that self-interest entails a willingness to compromise with others. While it might, it is not necessary that it do so. Nor is there in self-interest any reason why one *should* be concerned for others, nor even concerned to protect one's own life. Rawls' attempt to provide a version of social contract ethics which is not based on the arbitrary whims of power is no more successful. To make it work, he has to bring in something like Hume's benevolence and then is stuck with two irreconcilable principles. Although his conclusions, his "principles of justice," are acceptable at least as minimum moral guides, he provides no reason why we should accept these conclusions; his first principles of self-interest and benevolence contradict each other. If we wish to accept his conclusions, we must find other principles to justify them.

While this failure may seem surprising and even shocking to us since Rawls' understanding of justice as equal liberty, helping the least advantaged, and equal opportunity are so close to our cherished democratic ideals, it is really the inevitable result of any theory of morality that chooses the passions for its foundations. Since the passions are in themselves nonrational, the morality built on such foundations will also be, at bottom, nonrational.

If, following the social contract theory, one insists on basing morality on the passion of self-interest, then one cannot conclude with real universal directives, for universality has its origins in reason. In fact, any theory based on passion faces the same problem. One can speculate about whether a passion is universal or not, but the verification will always be particular and individual. Only the individual experiencing an emotion knows what the emotion is. As physical events, emotions involve particular matter in motion. As Westermarck pointed out, if ethics is based on emotions, then there is nothing which could make it universal since even the individual person experiences different emotions in response to the same thing at different times.

Even if it were possible to verify a universal passion, whether benevolence or self-interest, one would not be a step closer to justifying moral responsibility. For one thing, the fact of a passion does not logically imply any obligation to consistently follow that passion. For another, if passion rules, then we are not free to respond to any obligation anyway.

Morality, therefore, must have its foundations in reason, or it must cease claiming any universal applicability; that is, it must cease to make any recommendations about what ought or ought not to be done, for the word "ought" implies some notion of universal law and obligation. No such obligation can be derived from the simple facts of our emotional life in its response to pleasure and pain.

4

All's Well That Ends Well: Utilitarianism

We have seen how emotivism and egoism both fail to provide adequate foundations for moral responsibility. Whether one's passion is benevolent like Hume's or selfish like Hobbes' does not matter; for if morality is based on passion, then its principle is subjective and particular and hence unable to provide any objective and universal criterion for making moral decisions. Jeremy Bentham, the father of modern utilitarian theory (recall that Epicurus was something of a utilitarian), recognized this problem and thought that it could be rectified. To his mind, the trouble with Hobbes and Hume was that they did not stick closely enough to the scientific method. Their mistake was getting sidetracked into an analysis of the murky realm of emotion. When Bentham speaks of "moral science,"[1] he means exactly what he says. Not only does science set the parameters for the kinds of answers which will be acceptable (ones which assume the purely material nature of the human being), but the very method used in moral decision making must be the scientific method. This means that only the most objective evidence will be allowed. According to Bentham, ethics cannot be a matter of emotions such as "sympathy and antipathy"[2] (roughly Hume's and Hobbes' respective principles), for these are not objective. Emotions are private and internal and thus not verifiable. What we need are public facts which can be treated in terms of quantity alone so that our conclusions will be acceptable under the strictest demands of scientific rigor.

PLEASURE, PAIN, AND MORALITY

Where are these facts to be found? Bentham insists that they are not to be found in any kind of motive, but in the consequences of actions. Following strict scientific method, our hypotheses about the rightness or wrongness of an action are to be verified by the action's consequences. Along with Hume and Hobbes, Bentham denies that practical reason could be a direct motive of the will, and for the same reasons: since the objects of practical reason (good and evil, justice and injustice, etc.) are not verifiable by sense experience, they are illusory. However, Bentham thinks that the same kind of argument can be made against the emotions as motives; they, too, fail to measure up to strict scientific demands for verification. No more can benevolence (sympathy) and egoism (antipathy) be directly measured than good and evil, or justice and injustice. Besides, as motives, they precede the moral act and therefore are not, properly speaking, part of the moral act at all. If one wishes to examine morality objectively, one cannot afford to get lost in the cloudy region of subjective feeling. One needs clear facts to measure and tabulate. These facts are the consequences of actions in terms of pleasure and pain taken in their most physical (and hence most clearly measurable) form.

Principle of Utility

Thus, the project of utilitarianism is to measure and tabulate the pleasures and pains any action is likely to cause and to recommend those actions which will bring pleasurable results and disapprove of those which will bring painful results. So long as an action will bring about good consequences, that action may be done (and presumably ought to be done) regardless of motives, whether these be intentions or feelings. Bentham thinks that this principle is applicable not only to the tabulation and promotion of the individual's happiness, but also of the community's. As a disinterested gatherer of pure scientific fact, one is not more interested in the individual's happiness (even one's own) than in the happiness of the community.

> By the principle of utility is meant that principle which approves or disapproves of every action whatsoever, according to the tendency which it appears to have to augment or diminish the happiness of the party whose interest is in question; or what is the same thing in other words, to promote or to oppose that happiness. I say of every action whatsoever; and therefore not only of every action of a private individual, but of every measure of government.[3]

That some concern for consequences is an element in moral decision making seems noncontroversial, and there is much to recommend Bentham's turn from feelings to consequences. For one thing, the shift from subjective to objective criteria holds out the promise of moral principles applicable to all, of the universality implied in any notion of obligation or responsibility. For another, the disinterested promotion of the happiness of all people certainly sounds like a responsible and commendable activity. In fact, such an obligation to act for the common good has always been a central precept of traditional morality. Even the egoist would recommend taking into consideration the results of one's actions; "look before you leap," as the saying goes. What is controversial is whether consequences are the *only* legitimate elements in moral decision-making, and also whether the obligation to enhance the common good is compatible with Bentham's insistence on scientific method.

Scientific Method

As a first step in our analysis, it is important to underline the point that by happiness Bentham means pleasure and freedom from pain, and he means these in their most basic physical sense. In order to be true to his scientific method, he has to insist on this. Were he to deviate into notions of pleasure and pain understood as purely emotional or mental states, he would be entering the illusory world of nonexistent entities. If the word "good" has any meaning, it means pleasure; if the word "evil" has any meaning, it means pain.

In keeping with his insistence that morality be evaluated scientifically, Bentham's procedure for measuring and tabulating pleasures and pains is purely quantitative. Without going into a detailed analysis, let me mention the elements of this hedonistic calculus and make some general remarks about them. Although his system differs from Hobbes' and Hume's in the ways we have mentioned, there are also some striking resemblances to the ideas of his predecessors. On the importance for every legislator to know how to tabulate pleasures and pains, Bentham writes: "It behooves him therefore to understand their force, which is again, in other words, their value."[4] Here is Hobbes' might-makes-right theory applied on the microlevel of particular pleasures or pains. What makes a pleasure or pain valuable is its force, its quantifiable aspects.

As for the calculus itself, there are seven elements, placed in three categories.[5] The first four elements characterize any particular pleasurable or painful consequence of an act. They are its intensity, duration, certainty or uncertainty, and propinquity or remoteness. The next two elements refer to tendencies of a particular pleasurable or painful consequence to be followed by others like or unlike it. These are fecundity and purity, the first referring to the tendency of the consequence to be followed by pleasures or pains of the same kind, the second referring to the tendency of it not to be followed by the opposite kinds. In making these two general divisions, Bentham is following Hume's distinction of the two secondary roles of reason: reason can establish the facts, and it can understand cause and effects so as to be able to predict consequences. The four elements in the first division tabulate the facts about any particular pleasure or pain, using strictly quantitative terms.

The two elements in the second division deal with questions of probability, again an aspect of mathematics but different from the straightforward weighing and measuring of the first division. The last element of the hedonistic calculus is its own category. This is "extent" and refers to the number of people who are affected by any action.

To know whether an act is to be approved or disapproved, one need only go through the seven steps of the calculus. All this can be done in very scientific, quantitative fashion.

> Sum up all the values of all the *pleasures* on the one side, and those of all the pains on the other. The balance, if it be on the side of pleasure, will give the *good* tendency of the act upon the whole, with respect to the interests of that *individual* person: if on the side of pain, the *bad* tendency of it upon the whole. . . . *Sum up* the numbers expressive of the degrees of *good* tendency, which the act has, with respect to each individual, in regard to whom the tendency of it is *good* upon the whole: do this again with respect to each individual, in regard to whom the tendency of it is *bad* upon the whole. Take the *balance*; which if on the side of *pleasure*, will give the general *good tendency* of the act, with respect to the total number or community of individuals concerned; if on the side of pain, the general *evil tendency* with respect to the same community.[6]

The conclusion, implied but not stated, is that, if the final balance is more pleasure than pain, then the act should be done; but if the final balance is more pain than pleasure, then the act should not be done. I have quoted this passage at length to impress upon the reader the depth of Bentham's insistence on ethics as a quantitative analysis of physical pleasure and pain. The whole calculus is a matter of sums and balances—hard data.

While some concern for consequences seems essential to moral decision making, the logistics of tabulating all the pleasures and pains in their many quantitative dimensions and doing this for all the people who might be affected by the act being considered are daunting. One might very well ask how it is possible to go through such a procedure. Who has the time or resources? How would one know when consideration of all relevant pains, pleasures, and people has been made? And are not consequences subject to differing interpretations, depending on what the interpreter wishes to emphasize? All these difficulties seem to make the utilitarian project of moral evaluation extremely cumbersome and imprecise. While Bentham might very well agree that these are difficulties, he would answer that there is no other choice. Motives of the rational will and the emotions must be rejected as immeasurable and hence unscientific. All we have left is consequences. We must simply do our best to perform the calculus and follow its directives.

In addition to such problems of logistics, two general questions about Bentham's scheme readily arise. First of all, is morality really able to be explained in purely quantitative terms? It seems difficult to believe that the moral character of actions can differ only in quantitative ways and that intentions are irrelevant in the evaluation of an act. Secondly, why is it that one should consider other people's pleasure and pain in the calculus? Since pleasure and pain are always particular to individual experience (one cannot experience another's pleasure or pain in any direct sense), how is it that one is moved to take into account other people's pleasure and pain?

Quantitative Morality

In answer to the first question, Bentham would say that he is constrained by a faithful reading of the exigencies of scientific method to adhere to strictly quantitative modes of interpretation. To enter into a consideration of motives, rational or emotional, would be to depart from the requirement that all hypotheses be verifiable by sense experience.

Yet it seems absurd to say that intentions do not matter at all in judging an action to be good or bad. Consider a couple of examples. John plans to kill Peter, who is a rival for the affections of the woman John loves. Peter is rather a cad and a habitual drunkard. One day John lies in wait and shoots Peter as he walks in the local woods. Peter is not killed but only critically wounded. Nearly dying, he experiences a conversion of sorts, waking up to the joys of living and deciding to share this joy with other people by helping them. In addition, he falls in love with his nurse; they marry; they raise two wonderful children. Peter remains a faithful husband, a loving father, and becomes a model citizen dedicated to the common good. Judging by the consequences alone, John's act is good. But does it make any sense to say that the intended murder is good? The act for which John is responsible (the intended murder) does not become the least bit better because its consequences are good.

Or consider an example of an action with bad results. Ben sees a woman standing by the side of a stalled car on a cold and rainy night. He stops to help and is able to get her car running. Ten minutes later the woman is broadsided by some teenagers running a red light, suffers intense pain, and dies, leaving three small children without a mother. Looking merely at the consequences of the act, one would have to say that the net balance of pleasure and pain was on the side of pain, thus making the act bad. Had Ben not stopped, the woman would not have been killed at that intersection. But does it make any sense to ignore Ben's intentions and look only at the consequences of his act? It seems absurd to say that the bad consequences made his act morally bad.[7]

Concern for Others

Bentham's response to the second question (why consider other people in one's calculus?) would also be based on the same strict adherence to the scientific method. Hume would have said that one cares for other people because of a benevolent impulse, a natural love for humanity. Hobbes, on the other hand, would have said that one cares for other people because one has a natural passion directed toward self-interest and that caring for others is in one's long-term best interests. But these two routes are not open to Bentham, for he rejects any explanation in terms of motives of the will since they cannot be measured scientifically. Bentham's position is that the scientific facts alone are enough to indicate that one should care for others. It is true indeed that sometimes one's contemplated action will clearly cause more pain to others than pleasure to oneself. Take, as an example, the action of killing a classroom full of second graders. By using the hedonistic calculus and applying it to all parties in questions—parents and families of the students as well as the students themselves on the one side and the killer on the other, it is quite clear that the balance of such an action would be painful. Since, as a scientist, one has a purely disinterested concern to know the facts, every applicable piece of data—that is, every pleasure or pain—is to be tabulated and a balance struck. When this is done for our example, pain will outweigh pleasure, and hence, according to Bentham, the action should be disapproved. This disinterested attention to the facts is, of course, one of the necessary elements of good scientific research and, as such, is to be commended.

But here is the rub: How can a disinterested tabulation of facts lead to the very interested commitment to doing what is "better," that is, what brings about the greatest possible pleasure and freedom from pain? How is it that facts alone (and facts alone are what the hedonistic calculus claims to be considering) can lead to the conclusion that this action should or should not be approved? Again, Hume's insight into the impossibility of getting obligation from facts reveals the ultimate bankruptcy of any ethical theory which claims to take only physical facts into consideration. A tabulation of facts cannot provide any reason why one should care about promoting pleasure and diminishing pain. If one insists on considering only quantitative pleasure and pain in one's analysis, then one must be content to report on what *is* the case without in any way attempting to judge what *ought* to be the case.

UTILITARIANISM OF J. S. MILL

It so happens that a direct disciple of Bentham, J. S. Mill, took up these very two issues, namely, whether a purely quantitative approach is sufficient and how or why the calculus should extend beyond the self to others. But, before looking at how Mill dealt with them, it is important to establish him as a utilitarian in the tradition of Bentham. Mill does claim to accept the very same principles as his master.

> The creed which accepts as the foundation of morals "utility" or the "greatest happiness principle" holds that actions are right in proportion as they tend to promote happiness; wrong as they tend to produce the reverse of happiness. By happiness is intended pleasure and the absence of pain; by unhappiness, pain and the privation of pleasure. To give a clear view of the moral standard set up by the theory, much more requires to be said; in particular, what things it includes in the ideas of pain and pleasure, and to what extent this is left an open question. But these supplementary explanations do not affect the theory of life on which this theory of morality is grounded—namely, that pleasure and freedom from pain are the only things desirable as ends.[8]

Consequences in terms of pleasure and pain are the *only* criteria to be considered. In this Mill shows himself to be a direct disciple of Bentham. It is in the "much more requires to be said" that Mill departs from his master's teaching. It is in how Mill answers the two difficulties raised by Bentham's analysis that he differs from his master.

Quality of Pleasure and Pain

As for limiting utilitarian reasoning to merely the quantitative aspects of pleasure and pain, Mill says there is no reason for such a restriction. In moral decision-making, the quality of pleasure is equal in importance to the quantitative aspects, and perhaps even more important. There are different kinds of pleasure as well as different amounts, intensities, durations, etc. Here Mill follows in the footsteps of the ancient philosophers Epicurus and Lucretius, who said that pleasures of the mind are to preferred to pleasures of the flesh. The Epicurean life has as its ultimate goal tranquillity, and the pleasures of the mind are more apt to lead to such a state than the more intense sensual pleasures. As Mill himself notes, "There is no known Epicurean theory of life which does not assign to the pleasures of the intellect, of the feelings and imagination, and of the moral sentiments a much higher value than to those of mere sensation."[9] And this higher value is not just in terms of the hedonistic calculus—less fleeting, more certain, etc.; the higher pleasures are better in kind. Thus, Mill has in mind a hierarchy of pleasures, with sensual pleasure at the bottom and the pleasures of the mind at the top. The hierarchy might look something like this:

moral pleasure	(best)
intellectual pleasure	
imaginative pleasure	
sensual pleasure	(least good)

According to Mill, although sensual pleasure might rate very high in terms of quantity, intensity, certainty, etc., a very small amount of less intense moral pleasure might be more valuable. Bentham, of course, would cry out that bringing qualitative terms into utilitarianism is a violation of its scientific foundations. But most people are rather inclined to agree with Mill that there is more to happiness than just quantitative aspects of pleasure, and that wisdom and virtue, although perhaps quantitatively less significant in our lives than sense pleasures, are often treasured above sense pleasures. It may even appear that Mill is taking into account that element of intention which we noted as essential to the moral character of an act.

The problem with this theory of differing qualities of pleasure is that it is incompatible with Mill's own avowed allegiance to the principles of utilitarianism. While holding that pleasure and freedom from pain are the only things valued as ends, it is impossible for Mill to justify his hierarchy. If one wants to say that one kind of pleasure is intrinsically better than another, then one must be able to point to some criterion by which one makes the judgment. But if one is a utilitarian, then the only thing "better" can mean is "more pleasurable." Thus, the criterion can only be pleasure. But to say that moral pleasure is more pleasurable than sense pleasure is no help at all, for it is unclear what kind of pleasure is being taken as the standard in the phrase "more pleasurable." Either one takes a common denominator and is back with a merely quantitative analysis of pleasure or one is adrift in a sea of endlessly vague distinctions without differences.

Mill tries to answer this difficulty by offering another, supposedly more objective, criterion for discernment. He says that among pleasures, that one is best which most of the people who have experienced all the various kinds say is best. However, this is a very weak criterion for two reasons. First of all, it reverts to a quantitative methodology in the end: the majority of those who have experienced both kinds of pleasure know best. It is no advance on Bentham's theory on this score. Secondly, and more generally, the criterion fails to provide each individual with the principles by which to act in a morally correct way. How is the person who has not experienced the higher pleasures going to be able to judge that they are better? Such a person obviously cannot so judge, yet must make decisions about personal actions. Without full knowledge of the hierarchy, he or she is, through no personal fault, bound to be mistaken and hence immoral.

Thus, the idea of a qualitative hierarchy of pleasures is incompatible with the first principles of utilitarianism as laid down by Bentham. Mill's attempt to put a new twist (actually, an old Epicurean twist) on Bentham's hedonistic calculus fails.

Concern for Others

As for the second question, which asks why one should be concerned with other people's pleasure and pain, Mill in one place gives an answer very much like Bentham's, but elsewhere and more prominently diverges from his master's thought. First consider his answer which is in line with Bentham's position.

> No reason can be given why the general happiness is desirable, except that each person, so far as he believes it to be attainable, desires his own happiness. This, however, being a fact, we have not only all the proof which the case admits of, but all which it is possible to require, that happiness is a good, that each person's happiness is a good to that person, and the general happiness, therefore, a good to the aggregate of persons.[10]

Mill claims that it is just a fact that the general happiness, as a quantitative sum of particular individual states of happiness, is greater than any particular individual's happiness. But there is a problem with translating this true statement of fact into moral obligation. For in the first place, while the general happiness may be a good to the aggregate of persons, this fact does not imply that it is a good for any one individual; and in the second, from the fact that there is more possible happiness in the many than in the individual, there is no logical implication that the individual ought to be concerned to promote the happiness of the many. As to the first point, Bentham himself denies any real being to the community. "The community is a fictitious *body*, composed of the individual persons who are considered as constituting as it were its *members*. The interest of the community then is, what?—the sum of the interests of the several members who compose it."[11] There is no real entity "the community" for which the general happiness is a concern. There are only individuals concerned with maximizing pleasure and minimizing pain; and the only pleasure and pain which the individual can directly and scientifically verify is his or her own. As to the second point, which is even more devastating than the first, there is the Humean insight that whatever the facts may show, no obligation follows from them. The fact that more happiness will follow from this action than from its alternative in no way implies that one ought to choose the former.

Since the purely scientific "facing the facts" cannot move the will to choose one way or another, it seems that the ideal scientific analysis of consequences must slide either into a Hobbesian self-interest or into Humean benevolence. Some utilitarians have explained the transition from concern for self to concern for others on Hobbesian grounds, or at least have tried to find a way to reconcile self-interest and concern for others. For example, Henry Sidgwick wrote about "the vital need that our Practical Reason feels of proving or postulating this connexion of Virtue and self-interest, if it is to be made consistent with itself." [12] Mill, however, does not try to reconcile the two opposing feelings but follows Hume. Human beings are endowed with a natural inclination to be kind to each other. "As between his own happiness and that of others, utilitarianism requires him to be as strictly impartial as a disinterested and benevolent spectator." [13] Bentham, of course, would be horrified at either move, for he had expressly rejected "sympathy and antipathy" as being adverse to the principle of utility. All motives are immeasurable, whether they be of reason or emotion. Therefore, all motives are illusory except as interpreted in light of the consequences of actions. These consequences are facts; the subjective feelings of the individual (as unable to be publicly verified) are inadmissible as evidence. Here again Mill fails to be consistent with his principles. If consequences alone are to be the criteria for moral judgments, then he has no business introducing motives which, as moving the will to action, exist prior to the consequences.

Mill's theory about why we are kind to others raises the same questions as Hume's. Is it, in fact, true that we have a natural benevolent feeling? If so, what are the chances of it overcoming the raging passions of self-interest? The answer to the first question is that it is debatable, as there is a good deal of evidence which counts against it. To the second question, it would seem highly improbable that the quiet, peaceful passion of benevolence would overcome the wild and warlike passions of self-interest. Beyond these questions, there is the more foundational objection that there is simply no answer available to the adherent to scientific method as to why one should follow the benevolent impulse, nor why one would be wrong not to follow it. In short, no universal element of obligation follows from Hume's (and now Mill's) principle of natural benevolence.

RULE UTILITARIANISM

The promises for universality in moral guidance which Bentham thought he had found in scientific objectivity and Mill in a benevolent feeling both fail to deliver. There is, however, another strain of utilitarianism which has appeared on the contemporary scene, which tries to provide universality in a different way. This is called rule utilitarianism (to be distinguished from the act utilitarianism of Bentham and Mill) and its chief exponent is Richard Brandt.[14]

Rule utilitarianism tries to provide the universality required for ethical responsibility by introducing a rule of behavior between the individual and the consequences of his or her act. Instead of the individual calculating the consequences of pleasure and pain for any particular act in order to determine whether that act should or should not be done, the individual looks to a rule which is established to provide the best general consequences. The idea is that the rule removes some of the arbitrariness of the decision-making process. For example, on the act utilitarian model, it would be possible to argue that, even though one has agreed to pay $100 to get one's car fixed, one need not pay up when the work is done since the $100 could be better spent relieving starvation in Africa. However, on the rule utilitarian model, one would focus on the general consequences of everyone breaking promises. Since pandemonium would result, and this certainly is not a good general consequence, one would decide to keep one's promise rather than send the $100 to Africa.[15]

Foundation of the Theory

This sounds like a sensible correction of the utilitarian theory since it firmly focuses the utilitarian concern on the happiness of the community. But does it have the foundations to support such a refocusing? Again, the question is why one should be concerned with the good of the community. What is it about the fact that the consideration of the common happiness involves more net quantity of pleasure and pain than the consideration of any individual's happiness that justifies the universal requirement that one ought to care more for the community than for oneself? So long as reason is restricted to its theoretical role of establishing the facts and judging probabilities of a particular means leading to a particular end or of an effect following from a cause, there is no way to generate obligation. And, in fact, Brandt rejects practical reason with its focus on intentions just as vociferously as Bentham. It does not matter whether the agent thinks the act is right or wrong. One cannot be excused for intending a good act that went bad or blamed for intending an evil action that turned out good. Morality is still to be just a matter of the facts.

> It [rule-utilitarianism] makes rightness and wrongness a matter of the facts, and totally independent of what the agent thinks is right, or of what the agent thinks about the facts, or of the evidence the agent may have, or of what is probably the case on the basis of this evidence.[16]

Brandt is still seeking the ideal conformity to scientific method. Only publicly verifiable consequences are to be taken into account. Facts alone tell us what we should do. But facts alone can never imply obligation.

Hence Brandt's form of utilitarianism, although apparently promising a foundation for universal responsibility by introducing the notion of rules, fails to provide any basis for moral obligation at all. The only morally significant difference between this system and that of Bentham is that it seems to distance morality further from the individual agent, for now one's job is not to consider the consequences oneself, but merely to conform to some rules handed down on authority. The autonomy of the individual moral agent is thus completely swept away, to be replaced by some scientifically formulated calculus of the best general consequences—a formulation which, stemming as it does from facts alone, can never tell the individual why he or she ought to follow the rules.

Majority Opinion

Sensitive to some of these criticisms, Brandt revised his theory in *A Theory of the Good and the Right.* While still supporting a form of rule utilitarianism, the formulation is changed. Recognizing the objection that any set of rules might indeed interfere with a person choosing what is best for all in a particular situation, Brandt moves to a more flexible structure, one that would take into account different societies and different groups within those societies. The influence of Rawls is evident here, and Brandt freely admits this influence in the Preface. While critical of many of Rawls' points (particularly the influence of benevolence in making the "veil of ignorance" work),[17] he adopts Rawls' point about the rules of ethics being based on what fully rational people would support. Since he does not count on the fact that people are benevolent, he does not claim that all people would agree to these rules. Rather, the rules would be based on the opinion of the majority of rational persons.

> My defence, in brief, is this: a set of moral motivations is justified if it is what it would be if facts and logic were brought to bear on its 'choice' to a maximal extent—that is, if fully rational persons would tend to support it in preference to any other system and to none. I have argued that when we have identified such a system of motivations, we have found one which is 'justified' for us in the only sense in which a moral system can be justified at the present time. Further, I have proposed (Chapter 10) that we define 'is morally obligatory' as 'would be called for by the moral system which is justified, and which fully rational persons would most tend to support.'[18]

The code is to be limited to the society at the present time (a principle of social contract ethics), and is to motivate members of the society to act in ways most acceptable to fully rational persons (even if the members themselves do not understand why they should be so motivated).

Thus, while certainly more subtle than his earlier formulations of rule utilitarianism, this treatment has the same problems and tries to meet them by borrowing principles outside the facts of consequences alone. Indeed, Brandt calls his theory a "pluralistic welfare-maximizing moral system."[19] In it he makes use of principles from egoism, act utilitarianism, and utilitarian generalization. And, as with any theory which tries to combine principles, it is not clear which principle should be invoked at which time. The answer that it depends on the majority opinion of rational persons is a consensus view ultimately more appropriate to social contract theory than to utilitarianism.

SCIENTIFIC APPROACH

So it is that Bentham remains the most consistent utilitarian. Once one chooses to begin with sensible facts alone and claim that only consequences of pleasure and pain are the kinds of facts that can be admitted to an objective science of morality, one's system, if consistent and coherent, must look something like Bentham's. Attempts to change it without changing the first principles result in systems less coherent and no better able to provide a foundation for moral obligation.

The great advantage which Bentham claims utilitarianism has over ethical systems based on emotions (Hume and Hobbes) is that it is more scientific. Dismissing emotions as subjective and nonverifiable, Bentham turns to the supposedly more objective realm of consequences. The tabulation of hard facts concerning projected pleasure and pain is to substitute for psychological hypotheses which cannot be verified.

A question may be raised at this point: Does Bentham succeed in providing a more scientific foundation for ethics? While one might agree that an analysis of physical pleasure and pain is more concrete than speculations about emotional states, the problem with utilitarianism as a moral theory, from a scientific point of view, is that it has no facts upon which to work.[20] Since the facts in question are future and therefore hypothetical, they do not exist; they cannot, in fact, be verified prior to the action being done. Yet logically, the hedonistic calculus is to precede the action, for it is to tell one whether or not the action should be done. The scientific ideal of a disinterested tabulation of facts cannot be performed for the simple reason that there are no facts to be tabulated. While one might, indeed, want to consider consequences in one's moral decision making, one cannot do so and remain within the strict bounds of scientific method with its requirement of verification. Thus, Bentham and his disciples do not really achieve a more scientifically objective system of ethical analysis. In fact, one might argue that theirs is less scientifically objective, for at least the psychological analyses of Hume and Hobbes are based on facts that are concurrent with or precede an action and therefore could be said to be the cause or explanation of that action.

Consequences of Actions

Of course, one could answer that Bentham's idea is that the hypothesis (hedonistic calculus in projection) is to be verified by a hedonistic calculus of the consequences, and only then would one have scientific knowledge about whether or not the act should be (more precisely, should have been) done. The obvious problem here is that such a scientific account of action is absolutely worthless for the moral agent trying to decide what should be done, for the agent cannot know whether or not the action should be done until after it has been done. Either motives do matter, and the thinking process and reasons for choice prior to the action are important; or one has a theory of decision making which is simply incoherent. Since utilitarians firmly reject the reality of rational motives, they are stuck with the latter explanation, which, as incoherent, is no explanation at all.

Perhaps Bentham was aware of this slippage between his profession of strict adherence to scientific method and the fact that his "facts" were future and hypothetical and therefore not real. In any case, he does have something to say about the causal explanation for our actions which is in line with his two predecessors Hume and Hobbes. The bottom line is that utilitarianism, like emotivism and egoism, is a determinism. Bentham freely admits this (well, perhaps not really freely) and even boasts of it.

Determinism

Because they cannot be weighed and measured, motives and intentions are ruled out of utilitarian ethics. But if motives and intentions are ruled out, then so are the reasons and purposes we have for acting. The decision-making process is reduced to the mechanics of weighing and measuring consequences of pleasure and pain, which are the true springs of action. But if one denies that reason is the origin of the decision-making process, claiming the origin to be in the realm of pleasure and pain, then one reduces moral decision-making to a kind of determinism. Biological drives and mere stimulus/response reactions to the environment move us to act, not reason and conscience. Granted, human reason is retained insofar as it can tabulate like a computer, but its role is a secondary one, still a tool of the passions. The notion of human reason as able to decide, once the facts are in, which course of action is better and therefore should be taken has been rejected in the best Humean/Hobbesian tradition. Decisions of value fall to one's reactions to pleasure and pain, and free choice is an illusion. We are ultimately at the beck and call of those things which cause us pleasure and pain. Let me quote the opening lines of Bentham's *An Introduction to the Principles of Morals and Legislation.*

> Nature has placed mankind under the governance of two sovereign masters, *pain* and *pleasure*. It is for them alone to point out what we ought to do, as well as to determine what we shall do. On the one hand the standard of right and wrong, on the other the chain of causes and effects, are fastened to their throne. They govern us in all we do, in all we say, in all we think; every effort we can make to throw off our subjection, will serve but to demonstrate and confirm it. In words a man may pretend to abjure their empire: but in reality he will remain subject to it all the while. The *principle of utility* recognizes this subjection, and assumes it for the foundation of that system, the object of which is to tear the fabric of felicity by the hands of reason and law. Systems which attempt to question it, deal in sounds instead of sense, in caprice instead of reason, in darkness instead of light.[21]

FOUNDATION FOR MORAL JUDGMENT

As we come to the end of our discussion of utilitarianism, it might be good to ask the same question we asked of emotivism and egoism: does it provide a solid, defensible foundation for moral judgment? Has utilitarianism succeeded in answering the relativist where emotivism and egoism failed? With all the claims at being public and objective and scientific, one would expect that utilitarian theory has at hand the means for rational justification of moral action. However, it is not so. Utilitarianism, like emotivism and egoism, fails in the end to provide a coherent justification of moral obligation.

The failure appears in two ways. In the first place, it is clear that for any theory which makes the sum of consequences its standard, there are no particular choices or acts which are right or wrong in themselves. So long as all turns out well in the end, the means taken to achieve that end are acceptable, whatever they be. Thus, killing innocent people is permissible if it leads to saving more lives in the end; lying is acceptable if it ultimately benefits more people than the truth; dishonesty is to be welcomed if it brings more pleasure than pain to more people. No act (or rule if one follows Brandt) can be judged right or wrong in itself, only in its relation to some idea of an overall net good.

In the second place, Bentham's theory is relativism insofar as it is an explicit determinism: pleasure and pain are our absolute masters (recall Hume's "reason is and ought to be the slave of the passions"). Consequently, we are not free. If we are not free, then we are not free to decide what we shall do. If we do not really decide what we shall do, then our actions are completely relative to our environment—to the experiences of pleasure and pain which we receive from the world. This is complete and utter relativism. Far from classical utilitarianism being the great light cast on moral science, it is unable to justify any obligation at all.[22]

CONCLUSIONS ABOUT PLEASURE / PAIN THEORIES

The last passage quoted from Bentham is a suitable one with which to close this first half of the book. It points out the common ending of all theories of morality which take pleasure and pain as their first principles. Would they be true to their principles, they all must end in determinism and the obliteration of all moral responsibility. Let us recall the common features that inevitably bring them all to this conclusion. As a primary assumption, they all adhere to the ideal of the scientific method, with its limitation of the legitimate use of reason to the theoretical functions of dealing with relations of ideas and matters of fact. Only what can be verified by the senses can be counted as real. In other words, emotivism, social contract theory, and utilitarianism all share a materialist foundation. Because of this, they are forced to choose pleasure and pain for the matter of their study of morality. But if pleasure and pain are the only principles, then one is stuck with a relativism born of determinism.

In the end, if pleasure and pain are our sovereign masters, then we have no choice in our activities. And if we have no choice in our activities, it is obviously absurd to suggest that we *ought to* act in such and such a way, or *ought to* refrain from doing such and such.

Moral Responsibility

Even if these theories based on pleasure and pain recommend (inconsistently) certain actions as better than others, the very fact that they deny practical reason any foundational role in ethics dooms their theories to moral irrelevance. For if it is true that one is absolutely restricted in one's thinking to the realm of theoretical reason (making statements about the way things are), it is impossible that one could validly conclude to any obligation at all (commands about the way things ought to be). As Hume so carefully pointed out, there is no getting "ought" from "is," no getting obligation from facts alone. Thus, if one restricts inquiry to those things subject to scientific method (theoretical reason applied to material things), then there is really nothing to be said about moral responsibility.

A consideration of the explanations of morality presented by Hume, Hobbes, and Bentham can, perhaps, make this point more easily understood. As we already mentioned, Hume and Hobbes take as their starting points the passions—in Hume's case benevolence, in Hobbes' self-interest. Through these principles, they explain why people do what they do. One might, therefore, say that their ethical theories are really psychological theories. But psychology is a theoretical science which describes human behavior. It makes no claim to be a moral science; that is, it does not prescribe what one ought to do, morally speaking. In actual fact, Hobbes treats psychological categories (passions or emotions) in a reductive manner, explaining them in terms of matter in motion (i.e., physics). But physics is even more clearly a theoretical science, telling us what is the case about material things, not what ought to be the case.

Bentham's method (and in some ways that of the other utilitarians) is akin to the theoretical science of statistics; it is fact gathering. One simply records the various aspects of some action's consequences in terms of pleasure and pain and then adds them up. Those acts with projected consequences of more pleasure than pain are labeled "good," and those with more pain are labeled "bad." But just as statistical analysis is a theoretical science, which describes a situation or tendency and does not say what should or should not be done, so Bentham's utilitarianism, if consistent, is merely a theoretical study of actions in terms of their consequences with no ability to prescribe or forbid.

Once again, from facts alone (whether they be psychological or physical) no obligation can be derived. Thus, if the only foundation for acceptable human knowledge of reality is the scientific method with its requirement of material verification (psychology, biology, physics, statistics, etc.), then there is no foundation for moral responsibility.

Evaluation

But is there any reason to assume that the only acceptable foundation for human knowledge is the scientific method? An attempt to justify the assumption might be made by saying that materialism requires this limitation of reason to scientific method; if only material things exist, then only a method which involves experiential verification can know reality. However, this attempt at justification ultimately fails, for (as we said in Chapter One) materialism itself cannot be proven to be true; in fact, it is a self-destroying assumption. For if all that is real is material, then the statement "all that is real is material" is not real, for it is not itself a material thing any more than good and evil, right and wrong, justice and injustice are material. It turns out that the most basic element of all reasoning—meaning (whether in the realm of theoretical reasoning or practical reasoning)—does not fit in a materialist system. Hence, if one speaks meaningfully of anything, whether moral obligation or even the reasons why moral obligation is a fiction, one refutes the idea of materialism and the restrictions it implies.

All this, of course, does not prove that moral obligation and responsibility are real, but it does show that the arguments from science against their reality fail and that efforts to erect moral theories based on science alone cannot succeed. Without first principles of obligation to serve as premises, no particular obligations can be proven. In the following chapters, we shall consider some of these first principles and the arguments based on them which specify moral responsibilities.

5

Duty Calls:
Kant's Formalism

From our discussions of emotivism, social contract theory, and utilitarianism, it is clear that moral obligation cannot be derived from any analysis of pleasure and pain. However hard one may try, one cannot get either freedom or obligation from physiological or psychological facts. It is equally clear that moral obligations are real: it really is wrong to kill, rape, enslave, or cheat. Therefore, there must be something else besides pleasure and pain which is the foundation for moral obligation. The obvious candidate is as close as our own discussion and is found at play in any discussion—reason. This activity, specific to human beings, rises above the particularity of material things to the universality of meaning. Because reason is not reducible to matter in motion nor therefore determined by physical laws, it allows for that freedom which is absolutely necessary for moral obligation. While adherents to the scientific method (Hume, Hobbes, Bentham, and their disciples) deny reason's role in moving us to action, their arguments have been found to be fallacious. What is needed is a reevaluation of reason and its place in morality. Since Immanuel Kant presents such a reevaluation in the face of the kinds of arguments given by emotivism, egoism, and utilitarianism, let us begin with him.

KANT'S REEVALUATION OF REASON

Immanuel Kant belonged to the generation of philosophers directly following David Hume. Here our historical and systematic analyses dovetail. Not only did Kant follow Hume chronologically; he also responded directly to Hume's philosophy. Although Kant agreed with Hume that our knowledge of the world must involve a component of sense experience, he disagreed with Hume's contention that reason is limited in its activity to relations of ideas and matters of fact. While Kant treasured the new science quite as much as Hume, he understood that the restriction of reason to scientific method alone leads to skepticism and absurdity. Kant saw that if materialism is assumed, all knowledge—even scientific knowledge—is undercut. Hence there must be something which is real but is not material—at the very least, reason itself. Because of this insight, Kant was not bound to rule out the traditional categories of morality, such as good and evil, right and wrong, justice and injustice. With no presumption that these categories are meaningless because they are not material, Kant was able to rethink the whole issue of morality, and what he found was that the only viable candidate for explaining moral obligation is reason. If we are at all responsible for our actions, this could only be because morality is primarily a matter of reason, for pleasure and pain move the will not according to free choice and responsibility, but according to determined patterns of behavior.

Hume had challenged traditional morality, with its notions of right and wrong, to justify itself. According to Hume, experience is the origin of all our ideas. Since notions such as right and wrong, justice and injustice are not copies of sensible natures which we have experienced, they are to be accounted illusions. Kant takes up this challenge. While Kant will agree that ideas of morality do not come from experience, he insists that these notions are real and not illusory. Kant begins with his own "fact," not indeed a materially verifiable thing, but an immediate, obvious, and irreducible aspect of being human: people do, in fact, think that some choices and acts are always right and others always wrong. How, Kant asks, can this fact be explained?

Kant, it could be said, turns the challenge around and asks Hume and the scientific tradition to account for the universal idea of moral obligation. The very idea of obligation does not seem to be reducible to benevolent feelings or self-interest. Sometimes we know we ought to do something even though we do not feel like doing it and it is not in our self-interest, and sometimes we know we ought not to do something which does attract or would benefit us. How is it that Hume himself could make his famous "is/ought" distinction if all that is real is "is"? Where did he even get the notion of "ought" in the first place? To say that such a notion and all the categories of traditional morality are just illusions seems rather farfetched, nor can science provide any sound reasons for saying this.

Kant's project is to show what the idea of duty entails and then to show that there are no good reasons to deny that the obligations implied by duty are real. In order to help the reader understand that he or she knows what the foundations of morality are and that they are not benevolent feelings, self-interest, or the consequences of actions, Kant presents some concrete examples.[1]

To aid the reader in seeing that duty is not reducible to self-interest (Hobbes' egoism), Kant asks the reader to consider the example of a grocer who returns the correct change to a child too young to know whether or not he has been shortchanged. The grocer's honesty can be understood as motivated in two ways, either by self-interest or by duty. The distinction can be exemplified through a consideration of two scenarios. In the first, the grocer gives the correct change out of self-interest; he figures that to do so will be good for business, or perhaps he reasons that not to do so might result in his being discovered by the parents, which would be bad for business. In the second, the grocer gives the correct change precisely because it is the right thing to do. He is honest out of duty, not out of self-interest. Even if his honesty would be bad for business in the short and long run, he would still give the correct change. This, Kant says, is clearly the morally superior act, and the difference is one of intention and not facts, for the facts are the same in both cases: there is just the act of the grocer giving the child the correct change. Whether or not the reader thinks that there is in actuality a grocer who acts purely out of duty (very likely there is not) is not the issue. Nor is Kant saying that the grocer who is honest out of self-interest is therefore bad. Kant is merely concerned to show the reader that he or she understands that acting out of duty is not the same as acting out of self-interest, and that acting out of duty is better.

To help the reader see that duty is not reducible to direct inclination (Kant's analog to Hume's benevolent impulse), Kant asks the reader to consider the motivation of someone who helps others. Again he asks us to consider two scenarios, and again there are no differences in facts between the two cases. In the first case, the altruist helps other people because it makes him feel good; it is easy for him to do so, and it gives him much pleasure. In the second case, the altruist helps others because it is the right thing to do, because it is his duty. He does not enjoy doing it or have Hume's natural sympathy for his fellow human beings; nevertheless, he does help people in need. Again, whether or not there actually is a case of an altruist who helps others purely out of duty is beside the point. Nor is Kant saying that the person who helps others because of a feeling of benevolence is a bad person. All Kant wants the reader to understand is that helping others because one recognizes it as a duty is different from helping others because of the pleasure it brings oneself, and that acting out of duty is the superior motivation.

The ability to differentiate duty from self-interest and direct inclination indicates the presence of a reasoned judgment of value. No possible explanation in terms of personal response to pleasure and pain, whether in the guise of self-interest or benevolence, can explain one's understanding of duty. To do one's duty is to do what is right and good precisely because one knows it to be right and good, not merely to serve oneself or indulge a feeling. The motives of self-interest and direct inclination are subjective and particular; the motive of duty, on the contrary, is objective and universal—what ought to be done regardless of personal interests or feelings. At this point Kant has not fully explained what duty means, but he has—by a simple appeal to common sense—indicated that it is not self-interest or benevolence.

Besides showing that the essence of morality (duty) does not consist in self-interest or direct inclination, Kant also carefully points out that consequences do not make a moral choice better or worse. In other words, morality is a matter of intention, not a matter of a hedonistic calculus of facts which result from an intended choice. Good consequences cannot change the moral quality of an evil act, nor bad consequences the moral quality of a good act. It is clear that an action of rape does not become the least bit better because it results in the birth of a child who grows up to win the Nobel Prize for Peace. Nor does a judge's acquittal of a man falsely accused of stealing become any less just and good because the acquitted man robs a bank two months later, which would have been impossible had he been convicted.

To underline this focus on intentions in morality, Kant says that a good will is the only thing good in itself.[2] Everything else can be misused, from money to power to intelligence. Even virtue can be misused, for the temperate villain is all the more dangerous for his self-control.[3] In all these cases what is being misused is good, but not good in itself, for then it could never be misused. A good will, however, is good in itself; it can never be misused precisely because the will is the user, and if the user is good, the good thing will be put to good use. Since the intention of the will makes an act good or bad, the requirement to have a good will is the center of moral obligation.

A consideration of the meaning of respect reiterates Kant's point. Just as it is impossible to understand duty in terms of self-interest or direct inclination, so it is impossible to say what one means by respect in terms of these passions. One does not respect someone because that person is useful or a pleasure to have around. The person may be both of these things, and one may be glad of it, but these are not reasons for respect. Consider someone who is merely useful, able to be manipulated in whatever way desired—the willing slave. Such a person would be very handy, no doubt, but not an object of respect. Or consider someone whom one likes merely because he or she makes one feel good. Although such a person might be very pleasant to have around, and one might enjoy the company, one's appreciation of this person would not be a matter of respect. The object of respect is something objective, somehow above the self, commanding recognition and commendation. But the usefulness and the pleasure received from another person are subjective in the sense that they are desired because they are useful and pleasing to oneself. Insofar as another person is just an appendage to oneself, that person cannot be respected, for there is really no one there to respect. What commands respect is a person's unyielding commitment to what is good and right. One respects a person who will not give up his or her allegiance to what is good *even* for the sake of serving one's own self-interest or giving one pleasure. As Kant says: "The object of respect is, therefore, nothing but the law—indeed that very law which we impose on ourselves and yet recognize as necessary in itself. As law, we are subject to it without consulting self-love; as imposed on us by ourselves, it is a consequence of our will."[4]

Here are Kant's two fundamental ideas regarding the nature of moral responsibility; and, indeed, they are principles of the general natural law tradition which will be the subject of the rest of this book. In the first place, the moral law is something objective and as such imposes itself on us; that is, it is not subject to our whims. Whether we feel like following it or not, we know that we ought to. This is the insight Kant has been stressing in his discussions of duty and respect. In the second place, and equally important, is the fact that this law is self-given; that is, one understands it by natural reason and freely chooses to follow or disobey it. Duty is not something ultimately imposed from outside which one follows either because one must or because one fears punishment. Moral responsibility is not what those whom we have previously examined said it is—the forces of pleasure and pain determining our actions—for such an understanding of morality denies freedom and the dignity of the individual human conscience. Nor is it what Epicurus, Lucretius, Hume, and Nietzsche thought that it was—the imposition of arbitrary decrees from a deity whom we obey because we hope for rewards or fear punishment. It cannot be this because, if it were, moral responsibility would be a matter of self-interest. But Kant has made clear to us that our concepts of duty and respect indicate that we know that moral obligation is not a matter of self-interest. Rather, moral obligation presupposes knowledge of what is right and wrong. Only if one knows what is right and wrong can one be expected to do what is right and avoid what is wrong. An ethics based merely on an external source such as religion, with no foundation in one's own natural reason, would be no ethics at all.

The rest of Kant's moral philosophy is really just an explanation in more precise terms of these commonsensical concepts of duty and respect. While the language becomes somewhat technical and therefore more difficult, it is worthwhile analyzing his distinctions, for they can help us to understand what he means by duty and to situate his moral position among those we have discussed thus far. Kant begins by saying that reason (that is, reason as it applies to action) involves two very different kinds of commands or imperatives.

Now all imperatives command either hypothetically or categorically. The former represent the practical necessity of a possible action as a means for attaining something else that one wants (or may possibly want). The categorical imperative would be one which represented an action as objectively necessary of itself, without reference to another end.[5]

In using the word "end" here, Kant is speaking the language of intention, not of time; by end he means something sought or the purpose one has in acting, not the final moment of an action or its future consequences. When speaking of some means to an end, the end is always more important than the means. For example, if one plans to travel to New York City to see an art exhibit, then the means one takes (bus, car, plane, or train) is of less importance than the end one has in mind (to see the exhibit). Some ends can also be means to further ends. For example, seeing the art exhibit might be the means for fulfilling the requirements of an art course.[6] In every case, the end which is intended is considered better than the means, for one only desires the means for the sake of the end. Let us turn to a fuller consideration of Kant's two kinds of imperatives.

Hypothetical Imperative

When Kant speaks of hypothetical imperatives, he is really only speaking more precisely about the nonmoral motives of the will which we have already discussed in our analysis of Hobbes and Hume; these nonmoral motives are self-interest and direct inclination. The requirement involved in these imperatives is conditioned by the end sought, and since the end is given by desire or passion (not universal practical reason), these are not moral imperatives. As Kant recognizes two nonmoral motives of the will, so he distinguishes two kinds of hypothetical imperatives.

Corresponding to the motive of self-interest are what Kant calls "problematic imperatives" or imperatives of skill. For example, if one wants to be cool on a hot summer's day, then one should go swimming. Or if one wants to eat pizza, then one should go to a pizza parlor and not a deli. There are an infinite number of these imperatives corresponding to the infinite number of things which one could desire and the many different ways one could achieve them. Whatever one happens to want or desire (wide open), there are certain ways (usually more than one) to get it.

Corresponding to the motive of direct inclination are what Kant calls "assertorial imperatives" or imperatives of prudence. Kant asserts that there is only one end which all desire out of direct inclination—happiness. "Happiness" here should be read the way Hume, Hobbes, and Bentham meant it—that is, as the satisfaction of desires, the presence of pleasure, and absence of pain. Happiness is the fulfillment of our nature in the sense of what we need and want—that is, our fulfillment as material beings.[7] Here, while there is only one end, there are an unlimited number of ways to find this end since every human being occupies a unique body, has a unique personality with its own peculiar talents and preferences, and acts in situations which are particular as to place and time.

The most important point to be made about the hypothetical imperatives is that they have nothing to do with morality, with the obligations of duty. Hypothetical imperatives are, in fact, perfectly compatible with the ethical systems we have already examined; for all the previous philosophers agreed that reason plays the secondary role of determining means to end, and this is precisely what hypothetical imperatives are all about. One is not wrong not to go swimming or not to go to the pizza parlor, for there is no moral obligation to cool off or to eat pizza. Nor is there any moral obligation to satisfy one's natural desire for pleasure.

As responses to felt needs to either pursue pleasure or to avoid pain, these choices are not free in the fullest sense of freedom which we examined in the first chapter—that is, the freedom to choose among ends. Although these imperatives have the appearance of allowing great latitude in choice, the choice is merely about the means to an end given by the passions. There is no choice about which end to pursue. In fact, when speaking of human beings and the assertorial imperative, Kant says that happiness is "one purpose which they not merely can have, but which can certainly be assumed to be such that they all do have by a natural necessity."[8] To the extent that we are material creatures operating under the laws of matter in motion as they figure in our responses to pleasure and pain, our choices are really determined. The materialist assumes that we are merely material creatures and so would explain our behavior as merely responding to the environment or genetic programming in the ways Kant describes through his hypothetical imperatives.

Categorical Imperative

Over against these hypothetical imperatives stands the categorical imperative. This is duty. It is the imperative of morality. Unlike the conditional quality of hypothetical imperatives, the obligation of this imperative is absolutely necessary, what Kant calls "apodyctic." There are no "ifs, ands, or buts" about the categorical imperative; it must be followed whether or not it is in one's self-interest or one has a direct inclination to pursue it. The necessity is not, like the assertorial imperative, a physical or animal necessity, but a moral necessity, based in reason. On pain of moral contradiction and absurdity, we must do what the categorical imperative commands.

Unlike the hypothetical imperative, this imperative is not defined in terms of success in choosing a means to achieve some desired end or maximizing pleasant consequences. Rather, it is about the agent's intention and is defined in terms of what is worthy of choice for its own sake. Unlike the hypothetical imperative where the end is given by passion or desire (as it is for Hume, Hobbes, Bentham, and their disciples), here the end is given by reason. Morality is not a matter of achieving good consequences but of having good intentions—not just a feeling of well-wishing, but a reasoned commitment to do what is good for its own sake. While Kant has already discussed this moral principle as duty, he goes on to explain this principle more fully in his famous three versions of the categorical imperative to which we now turn.

It is essential in understanding Kant's position that one keep in mind that these three versions are not three different and alternative ways of being morally good, but are parts, distinguished by analysis, of the single moral imperative—duty.[9] The first version gives the form of duty, which is its universality. The second gives the content to duty, which is the idea of humanity as an ultimate end to be respected. The third version combines the first two, thereby reaffirming the exclusion of self-interest and direct inclination from moral obligation. With this point in mind, let us proceed to an examination of Kant's three versions of the categorical imperative.

The first version focuses on the requirement that ethics be universal. That one recognizes duty as something imposed on oneself indicates that it must be universal. Were it just a matter of one's own particularity (subjective relativism), then one would not recognize oneself bound (that is, obliged) to do one thing rather than another. Kant's expression for this requirement of universality is: "Act as if the maxim of your action were to become through your will a universal law of nature."[10] If the principle behind one's choice to act could become a universal law of nature, then the act may be done. If it could not become a universal law of nature, then the act should not be done.[11]

Perfect and Imperfect Duties   Kant distinguishes two kinds of duties implied by this version of the categorical imperative—perfect and imperfect—reflecting two degrees of obligation. A perfect duty is one whose violation literally could not be a universal law of nature. One could not even conceive of a world in which everyone violated such a duty. An imperfect duty is less strict; it is a duty whose violation could conceivably be a universal law of nature but whose violation one would not want to be such a law. The universal violation of a perfect duty involves a contradiction—hence an impossibility; the universal violation of an imperfect duty does not involve a contradiction, but it conflicts with what one wills.[12]

The examples which Kant gives help to clarify what he means by perfect and imperfect duties. There is a perfect duty to oneself and a perfect duty to others. Likewise, there is an imperfect duty to oneself and an imperfect duty to others. The perfect duty to self is that one should not commit suicide. Kant's claim is that there could not be a world in which suicide were universally practiced by human beings as a way of benefiting themselves. Such a world would involve a contradiction in that the principle of self-preservation in human beings (self-love) would also be the principle of self-destruction. "One sees at once a contradiction in a system of nature whose law would destroy life by means of the very same feeling that acts so as to stimulate the furtherance of life, and hence there could be no existence as a system of nature."[13]

The perfect duty to others is that one should not make lying promises. There could not be a world in which everyone made only promises he or she did not intend to keep; such a world would involve a contradiction. A world in which lying promises were universal would be a world in which there were no lying promises at all; for if all promises were lies, then there would be no promises and hence no lying promises. Deception is possible only because people are used to trusting promises. If no promises were good, no deception would be possible.

The imperfect duties to self and others are concerned with avoiding actions which are in conflict with one's will. The imperfect duty to oneself is that one should develop one's talents. It is quite possible to conceive of a world in which people did not try to better themselves—some South Sea island where there was no disease and food fell from the trees year-round. Nevertheless, Kant thinks that one would not want such a world because one wills to achieve some goals which cannot be accomplished without developing one's talents. The imperfect duty to others is that one should help them. Again, one can conceive of a world in which no one helped anyone else (either the South Sea island world in which there was no need of help or the very different Hobbesian state of nature). However, one would not want such a world because one knows that sometime or another one will need help from others.

Thus, perfect duties are universal prohibitions which we have an absolute duty to uphold. Imperfect duties are universal recommendations which it would be meritorious to uphold.

Form of Duty   Now there is something odd and unconvincing about Kant's account of morality under this first version of the categorical imperative. For one thing, it seems strange that the ethical prohibition against murder should not be as strong as that against suicide. And yet, since murdering another for one's own good does not involve any contradiction, the first version provides no perfect duty against murder. For another thing, the justifications for the imperfect duties are out of line with the idea of duty itself. Both kinds of imperfect duty are justified in terms of self-interest: one should develop one's talents because it will be of help in reaching one's goals, and one should be kind to others because someday one may want their help. These recommendations are perfectly compatible with a Hobbesian approach to ethics.[14] In Kant's own system, they read like examples of his hypothetical imperatives, which are not imperatives of morality at all. Whether one's goal be some particular thing (problematic imperatives) or happiness (assertorial imperatives), one should develop one's talents and help others for one's own sake.

Beyond these problems, a close scrutiny of Kant's method of establishing these moral precepts shows Kant to be in violation of Hume's "no ought from is" thesis. Why is it that, because there could not be a world in which suicide or lying promises were universal (fact), one ought not to commit suicide or lie (obligation)? A theoretical contradiction does not imply a practical or moral contradiction. Kant is shifting categories here. While it may be theoretically impossible to have an animal whose first principle (self-love) is at once a principle of self-preservation and self-destruction, it is certainly not practically impossible for any individual human animal to commit suicide (since people do it). That it is morally contradictory to commit suicide—that is, that one cannot do so and at the same time be morally correct—has not been shown.

The first version fails by itself to establish moral obligation; the simple ability for one's maxim to be universalized is not a sufficient foundation for moral responsibility. Thus, it is essential to remember that in Kant's scheme the first version is only part of the overall explanation of duty. What the first version makes clear is that duty involves universality, which is essential to the idea of law and which rules out the particularity that is self-interest. The motive of self-interest by definition involves what is best for the individual self, but duty or obligation transcends the self. While the choice of means to end in problematic imperatives depends on the whim or passion of the individual (radical self-interest), the categorical imperative declares that the means taken to any end must pass the test of universal application. Thus, the form of the categorical imperative (universality) is given by reason.

Specific Content of Duty   However, to say that reason, as the source of universality, is the heart of moral obligation is not enough to explain what moral obligation is, for while reason is always universal, it can be either theoretical (addressing the way things are) or practical (addressing the way one ought to act). Since universality is not peculiar to duty, it is only a necessary ingredient in the explanation of duty, not an explanation sufficient in itself. Something else is needed, something which will distinguish the universality that is duty from the universality that is mathematics, or logic, or science. What is needed is something that will give specific content to duty.

This something would have to be essential and unique to moral obligation (practical reason), as distinct from the many disciplines of theoretical reason. Thus, it would have to be something having to do with what is good, rather than what simply is, for the object of practical reason is what is good. Kant asks whether there is any object of the will which is good in itself, and which therefore should always be accorded absolute respect.

Let us suppose that there were something whose existence has in itself an absolute worth, something which as an end in itself could be a ground of determinate laws. In it, and in it alone, would there be the ground of a possible categorical imperative, i.e., of a practical law.[15]

The question Kant is asking is whether or not there is anything that is an end in itself, something that should never be treated simply as a means to a further end.

Extension to All Human Beings   The human being (or any rational being) is such an end. Here Kant retracts, or at least reformulates, his claim that only a good will is good in itself. Now he says that every human being (who, in having a rational will, is the locus where what is good in itself—a good will—can exist) is an end in itself which must always be respected. Kant's second version of the categorical imperative reads: "Act in such a way that you treat humanity, whether in your own person or in the person of another, always at the same time as an end and never simply as a means."[16]

How does one know that every human being is an end that should be treated with respect? Kant says that the fundamental insight here is an insight into one's own status as an end. One knows oneself as an end, and knows that one is not to be treated merely as a means to the satisfaction of someone else's self-interest or pleasure. Since one knows this, and since there are no relevant differences between oneself and others which could warrant not treating them in the same way that one knows oneself should be treated, one is obliged to treat other people as ends, also.

> The ground of such a principle is this: rational nature exists as an end in itself. In this way man necessarily thinks of his own existence; thus far it is a subjective principle of human actions. But in this way also does every other rational being think of his existence on the same rational ground that holds also for me; hence it is at the same time an objective principle, from which, as a supreme practical ground, all laws of the will must be able to be derived.[17]

The question might well be raised here whether Kant runs into the same problem Bentham had in trying to extend obligation from self to others. If what Kant is talking about is merely a feeling one has that it would be unpleasant to be used by another, then we would have to say that he does fail in the same way that Bentham does. For the fact of a desire in oneself cannot lead to the obligation to respect the same desire in others (no obligation can be derived from fact). But this is not Kant's point. He agrees that, were it just a matter of feelings, there would be no apparent reason why it should be forbidden to treat even oneself as a means to an end. However, the truth is that one *knows* it is wrong to treat oneself this way (even though one may sometimes desire to do so). One knows that reason should not be sacrificed to desire. One knows this first in one's own case, and understands that it applies to every other example where reason and desire come into conflict.

Kant is not arguing from the particular theoretical fact that one is concerned for oneself to the universal obligation that one ought to be concerned for others. Rather, he acknowledges, as a universal self-evident principle, the obligation to treat all rational creatures as ends. The movement of the argument from self to others is a theoretical, genetic account of how one becomes aware of this principle and its extent, not a deduction of the moral obligation to care for others from self-interest. The insight is subjective first because one has a direct and immediate grasp of the fact that one is a rational and free agent. One becomes aware that other persons should be respected as ends by reflecting on the fact that there is no reason to doubt and every reason to believe that they, too, are rational and free. The priority of self to others is a temporal priority in the awareness of the very same principle—that rational beings should always be treated as ends in themselves. Thus, Kant's way of explaining why others should be treated as ends as well as oneself does not fall prey to the criticism of Hume that there is no deriving "ought" from "is."

While the first version focuses on the way duty differs from self-interest in its universality, the second version focuses on the way duty differs from direct inclination. Recall that the end of the assertorial hypothetical imperative is happiness understood as the object of natural inclination. As such an object, happiness is an end that we do not choose to seek, but which we seek automatically and necessarily because we are animals. Humanity as an object of respect, however, is an end recognized by reason, not direct inclination. Unlike Hume, who thought we had a direct inclination to treat human beings kindly, Kant holds that we *know* that every rational and free being is an end in itself, to be honored for its own sake, regardless of how we feel about that person or humanity in general. Thus, not only does reason provide the form of duty (universality); it also provides the content (humanity as an end in itself).

Besides grounding moral obligation on direct insight into the absolute value of any rational being, this second version of the categorical imperative avoids the odd implications of the first version which we found to be incompatible with real moral responsibility. On the terms of the second version, it would be just as wrong to murder someone else as it would be to commit suicide. In either case, one would be using humanity merely as a means to an end. Also, the imperfect duties to self and others are no longer explained in terms of self-interest, but can be understood as implications of the obligation to treat human beings as ultimate ends. If one is serious about respecting oneself as a rational being with ultimate value and dignity, then one is obliged to develop those talents which enhance that value and dignity. Again, if one is serious about respecting others as ends in themselves, then one is obliged to help them live lives befitting the dignity of being such ultimate ends. Thus, the second version provides a solid base for moral obligation—one's immediate awareness in oneself of the absolute value of a being with a rational will.

Autonomy   Kant's third version ties the first two together, taking universality from the first version and the idea of humanity as an end from the second. He calls this principle "autonomy"[18] (literally, self-given law): "According to this principle all maxims are rejected which are not consistent with the will's own legislation of universal law."[19] Kant claims that this is the most comprehensive formulation of duty. What makes this the best formulation? It might seem that placing the individual will as the source of morality is taking a step back into relativism. However, this is not the case. Kant is merely underlining what he said earlier about the object of respect: it reveals itself as something that both imposes itself and is self-imposed. To be a rational being is to be under the universal obligation of practical reason; and since reason is natural to every human being, every human being is the origin of that universal obligation.

What makes this third expression of duty superior to the others is that it distinguishes duty simultaneously and unequivocally from self-interest and direct inclination. If the law one follows is not self-given but given by another (heteronomy), then one has a further question which needs answering: why it is that one follows the law? If one follows it through fear of punishment or hope for reward, then one's motive is not duty at all but self-interest. If, on the other hand, one follows it because one knows it to be right, then what else is this than saying that the foundations for moral knowledge are in one's own reason—that the law is, in fact, self-given. The self-given nature of the moral law also clearly rules out direct inclination as its source. Direct inclination is a fact of our material nature which operates on us by natural necessity; it is not something that the self initiates or wills. To say that the moral law originates in the self is to deny that it originates in direct inclination, in some biological drive, or in any environmental condition, and to affirm its origin in reason. Thus, the principle of autonomy explicitly excludes self-interest and direct inclination (the hypothetical imperatives) from the idea of duty or moral responsibility.

DETERMINISM OR FREEDOM

At this point Kant has said all that he thinks there is to say regarding an explanation of what duty means. However, his work is not quite done, for if it can be shown to be a fact that we are not free to choose, then whether or not we have an idea of duty, we simply cannot perform that duty. In other words, if determinism is true, then duty is an illusion. To establish the reality of the will's autonomy, Kant needs to answer Hume's argument for the impossibility of morality having its origin in reason and the accompanying implication of determinism; that is, he must show that the assumed materialism and attendant determinism of Hume, Hobbes, Bentham, and their disciples is not a demonstrated conclusion of reason. Along with this, he must show that it is reasonable to affirm that we are free.

Theoretical Proof of Freedom

Thus, in the Third Section of his *Grounding for the Metaphysics of Morals*, Kant presents two proofs for the reality of freedom, a theoretical proof that freedom is possible and a practical proof that freedom is real. Let us look at the theoretical proof for the possibility of freedom first. The point Kant makes is very much like the one we presented in Chapter One, which showed that the scientific method is not the only legitimate use of reason. Kant understands that if all is reducible to matter in motion, then there is no such thing as freedom and hence no morality. Material things operate under physical necessity, having their causes outside themselves; they are subject to what Kant calls heteronomous (as opposed to autonomous) causality. The motions caused by gravity or electromagnetism are examples of heteronomous causality. The planets do not move around the sun by their own free will but according to the necessary law of gravity. If human choices were merely a matter of heteronomous causality (as Hume, Hobbes, and Bentham thought they were), then there could be no such thing as human freedom, nor any way to ground moral responsibility.

Against such a view, Kant claims that the very empirical method established by Hume implies that there must be a nonphysical reality beyond what is sensed. While it may be true that one's scientific knowledge depends on sense experiences, it is clear that one is not the source of these experiences, for they appear without regard to one's will. Therefore, one knows that there must be a world independent of sense experiences which is the origin of these experiences and which itself is not the object of the senses. This is the world of the understanding. Hence there are two points of view by which we can consider the world. If we consider the world as it appears to us through our senses, then it is a world of material causality determined by the laws of physics. However, if we consider the world as it is in itself, the world which is the origin of sense experience, then it is the immaterial world of the understanding which is not bound by the determining laws of matter in motion.

> This must provide a distinction, however crude, between a world of sense and a world of understanding; the former can vary considerably according to the difference of sensibility [and sense impressions] in various observers, while the latter, which is the basis of the former, remains always the same.[20]

This distinction which applies to the world can also be applied to human beings. Insofar as one is a material being, one belongs to the world governed by heteronomous physical laws. To this degree one is determined: if one steps out of a second–story window, one falls to the ground (the necessity of gravity); if one is cut or frightened, one feels pain (the necessity of cause and effect in one's neural system). However, insofar as one belongs to the world of the understanding—that is, insofar as there is a unified self and not just an unconnected flux of various experiences—it is possible that one is free; for this world of the understanding, since it is not a material world, is not subject to physical determinism.

This, however, is not to prove theoretically that one is free, but merely that freedom is a possibility. It is, in fact, impossible to give any theoretical proof of freedom. As a first principle of practical reason, freedom cannot be derived from theoretical reason (nor, of course, disproved by it either). Just as there is no deriving obligation from facts, so there is no deriving freedom, which is a prerequisite for obligation, from facts. However, the use of theoretical reason implies that freedom is possible. Freedom, if it is real, transcends the material world in which actions are determined by environmental conditions. Since the scientist must leave room for the immaterial reality of his own thought if he is to prove anything (or his ideas can carry no universality), he must admit the possibility of other immaterial realities, among which could be freedom.

Practical Proof of Freedom

The only proof of the existence of freedom is a practical proof. However, since freedom is a first principle of practical reason, like all first principles, it cannot be deduced from some more basic principle of practical reason. The only way to prove the existence of a first principle is by showing that its denial leads to absurdity. In Chapter One we showed that truth is a first principle of theoretical reason by showing that anyone bent on denying this had to hold that his denial was true, thereby either admitting the first principle or saying nothing at all. The same kind of proof is appropriate for revealing this first principle of practical reason.

> Now I say that every being which cannot act in any way other than under the idea of freedom is for this very reason free from a practical point of view. This is to say that for such a being all the laws that are inseparably bound up with freedom are valid just as much as if the will of such a being could be declared to be free in itself for reasons that are valid for theoretical philosophy.[21]

One is aware of having options and making choices. It is impossible to believe that one's conscious choices are actually made by another and not oneself; for then one would believe that the choices are both one's own and not one's own—a contradiction. The very fact of consciousness, of knowing oneself as an acting self, is impossible save on the assumption that one is free. If one really thought that one's choices were not one's own, then one would not even have the idea of "one's choices." The reason one cannot really believe in a world of perfect determinism is that such a world would involve no "one" to do the believing. Again, this is not a theoretical proof that one is free, that there is not (in Descartes' colorful phrase) an "evil genius" who deceives us into thinking that we are free when, in fact, we are not.[22] There is simply no way to disprove such a hypothesis theoretically (nor, of course, any way to prove it either). Relying merely on theoretical reasoning, we end up with a draw—no blood either way. Practically speaking, however, all the evidence supports the belief that our conscious choices really are our own—that we really are free.

Let me suggest a slightly different way of looking at the issue. While one can, of course, *say* that we are absolutely determined (as Bentham or, more recently, B. F. Skinner would have done), if we are, then we are not free to say it. And, as one normally would not believe or trust any statement from someone who had been hypnotized and programmed to say not what he or she really thinks but what some other person thinks, so there is no reason to believe the person who says that human beings are not free. Since, according to this person's own position, he or she is not giving a free and considered opinion of the matter, one is not bound in any way to take this opinion seriously. To use Kant's terminology, one is not required to consider such statements as issuing from a rational and autonomous agent since, by the speaker's own admission, he or she is not such an agent.

PRACTICAL REASON

Faced with the challenges of emotivism, egoism, and utilitarianism, Kant succeeds in showing us clearly that moral obligation cannot possibly be based on any of them. It is just as clear that we have some notion of moral obligation, for we understand the meaning of such words as "duty" and "respect" and "caring for someone for that person's own sake." In recognizing humanity as an ultimate end which should never be treated merely as an instrument for achieving some other end, Kant has put his finger on the very core of moral obligation. Like all first principles, this insight is not one which can be deductively proved, for such proof is always by way of something prior, and a first principle has nothing prior to it. Thus, the insight that a person is an end who must be respected as such regardless of the desires and self-interest of others or even of that very person is foundational to moral obligation in the sense that it is obvious, on reflection, to anyone who thinks about it.

There must be a first principle of practical reason, or there could be no conclusions of practical reason—no notions of duty or respect, no better or worse, no idea that feeding the hungry is better than killing innocent children. Since one does have notions of duty and respect and of right and wrong, and since one does know that feeding the hungry is better than killing innocent children, there must be a first principle of practical reason. In his explanation of this first principle, Kant focuses on the human being who, as possessing the rationality and freedom without which there can be no moral obligation, is an end in itself. Every human being is an ultimate good, never to be sacrificed to any other good.

> Persons are, therefore, not merely subjective ends, whose existence as an effect of our actions has a value for us; but such beings are objective ends, i.e., exist as ends in themselves. . . , for otherwise nothing at all of absolute value would be found anywhere. But if all value were conditioned and hence contingent, than no supreme practical principle could be found for reason at all.[23]

Evaluation

If there is a weakness in Kant's ethical theory, it is that his moral directives remain on a plane of high generality. It is true that he does move from very abstract and formal statements such as "the only thing good in itself is a good will" and "one should universalize one's maxims" to the more concrete duty that one must not treat any human being, oneself included, merely as a means to an end. However, what this implies for particular moral choices is hard to decipher. For what ways are improper ways to treat human beings? Kant cannot mean that one should simply refrain from treating people in ways that violate their will (in which case all acts done by consent would be permissible); for, although presumably one consents to treat oneself in all the various ways one does, Kant insists that one may not treat oneself merely as a means to an end. Even the suicide assents to the killing, and yet Kant clearly condemns this action. And what is it to treat humanity as a means but not "merely" as a means? About all that this would clearly rule out is suicide and murder. Even lying could be construed as being "for someone's own good." Thus, while Kant is excellent at refuting the claims of relativism and its various guises—emotivism, egoism, and utilitarianism—and he is certainly right in his basic insight that persons should always be respected, he is somewhat vague about specific moral precepts.

The difference between Kant and the natural law tradition as developed by thinkers such as Aristotle, Cicero, and Aquinas does not lie in their conceptions of the moral foundations, for all agree that morality is a matter of reason choosing between good and evil, not of passions reacting to pleasure and pain. It is in the greater clarity and comprehensiveness of the natural law position that the difference is to be found. The rest of the book will be devoted to this natural law tradition, both as it can be immediately grasped by one's reflective judgment and as it has been conceived by philosophers past and present.

6

Do Good and Avoid Evil: Natural Law

What may be most surprising about natural law ethics is just how basic, obvious, and commonsensical—in short, unsurprising—it is. Natural law ethics is not in the least esoteric. It does not presuppose some theory of knowledge based on exclusive adherence to scientific method, as do the theories of Hume, Hobbes, Bentham, and their disciples which we have discussed. Nor does it involve the technical language of Kant (even though Kant's basic insight of duty is in itself commonsensical). Even the chapter title "Do Good and Avoid Evil" will likely raise the response: "Of course, that's obvious, but so what?" This is precisely the point: obligation is obvious. If it were not, it would make no sense to expect everyone (or anyone, for that matter) to be responsible.

Nor, by this time, is the natural law position anything new to the reader. For one thing, our discussion of Kant has already introduced many of the central principles. But even before we looked at Kant, these principles were at work in our examination and criticism of the other ethical theories. In fact, any examination or criticism of actions or moral theories presupposes the principles of what we are calling natural law ethics, which is really just a name for our orientation toward what is good and our ability to make moral judgments.[1]

More radically still, the original desire of the reader to know what the foundations of moral responsibility are, or even whether or not there are any, presupposes some understanding of these basic principles. Recall some of the criteria mentioned in the Preface. For there to be any justifiable moral conclusions, there must be some absolutely certain, self-evident, moral principles. These principles must not be incoherent or contradictory. And finally, these principles must allow for freedom. All these criteria merely define what must be the case if there is any such thing as moral responsibility, if any choices or acts can be said to be right or wrong; and one recognizes these criteria as essential through one's immediate grasp of what it means to do good and avoid evil. If any actions are good (and therefore to be done and their opposites not done), then there must be certain, self-evident principles of good.

Whatever the principles are like, they must not be contradictory or they will cancel each other out. And finally, they must allow for freedom for the very obvious reason that only a free agent is able—and therefore may be expected—to do what is good and refuse to do what is evil.

The problems with emotivism, egoism, and utilitarianism are that they violate these basic criteria. In the first place, by insisting on the exclusive use of scientific method (a kind of theoretical reason), they deny that there are any first principles of moral responsibility (practical reason). But if there are no first principles of moral responsibility, then there are no valid particular conclusions of moral responsibility. This, of course, is the position of ethical relativism, which none of these theories can coherently refute. But recall that to prefer relativism as a theory of morality is contradictory, since relativism denies that there are any principles which can justify preferring anything over anything else. In trying to recommend theories of morality while refusing to allow practical reason its own first principles, Hume, Hobbes, Bentham, and their followers all fall into the fallacy of deducing obligation from fact.[2] Finally, through their assumption of materialism, these philosophers deny (or should deny if consistent) the reality of freedom; a consistent adherent to any of these positions must be a determinist. Ultimately, none of these theories is a theory of moral obligation at all, since it makes no sense to expect people to do what is good and avoid what is evil if they have no choice in the matter. All these criticisms are simply the voice of what I am referring to as natural law ethics.

The nonesoteric character of the natural law tradition is borne out by historical and anthropological studies as well. In a survey of the literature from east and west, north and south, from Confucius, Lao-tzu, and Buddha to the western pagans Plato, Aristotle, and Cicero, to the Eskimos and American Indians, to Babylonian, Ancient Egyptian, and Old Norse sources, one finds recurring themes of ethical obligation—such basic precepts as do not kill, do not lie, help others, honor elders.[3] And if one makes an anthropological survey of current primitive tribes, one finds the same thing to hold true—in all cultures the same basic goods are, in fact, honored.[4] Thus, the honoring of such fundamental human goods as life, honesty, friendship, family, and beauty is not the bailiwick of some narrow western, Christian tradition. On the contrary, the basic insights into human good upon which natural law ethics is founded are common to the whole human family.

Of course, the fact that most or all cultures have honored and do honor these goods does not imply that one ought to honor these goods, for, as has often been repeated, obligation cannot be derived from statistical fact. In other words, a survey of cultures which indicates that certain practices are the statistical norm worldwide does not, by itself, oblige anyone to follow these practices. Conversely, if a survey were to reveal that most people in the world think that it is permissible for a majority to enslave or eradicate a minority, this would not prove that such a policy is permissible. Thus, the purpose in making the observation that natural law ethics has been, and still is, the norm is not to present a philosophical proof, but to dispel the idea (which is all too prevalent) that the precepts of the natural law are limited to the Catholic, or the Christian, or even the western tradition.

Although the precepts of natural law ethics are found worldwide, it has been the western philosophical tradition descending from Socrates, Plato, and Aristotle which has ordered them into a coherent whole and which, not being content with observing that most people do follow these general precepts, has given arguments for why people ought to follow them. For this reason the philosophers considered in this chapter will be from the western tradition. However, in talking of this western philosophical tradition of natural law ethics, even here I am not referring to a narrow school of thought, but to a tradition of ethical thinking in which reason distinguishes between choices, judging some to be good and right and others to be evil and wrong.

COMPARISON WITH OTHER THEORIES

As we begin our analysis of the natural law position, it would be well to clarify a couple of points concerning the relation of natural law ethics to some of the theories we have discussed. The first concerns Hobbes and his use of the term "natural law." The second concerns the advisability of including Kant in the natural law tradition since Kant explicitly criticizes elements of the tradition, particularly the prominent place it gives to happiness.

Hobbes and Natural Law

Recall that Thomas Hobbes speaks of natural laws as the foundations of his ethics. From what has been said already, it should be obvious that Hobbes is not a member of the natural law tradition being discussed in this chapter. To understand the difference, we have only to consider the meaning of "law" and "natural" in each case.

First, consider the difference between the notion of law for Hobbes and for the natural law tradition. Hobbes' understanding of law is taken directly from his model of physics, as is the whole scope of his moral and political philosophy. Such laws are the mechanical rules for matter in motion. It should be clear from our discussion of moral law in Kant that the natural law is a law of obligation, not physical determination. Thus, it is a law that we *can* break, but which we *ought not* to break. While we can hardly break the law of gravity, we certainly can (and do) break the moral law. In fact, it would make no sense to say that we ought or ought not to do something if the choice were not in our power. It would be like telling someone that he or she ought to free fall at the rate of 32 feet per second or ought not to bleed when cut. Since one has no choice in either matter, such commands would be senseless. The natural moral laws are not physical laws, but rather—like the laws of the land—they can but should not be broken.

Secondly, consider how the meaning of natural differs in each case. Nature, for Hobbes, is equivalent to material nature. Thus, natural applied to human beings refers to our nature as material—that is, to our pleasures and pains, to our needs and passions. For Hobbes the human being is merely an animal and hence directed by precisely the same mechanisms of genetics, instincts, and environment as guide other animals. In his deductivist materialism, this all comes down ultimately to the interactions of matter in motion—to mechanism. On these terms, it is indeed impossible for anyone to break the natural law, since it is nothing other than physical law. In natural law ethics, however, nature is not equivalent to material nature; it includes all aspects of created reality. Thus, applied to human beings, natural refers to our nature as rational and free, as well as material. For the natural law tradition, the human being is defined as a rational animal, and the rationality extends to the knowledge of right and wrong as well as to the ability to calculate relations of means to end and cause to effect. Natural law refers to the obligation of human beings to apply reason to choices. It is reason's call to pursue what is good and avoid what is evil, not a mechanical determination of one's actions.

Kant and Natural Law

Having distinguished between the meaning of natural law in Hobbes and the tradition, let us turn to the apparent disagreement between Kant and the adherents to natural law ethics. There is no question that Kant explicitly rejects, at times, the natural law tradition stemming from Plato and Aristotle and further developed by the Stoics and the Medievals. All these philosophers of the tradition agree in saying that happiness is a first principle of ethics. They hold happiness to be the ultimate end which human beings seek, and morally correct behavior is understood as that which brings real happiness. Kant, however, denies that happiness is a moral principle, relegating it to the realm of the hypothetical imperative where the requirement to choose some means rather than others to reach happiness is a counsel of prudential self-interest, not duty. In order to clear up this controversy, two important points need to be made. The first concerns the meaning of happiness; the second has to do with whether happiness is a principle of theoretical or practical reason or both. Let us consider the meaning of happiness first.

If happiness is understood as tranquillity, the fulfillment of pleasure and peace of mind (the meaning it had for Epicurus, Hume, Hobbes, and Bentham), then Kant is certainly correct in his rejection of this principle as the foundation for ethical obligation, and the natural law tradition would completely agree with this rejection. However, this is not the meaning of happiness as understood by the tradition. Happiness is not just a feeling of bodily and psychological comfort. Rather, it is also, and foremost, an activity of wisdom and virtue in which one chooses and acts in conformity with reason's demands. Just as it is for Kant, the exercise of reason is the central feature of ethics within the tradition. Human happiness is grounded on the use of reason as it knows the truth and as it chooses in conformity with what is right. While it is understandable that, given what happiness meant in the philosophical discussions of his time, Kant would reject happiness as a moral principle, happiness means something quite different in the natural law tradition. Had Kant sufficiently understood this, he might well have recognized the natural law tradition as the ally it really is to his position, rather that the enemy he thought it was.

The second point concerns the understanding of happiness as a principle of theoretical or practical reason. For Hume, Hobbes, and Bentham, happiness is clearly a principle of theoretical reason. It is a way of describing the mechanism of human activity. It is not that human beings *ought* to seek happiness; it is merely a fact that people *are* motivated to seek happiness. Kant adopts this definition of happiness in his analysis, for although he counts happiness as the principle of an imperative (the assertorial hypothetical imperative), the imperative is not one which we are free to choose or not to choose; it is necessary physically, biologically, and psychologically that we seek happiness. This desire for happiness is simply the way human beings are made and has nothing to do with moral responsibility and choice. Although the natural law tradition means by happiness something quite different from what Hume, Hobbes, Bentham, and Kant mean by it, the tradition does sometimes consider happiness as a principle of theoretical reason—the first principle in describing how the human will is, in fact, moved to choice and action. Used in this way, it is a psychological or metaphysical principle and not a principle of moral obligation.

However, happiness is also considered by the natural law tradition to be a principle of practical reason in the following way. Happiness is the fulfillment of one's human nature. This involves fulfilling not just the exigencies of being an animal, but also, and more importantly, the exigencies of being rational—including the full participation in intelligible good. Here happiness is an end not given by passion or inclination, but by reason. The full participation in happiness means the perfection of one's humanity; to use Kant's terminology, it is to fully respect oneself as an end. Understood in this way, happiness is not an alternative to moral obligation, but the fulfillment of that obligation. It is thus a principle of practical reason as well as one of theoretical reason.

Theoretical and Practical Reason

From this discussion, one can see how essential it is to distinguish between theoretical reason and the laws it formulates, which do not and cannot provide the foundation of moral obligation, and practical reason and the laws it formulates, which do. Kant made this distinction between theoretical and practical reason, and we have discussed his explanation, but the point was made long before his time by Aristotle and more systematically by Thomas Aquinas, whose analysis I shall be following here.[5] The main distinction is based on the insight that there are two realms with which reason is concerned: the realm of what is (being and truth) and the realm of what is good (value and obligation).

Object of Theoretical Reason   Theoretical reason is concerned with what exists and what is true. The root of the word theoretical is taken from the Greek word meaning "to see." Thus, theoretical reason "sees" what exists and what is true. Unlike Hume, Hobbes, Bentham, and their disciples, however, Aristotle and Aquinas do not limit theoretical reason to relations of ideas and matters of fact. Besides knowing mathematical truths and applying the scientific method to material reality (matter in motion), theoretical reason also has insight into the natures of things, their orientation to perfection, and their ultimate purpose.

Here it is necessary to take a brief excursion into the realm of theoretical reason. While such a digression might seem out of place in a book on ethics, it is important for two reasons. In the first place, while no proposition of theoretical reason can by itself provide moral obligation (as seen in our examination of Hume, Hobbes, and Bentham), still theoretical propositions are part of every specific moral argument. A proper understanding of what counts as known about reality is therefore essential to formulating specific moral obligations. In the second place, the good of knowledge, to which human beings are naturally oriented, has been arbitrarily truncated by assumptions of materialism. Not only has the moral dimension of meaning—virtue, justice, duty—been denied without good reason, but also theoretical dimensions of meaning irreducible to the quantifiable elements of matter in motion have been arbitrarily rejected, under the specious argument from science that they cannot be real because they cannot be verified by sense experience. To recover an understanding of these arbitrarily rejected dimensions of theoretical meaning is to restore the good of human reason. As Aristotle formulated these theoretical dimensions of meaning neatly in his doctrine of the "four causes,"[6] let us consider his analysis here.

Aristotle's Theory of Explanation   Aristotle developed his theory of explanation in response to questions we naturally raise about the things we experience. In answer to the question "What?", he assigns two causes: the material cause which explains the stuff from which something is made, and the formal cause which explains the thing's shape or structure, that which it shares in common with other things of the same kind. In answer to the question "Why?", he again assigns two causes: the moving cause (also known as the efficient cause) which explains how the thing came into being, and the final cause which explains the ultimate purpose of that thing in the order of the universe. Consider the example of a ship: its material cause is wood (or fiberglass or steel); its formal cause is the structure that we call ship; its moving cause is the shipbuilder; and its final cause might be transportation or pleasure or monetary gain. Aristotle holds that these causes apply to natural things as well as artificial, manufactured things.

Scientific Method   In its explanation of nature, the scientific method adopted by Bacon, Hobbes, and Hume accepted only the material and moving causes as legitimate explanations since these things can be measured; they rejected formal and final causes and the idea of a first moving or efficient cause of the universe because these could not be verified by scientific method. Thus, they denied that things have intrinsic essences and tendencies or that there is any overall order and purpose to the universe. In short, they denied the legitimacy of metaphysics which, according to Aristotle, is theoretical reason in its highest activity.

Metaphysics   Metaphysics examines the structure of things (formal causes) and the relation of things to each other and ultimately to the whole universe and its first principle (efficient cause) and ultimate meaning or purpose (final cause). Metaphysics culminates in the knowledge of the first principle of all reality—the ultimate explanation which Aristotle calls God. Since the reasons Bacon, Hobbes, and Hume had for rejecting explanations for reality in terms of formal and final causality are no good (the assumption of materialism is self-refuting), there is no reason to ignore metaphysical explanations of things.

However, although metaphysics differs from the hard sciences in dealing with real objects which are not in themselves material, like them, it is a theoretical discipline. As such, it is no more able to provide foundations for moral obligation than is the scientific method. Since its propositions are indicative ("is" statements), there is no deriving the imperatives of moral obligation ("ought" statements) from them.[7]

Objects of Practical Reason   The object of practical reason is what is good. The word practical comes from the Greek word "praxis," which means activity. Thus, practical reason is concerned with what is to be done. Now there is a sense in which Hume and company have some limited notion of practical reason, for they allow reason to play a secondary role in decision making: reason can deal with questions of means to ends. This kind of practical reasoning tells us how to go about getting what we desire. Indeed, this is what the modern mind first thinks of when it hears the word "practical." However, it is not the primary meaning of practical for the natural law tradition. While this ability to recognize appropriate means to specific ends is indeed one of the activities which Aristotle and Aquinas would call practical, the fundamental activity of practical reason is to know what is good and that one should pursue it. This activity is precisely what is rejected by Hume and company. For them good is equivalent to pleasure and is an object of passion, not reason. But if motivation is merely a matter of passion, then there is no such thing as moral obligation. Passion operates beneath the level of reasoned choice, and one cannot be obliged to do something which is not open to choice—something, in other words, which is inevitable. If moral requirements of any sort can be held to be real, then ethics must be based in reason, and if in reason, then in practical reason understood as the ability to know and choose intelligible goods.

First Principles   Since theoretical and practical reason have different objects—the knowledge of "what is" and of "what is good," respectively—they will differ in some fundamental ways. Both operations of reason argue from premises to conclusions in logical form, but their first principles are distinct, and their conclusions differ accordingly. While theoretical reason's conclusions are indicative, stating what is real and true, the conclusions of practical reason are imperative, telling us what ought and what ought not to be done.

Hume was right when he said that it is impossible to get obligation from fact. The principles of practical reason cannot be derived from the principles of theoretical reason. But he was wrong in not understanding that practical reason has its own first principles which are real commands of reason.

The first principle of theoretical reason states that something cannot *be* and *not be* at the same time and in the same respect. This is the so-called law of noncontradiction. This principle is completely obvious, self-evident, and noncontroversial. Controversy (reasoned disagreement) is possible only if the principle is accepted. Indeed, all thought presupposes the principle. To disagree with it, one must use it (or one's disagreement can be construed as, also and simultaneously, agreement).

The principle which holds the same foundational position in practical reason is the imperative which commands that good is to be done and pursued and evil avoided. All our choices make use of this principle. Even objections to this position must make use of it. For if one wishes to disagree with it, one can only do so in the form "it is not good to do good and avoid evil," but then, of course, one has made use of the principle, or one has said nothing at all. Every deliberative action, every intentional choice implies acceptance of this principle. Thus, moral obligation does not receive its first principles from theoretical reason—scientific or metaphysical—but has its own principles. While it is true, of course, that the command "do good and avoid evil" relies on the law of noncontradiction in the same way that every utterance must if it is to be other than nonsense, the command does not rely on the law of noncontradiction for its content. Prior to the formulation of the imperative in words is the human being's orientation toward good, which is what is meant by the first principle of practical reason.

For both theoretical reason and practical reason, there are other self-evident principles which follow from the first principle. Thus, for theoretical reason, given the understanding of "equality," and of the words "whole" and "part," one knows immediately and with absolute certainty that two things equal to another are equal to each other and that the whole is greater than any of its parts. Parallel to these declarative statements of theoretical reason, which are immediately grasped as true, there are imperatives of practical reason based on understanding what the word "good" means. As soon as one understands what such words as "life," "friendship," and "knowledge" mean, it is self-evident that life, friendship, and knowledge are good and therefore should be pursued, promoted, and not violated.

Choice of Goods   One might ask: Why pick these goods among all the possible goods that could be pursued? After all, everything that exists or even appears to exist can be the object of choice and hence can be called good. There are two characteristics which the basic goods have and other goods do not. First of all, they are self-evidently good—that is, knowing them to be good does not depend on knowing something else to be good. Secondly, they are good in themselves, not aspects of more fundamental goods. Most of the things which we call good are either explained by some more ultimate good (as food and clothing are means to the more basic good of life) or are instances of a more basic good (as the solution to any particular problem is an instance of the good of knowledge). It is these basic goods combined with the basic imperative—do good and avoid evil—which form the foundation for concrete ethical obligation.

The list of such basic human goods varies somewhat within the tradition. Aquinas includes life, procreation, knowledge, and orderly social life. A slightly different list is given by Cicero (by whom Aquinas was certainly influenced): life, procreation, knowledge, friendship, quest for excellence, and beauty. John Finnis, a contemporary natural law philosopher, presents the following: life, knowledge, play, aesthetic experience, sociability, practical reasonableness, and religion.[8] What is common to these lists is that they are intended to cover all the things that human beings naturally recognize as self-evidently and irreducibly good. As first principles of practical reason, these basic goods cannot be proven to be basic by something more fundamental. In the realm of what is choiceworthy, these are the irreducible elements.[9]

Since both the basic goods and the imperative "do good and avoid evil" are self-evident, the norms which follow from their combination are also self-evident. Thus, every human being is morally obliged to honor such basic moral precepts as do not kill, do not commit adultery, do not lie, and do not steal.

MORAL RESPONSIBILITY

At the close of Chapter Five, we suggested that natural law ethics supplies some of the specifics missing from Kant's analysis of obligation, offering guides to a morally responsible life which are at once more concrete and more certain. Let me offer now a brief account of what was meant. Natural law agrees with Kant that morality is fundamentally based in reason and that one is obliged to do what is in accord with duty (to do what is good and avoid what is evil). Where natural law ethics shows an advance on Kant's theory is in spelling out what counts as fundamentally good. Both understand that there are some instrumental goods (lesser goods) which can be used to achieve greater goods or can be sacrificed for the sake of greater goods. For example, money can be spent to buy food and plants can be sacrificed to feed human beings. And both understand that there are some goods which must be honored as ends and never sacrificed for other goods. However, when it comes to an explication of what counts as fundamentally good, or good in itself, Kant gives us only the general idea of the human being. What the natural law does is specify what it means to be a human being by spelling out the dimensions of human fulfillment. These are the fundamental human goods—such things as life, knowledge, friendship, family, beauty, and religion.

Ends and Means

As Kant understood, whatever is known to be good in itself should be treated as an end and not merely as a means (that is, as if it were not good in itself). This is the fundamental moral requirement. Applying this principle to the natural law specification of fundamental human goods, we end up with the requirement that ultimate human goods should be treated as ends and not merely means to further ends. In other words, one is never to intend the violation of basic human goods. To do so is to be in practical contradiction: it is to value something as good without qualification and then to qualify it—not to value what one values.

In addition to specifying what it is to honor humanity, distinguishing the different dimensions of human good also clarifies the prohibition against treating humanity as *merely* a means to a further end. As Kant's reason for respecting human beings lies in their possession of a rational will, the only clear violation of humanity (treating humanity merely as a means) would be murder—the destruction of the rational will. By specifying a number of basic human goods, the natural law position extends the range of the prohibition considerably. Not only must one not kill another human being (violation of the good of life), but one must also not violate any human being's participation in any of the basic goods (in knowledge, play, beauty, friendship, practical reason, or religion). To do so would be to treat basic human goods (understood as essential dimensions of humanity) *merely* as means to other ends. The specification of human goods thus preserves the fullness of what it is to be human from arbitrary violation.

What is good in itself is an end to be respected. As such, it is not to be violated or sacrificed for the sake of some other good. Just as one would say that human beings as ends are not to be sacrificed for other ends (even other human beings), so the basic goods as ultimate ends are not to be sacrificed for other goods (even other basic goods). Thus, human life must not be sacrificed to increase knowledge; betrayal of friends to save one's life is wrong;

families must not be sacrificed in the name of social order; one should not lie in order to better provide for one's family. The primary command of the natural law is that one should never intentionally choose against a basic good, that one may not sacrifice one basic good for the sake of another. As Bruno Schüller puts it:

> Moral goodness is jealous. . . . It lays claim to the *whole* person, his whole heart and his whole will. Therefore we can decide for moral goodness only if, insofar as it lies in our power, we are willing to let it determine all our words and deeds. In other words, moral goodness is *indivisible*. Aristotle and the Stoics express this in their teaching about the solidarity of all particular virtues. No one can opt simultaneously for justice and *against* fidelity as basic moral attitudes.[10]

One is obliged to do good and avoid evil. This being so, one cannot be justified in choosing to violate any of the basic goods. This principle is absolute.[11]

Differing Moral Conclusions

What is not absolute, and what explains the fact that (unlike the conclusions of theoretical reason) moral conclusions can differ legitimately for different people, is the situation within which a choice is made. The exact same principle may yield different conclusions in different situations.[12]

Killing   This point can easily be seen by considering the two cases of premeditated killing and killing in self-defense. The first is obviously wrong, and the second morally permissible. But the fact that one is wrong and the other is right does not prove that ethics is relative, that it is sometimes right to intentionally seek to destroy the good of life. Quite the contrary, it is precisely because the principle that one should honor and not violate the good of life does not change that the judgments of the two cases can be different and yet both be justifiable. In the first case, the death of the other person is directly intended, and therefore the choice and act are wrong. In the second case, provided it really is killing in self-defense, the death of the other person is not directly intended. What is intended is the preservation of life—one's own life in this case—and therefore the choice and act are permissible.

One other qualification is necessary if killing in self-defense is to be morally acceptable: the killing should be the last resort. In other words, one should use the least force necessary in defending oneself. This qualification is really just a specification of intention, for if one uses more force than is necessary (say one kills when one knows that wounding would have been sufficient to ward off the attack), then it is quite clear that one really does intend that the other person should die, and this, as a direct violation of the good of life, is always wrong.[13]

Thus, what distinguishes, morally speaking, one situation from another is not the facts of the situation, nor the ultimate balance of good and bad consequences, but the object intended. It is because the facts of the situation lead us to believe that the taking of life is intended in one case and not intended in the other that we censor the first and permit the second. Understood this way, murder and killing in self-defense are two different acts, not one act that is sometimes right and sometimes wrong. Aquinas makes this point clearly in distinguishing between the marriage act and adultery. As physical act and as able to generate an offspring (their theoretical descriptions) they are the same, but in intention (which distinguishes them morally) they are radically different And so Aquinas says that, from an ethical point of view, the two acts belong to different species and that the act of adultery is always wrong.[14] We do not have one act which is sometimes permissible, but two acts: one permissible, the other forbidden.

Truth   Take, as another example, two cases of telling an untruth. In the first, one is asked where one's friend is by a judge in a court of law; in the second, one is asked the same question by a maniac who, wielding a knife, is threatening to kill the friend. In both cases one says what is untrue—that the friend left town last Tuesday without revealing his destination. It is clear that telling the untruth in the first case is immoral, while in the second it is not But again, this is not due to a change in the principle but in the situation. The good at stake is the good of orderly social life (friendship), for if we lie to one another, all community life is at an end.[15] In the first case, there is a legitimate authority asking the question, and the context is the pursuit of truth for the sake of the common good. To say what is untrue would be a violation of one's obligation to that common good.

In the second situation, however, there is no legitimate authority, and the context is not the pursuit of truth for the sake of the common good. One's untruth is not a violation of the common good; on the contrary, it advances the common good by avoiding a crime. However, one might ask whether the untruth is nevertheless a violation of what is owed the assailant as a fellow human being. While the assailant is clearly not interested in promoting the good of orderly social life (friendship), this does not imply any forfeiture of the right to be treated as an end, so that one may disregard the basic goods in dealing with criminals. Such a conclusion is compatible with social contract theory, perhaps, where obligation is based on covenants, but not with natural law ethics. As goods are more fundamental than rights (one can only have a right to something good), someone else's loss of a right does not permit one to violate a good. Since one has a real obligation to help one's fellow human beings, one has an obligation to help this human being. However, to fulfill the assailant's request will not help the assailant. To give the information is not only to be party oneself to the crime of murder (if the threat is carried out) and so to disregard one's responsibility to the murdered person and the community, but it is also and more immediately to disregard one's responsibility to this person who will murder if given the requested information. For the assailant's own good one must not allow him or her to kill another.

Not only must we not do evil, but we must also prevent evil from happening. Thus, one honors the good of orderly social life (friendship) both in preventing harm to other members of the society and also in preventing harm to this member, the most serious harm of making oneself evil by intentionally violating fundamental human goods. Now if it were possible to prevent the evil action without telling an untruth, then one should not tell the untruth, since in itself such an act violates the common good. As Aquinas said in his article on killing in self-defense, not only should one not intend to violate the good in question, but one must also use the least force necessary. In this case that might mean disarming and subduing the assailant (if possible) or better yet (if possible) using rational argument to convince the assailant that the action is wrong and should not be done.

Thus, the particularity of factual elements plays an important part in ethical decision-making. Again, this is not to say that the locus of moral significance in an act is the facts which describe its context. The complicated set of situational facts helps one judge, after the fact, whether or not the intention was good. This judgment is not to be based on some overall net balance of good consequences over bad ones (which calculation cannot be done), but in rightness of intention. For anyone deliberating about whether an act should be done, the moral point is never to do any act which intentionally violates a basic good. Some acts do this (intentional murder, adultery); others do not (killing in self-defense, sexual intercourse within marriage). The latter are permissible; the former are always wrong. Thus, while the situation can affect the way the principles of the natural law are applied, this fact in no way destroys the absolute character of the basic moral precepts themselves.

RELATIONSHIPS AMONG TRADITIONS

I am including within the natural law tradition people as diverse as Kant and Aristotle, as well as Plato, Cicero, and Aquinas. Can these all be said to share the same fundamental insights into morality, or should we separate their philosophies into different camps? It is quite common to distinguish deontological ethics (Kant), natural law ethics (Cicero and Aquinas), and virtue ethics (Aristotle and perhaps Plato—although people are not too sure where to put Plato). And there is some vociferous disagreement over which of these three theories is the most important. One major point of contention is the question of whether or not natural law is equivalent to duty ethics.[16] Another is whether morality should be understood as primarily a matter of law (whether duty ethics or natural law ethics) or of virtue.[17] In what follows, I intend to show that, while the emphases of these philosophers differ, they are in fundamental agreement about the foundations of moral responsibility.[18] Discussing their different emphases while showing their common ground may serve to fill out what is meant by natural law ethics as well as to defuse some controversy. Sometimes disagreement is more a matter of semantics than of real content. As Newman said,

> Half the controversies in the world are verbal ones; and could they be brought to plain issue, they would be brought to a prompt termination. . . . This is the great object to be aimed at in the present age, though confessedly a very arduous one. We need not dispute, we need not prove—we need but define. At all events, let us, if we can, do this first of all; and then see who are left for us to dispute with, what is left for us to prove.[19]

Natural Law Ethics

Let me take a moment to define what I mean by natural law ethics, for the term is being used ambiguously here—as the general notion of ethics founded on reason and as a specific theory of basic human goods and the first principle of practical reason (do good and avoid evil). One may well ask why not call this ethical tradition duty ethics or virtue ethics if they all have the same foundation. My contention is that natural law ethics in the specific sense is a necessary foundation for moral responsibility. While in no way antithetical to duty or virtue ethics, it is more specific and subtle than duty ethics (as we have already argued) and essential to virtue ethics since good habits logically require (at some stage) a knowledge of what is good. Thus, my purpose is not to deny the insights of duty or virtue ethics but to preserve them. This can only be done by specifying human good in the way that natural law ethics does. At the same time, I am concerned to show that the moral life is founded on practical reason as Kant insists and that its fullness requires virtue. To consider Cicero or Thomas Aquinas as adherents to natural law ethics is to take some such view as this of the ethics of reason, for both include

extensive discussions of obligation and virtue along with their treatments of
the basic goods.

Plato

In our examination of this natural law tradition, let us begin at the beginning, with Plato. While Plato centers his discussion on the cardinal virtues
(wisdom, justice, courage, and temperance) and thus could be called an
adherent to virtue ethics, he is really quite like Kant, for Plato insists on the
purity of intention as the center of ethics. Thus, in his *Crito*, Plato rejects
emotivism, self-interest, and consequences as moral guides in favor of reason
and doing what one knows to be right. The situation in the dialogue is that
Socrates is in jail on trumped-up charges, awaiting execution. In response to
Crito's eager encouragement to escape, Plato has Socrates reply: "My dear
Crito, your eagerness is worth much if it should have some right aim; if not,
then the greater your keenness the more difficult it is to deal with."[20] There is
nothing intrinsically bad about emotion; in fact, it is good if it follows and
supports reason. But reason must guide so that emotion is for the good; if
emotion supports what is wrong, the stronger it is, the worse the action will
be. And in the following rhetorical question, Socrates clearly rejects social
contract and utilitarian ethics. "Above all, is the truth such as we used to say
it was, whether the majority agree or not, and whether we must still suffer
worse things than we do now, or will be treated more gently, that nonethe-
less, wrongdoing is in every way harmful and shameful to the wrongdoer?"[21]

Thus an evil choice—even if it feels right, and/or agrees with majority
opinion, and/or brings about good consequences—is always wrong; and its
wrongness is bad for the agent. In other words, whether or not one's evil
choice hurts others, it is always self-destructive. To act unjustly is to harm
oneself. Conversely, to act justly is to better oneself. Now this point, central
to the natural law tradition, might appear to be a species of the Hobbesian
argument from self-interest; i.e., it is in one's self-interest to be good. Plato
did, in fact, argue that the egoist claim that one is best off having complete
power to do anything one wants (steal, rape, and kill) is false. Plato has
Socrates argue in the *Republic* that such a person who achieves mere satisfaction of desires through unconstrained power, far from being the happiest of
all human beings, is the most miserable.

Plato and Hobbes

However, the notions of self-interest espoused by Hobbes and Plato are as different as their two notions of self. Self-interest on the Hobbesian model is

based on the notion of the self as determined by the passions, where happiness is pleasure and freedom from pain. Self-interest as applied to Plato's argument is based on the understanding that the self is rational and free, able to know and do what is just. To act unjustly is to do what one knows one should not do. It is to create contradiction and confusion in the self; and to live with one's soul in such a state is to live a miserable existence.

Ultimately, the term self-interest (understood as the opposite of an interest in others) is really inappropriate when applied to Plato's notion since what is of self-interest in Plato's sense is also for the good of others. To really care for oneself is to be just and wise and temperate and courageous (the four cardinal virtues). But being just and wise and temperate and courageous is also good for the community. In short, there is no either/or in Plato's understanding of morality: what is good for the self is good for others and *vice versa*.

Plato and Aristotle

Aristotle says something very much like Plato where, in his discussion of friendship, he addresses the question of whether or not one should be a lover of self.[22] His answer is "no" and "yes," depending on what one holds to be good. If one places the lesser material goods (riches, power, and fame) above the greater common goods (friendship, truth, and justice), then one should not love oneself, for to do so is to further ruin the community and oneself. However, if one places the common goods above the material goods, then one should love oneself, for to do so is to further perfect the community and oneself. Material goods are competitive goods; one person's share of them decreases as someone else's increases. The same is not true of the common goods such as knowledge and beauty and friendship. With these, the more one person has, the more others can have. The more one person grows in wisdom, the more there is for everyone else. One person's work of art increases the store of beauty for all. As one makes more friends, the community of friendship widens for others, as well. While the material goods tend by their nature to be divisive, the common goods tend to promote community and peace. Provided that one chooses the real goods for oneself (those which are lasting and good for all human beings) and that one means the real self (the rational being who creates his or her character through choice and action), Aristotle concludes that one should be a lover of self.[23]

Plato, Aristotle, and Kant

While Plato and Aristotle argue for cardinal virtues as principles of moral perfection, recall that Kant (when discussing his point that the only thing good in itself is a good will) rejects the idea that the virtues could be considered good in themselves. After all, they can be misused; a temperate thief is a greater danger than one who might be distracted from crime by the lure of other pleasures. Thus, Kant rejects the virtue ethics of the ancients which is central to their understanding of happiness. However, Kant is mistaken in his understanding of the classical doctrine of the virtues. Neither Plato nor Aristotle would admit that there could be such a thing as a temperate thief. Virtue is a whole; to be virtuous is to be wise, just, courageous, and temperate.[24] To be unjust is to do what one knows one ought not to do, and to do this is not to be in control; hence, it is to be intemperate. To face danger unguided by wisdom is to be rash, not truly courageous. And to be intelligent without justice is to be merely cunning, not wise. Thus, for Plato and Aristotle all real virtue involves justice—that is, doing the right thing for its own sake. Hence, understood properly, there is much less distance between the virtue ethics of the ancients and Kant's ethics of duty than the latter thought.

The closeness of the two positions can be underlined in a very clear way by comparing Kant's explication of the three motives of the will with Aristotle's account of the three kinds of friendship. Recall that for Kant one may be motivated by self-interest, direct inclination, or duty; and it is only when acting out of duty that one's act has any moral worth. Aristotle says that friendship may be for the sake of utility, pleasure, or virtue.[25] The last kind, which he also calls perfect friendship, means that one cares for the friend for the friend's own sake. What is this but the recognition that the friend is an end who should be honored for his or her own sake and who is not to be treated as a means to satisfy one's desire for utility (self-interest) or pleasure (direct inclination)? The parallel is perfect, illustrating the point that Aristotle, known as a practitioner of virtue ethics, understood quite as well as Kant that morality is a matter of intention, and the best intention is to treat others as ends and not as means to other ends.

Of course, it is true that Aristotle's ethics does turn around a discussion of the virtues. His definition of virtue as "a habit, disposed toward action by deliberate choice, being at the mean relative to us, and defined by reason and as a prudent man would define it"[26] has been criticized by some adherents to the natural law position for not providing very strong moral guidance.[27] For if being good is some kind of a mean on a sliding scale between two extremes, how is this different from having one's own personal values (i.e., relativism)? And Aristotle's claim that the good person is the measure of ethical judgment and that what one has to do is simply follow that person raises the problem of finding and recognizing the good person, which might be hard to do (1) since few human beings are really good and (2) because it is impossible to recognize when one has found something without knowing what one is seeking.

However, a focus on this definition of ethics as the center of Aristotle's theory would be a mistake. For one thing, Aristotle distinguishes between virtue in the full sense, which belongs to the mature person who not only does the right thing but knows that the action is right, and the virtue of a child, which is mostly a matter of imitation without knowledge.[28] This is very much like the distinction Kant makes, in his examples of the grocer and altruist, between acting from duty (real moral worth) and merely in conformity to what duty demands (morally neutral). For another, in this definition Aristotle is only talking about virtues such as temperance and courage, where the application of habit and mean are most appropriate. The definition does not apply equally to a discussion of justice or wisdom, where the focus is more clearly on reason's judgment than on the development of good habits. Aristotle makes it very clear that an acceptable mean cannot be found for every action.

> Not every action nor every feeling, however, admits of the mean, for some of them have names which directly include badness, e.g., such feelings as malicious gladness, shamelessness, and envy, and, in the case of actions, adultery, theft, and murder; for all of these and others like them are blameworthy for being bad, not [just] their excesses and deficiencies. Accordingly, one is never right in performing these but is always mistaken; and there is no problem of whether it is good or not to do them, e.g., whether to commit adultery with the right woman, at the right time, in the right manner, etc., for to perform any of these is without qualification to be mistaken.[29]

This is pretty strong medicine, as strong as anything Aquinas or Kant or the Bible says about the moral law. In addition to this passage, there are passages in the *Nichomachean Ethics* which make reference to other fundamental human goods—such as life, procreation and family, friendship, knowledge, and religion—and the obligations based on these goods.[30]

Thus, the idea that the virtue ethics of Aristotle is somehow an alternative to Kantian or natural law ethics, since it is based on different foundations, is simply mistaken. Yes, there is a difference in emphasis: Kant does stress the formal structures of moral imperatives more than Aristotle, and Aristotle does focus on the development of the virtues, providing subtle distinctions about the relationship between what is good and what is pleasant that go far beyond what Kant has to say. However, when it comes to ultimate foundations, they agree that intention is central, and that there are some choices that are simply wrong in themselves. As Aristotle puts it, "the main principle in virtue and in character lies in intention."[31]

SYNTHESIS OF CICERO

The Roman philosopher Cicero did not think he had to choose between the ethics of duty, natural law, and virtue. In a letter to his son (*On Moral Obligation*), Cicero begins with some basic principles of obligation and duty, proceeds to discuss the range of basic goods, and then relates these to the cardinal virtues. Cicero openly states that the best moral philosophers are the Academics (followers of Plato), the Stoics, and the Peripatetics (followers of Aristotle). His position is an original synthesis of the elements of each—drawing mainly upon Plato for the basic idea of duty, on the Stoics for the notion of a natural law, and on Aristotle for an understanding of the virtues.

Obligation and Good

In the opening section, Cicero claims that morality is about obligation (duty), which covers "personal matters as well as those affecting others."[32] Thus, ethics is not just a way of mediating between people and settling disputes as the adherents to social contract theory hold. And, like Plato and Kant, Cicero rejects the idea that it is by utilitarian or emotional standards that morality is established. All ethical theories based on pleasure and pain fail to ground any obligation and are antithetical to virtue. "The man, for example, who considers pain the greatest evil can never be brave, nor can someone who considers pleasure the greatest good ever show self-control."[33] Not only is it impossible to derive virtuous behavior from pleasure and pain, but those who believe we are guided by pleasure and pain really have no business making any ethical judgments at all.

> These sects [those who think that pleasure and pain are the first principles of our actions], therefore, if they are to be consistent, are in no position to pronounce on moral obligation, since any rules which are to be reliable, lasting and in accordance with natural law, can only be laid down by those who consider that moral excellence should be sought solely, or at any rate primarily, for its own sake.[34]

Having firmly established that morality is a matter of obligation and of pursuing what is good for its own sake, Cicero goes on to list a number of basic human goods: life, procreation/family, community on all its levels, knowledge/truth, excellence in one's choices, and beauty. They are the goods of human nature, those things which are self-evidently and ultimately good to a conscious and reflective person. Their goodness is not a matter of convention, nor something established by majority opinion. Speaking of any of these basic goods, Cicero writes: "Even if its goodness were not recognized, it would still be good; for whatever we can say in all truth is commended by its own good nature, even if not approved by any man living."[35]

Natural Inclinations and Morality

One of the criticisms often leveled at natural law ethics from some members of the Kantian (deontological) camp is that natural law derives its precepts from psychological, biological, or physical drives. Were this the case, the Kantian would claim that only hypothetical imperatives could be derived, based on desires and not the dictates of reason. What is more, such a procedure would falter on Hume's insight that one cannot derive obligation from fact. While such a theory of the derivation of morality from such drives may have been true for some of the Stoic philosophers,[36] it is certainly not true for Cicero nor for Thomas Aquinas. It is true that they sometimes talk about natural inclinations (such as an inclination to live, to procreate, to know the truth, and to live together), but that they intend these inclinations to be read as premises for moral obligation is certainly not the case. The assumption that such a law of inclinations is the origin of all our actions would rule out freedom, for inclinations are subrational. Rather, Cicero and Aquinas always insist that reason should guide us, not inclination.[37] We *know* that life, procreation, knowledge, friendship, etc., are good and should be promoted and not violated, whatever the discussion may be concerning our psychological, biological, or physical relationships to these goods. This criticism does count against Hobbes' natural laws carrying any real obligation, for Hobbes' natural laws are ultimately reducible to physical laws; but the criticism fails when addressed to natural law as understood by Cicero and Aquinas. For Cicero and Aquinas the natural law is not the mechanical directives of our passions, but the dictates of practical reason which we are free to follow or not as we will.

In addition to affirming both duty and the basic goods as principles of ethics, Cicero underlines the intimate connection between the basic goods and the virtues. In the very act of listing the fundamental human goods, Cicero links them with the cardinal virtues (wisdom, justice, courage, and temperance)[38] which will be the focus of his discussion for the rest of the letter. The perfect honoring of the good of knowing the truth is wisdom. The perfect honoring of the good of community on all its levels is justice. The uncompromising search for excellence is an act of moral courage. And the highest instantiation of beauty in this world is the ordering of one's choices and actions through temperance. Thus, there is no fundamental option between honoring the basic goods of the natural law and perfecting oneself in virtue. The very honoring of the goods is the beginning of the virtues, and the virtues help one to more perfectly participate in the goods.

Foundation for Good Conduct

It is in this complementary support that the real difference between the basic goods and the virtues lies. The rational foundation for good conduct is found in the obligation to promote and perfect these basic human goods and to avoid acting in ways which dishonor or destroy them. Thus, for a complete explanation of what ought to be done and why, or what ought not to be done and why not, one must finally have recourse to the fundamental principles of human perfection—the basic goods. However, it is not enough to know what is good and why; to be morally excellent, one must also be able to do what one knows ought to be done. This consistent tendency to judge correctly and to do what is right is what is meant by virtue. Virtues are like habits: one acquires them by doing them. To become virtuous, one must practice being virtuous. Beyond hearing and understanding what is right and good, one must do what is right and good and do it consistently so that one becomes the kind of person who reliably acts in a morally excellent way. Thus, the basic goods and the virtues are not alternatives in some kind of competition for one's moral allegiance. Rather, they are two essential aspects of morality, both requiring one's attention. Would one be fully moral, one must know what is right and why it is right, and one must do what is right.[39] One must be well grounded in the natural law, and one must be virtuous. The natural law provides the content; the virtues provide the stable disposition for putting the principles of natural law into practice.[40]

FREEDOM AND NATURAL LAW

As we ended the first half of the book with the conclusion that all ethical theories which take pleasure and pain as first principles must embrace determinism (the denial of free choice), let us conclude this chapter on natural law by returning to the question of freedom. For while it is commonly thought that natural law ethics, with its moral absolutes, unduly restricts freedom, the truth is just the opposite; natural law ethics offers the widest scope for free activity of any theory of ethics.

In the first place, only by recognizing practical reason as central to human choice can there be such a thing as freedom of choice at all. And so, taken at their word, relativism, emotivism, egoism, and utilitarianism, insofar as they reject the reality of practical reason, reject freedom of choice. By placing reason at the center of morality, natural law ethics insists on the reality of free choice.

In the second place, natural law ethics does more than just allow for the possibility of free choice; it provides for the greatest latitude of good choices and so gives to the individual agent much greater personal freedom and responsibility than other ethical theories. While it is true (although inconsistent with their first principles) that egoism in its social contract form and utilitarianism seem to transcend mere emotional response by granting some degree of reasoned choice, their methods are far more restrictive of freedom than is the natural law injunction to honor and not violate basic human goods. If one adheres to Hobbes' idea of the social contract theory, one is obliged to do what the majority as bearers of power think is right, regardless of whether one's own reasoned judgment concurs. And if the utilitarian injunction to maximize consequences is taken seriously, then there is only one correct choice in any situation, for only one choice or action will, in fact, bring about the highest possible balance of pleasure over pain. Every choice but one will be a bad choice. To make that one right choice, one needs to be able to calculate the consequences of one's action on all those who are affected by it, near and far, now and in the future—a virtually impossible task. The upshot is that if social contract theory is right, the locus of morality shifts from the judgment of the individual conscience to social arbitration and compromise, and if utilitarian theory is right, we are all condemned to immorality since we cannot know the act with the best consequences.

Natural law ethics is not subject to such restrictions on freedom. As we stressed repeatedly in our discussions of Kant, the individual is a unique center of reason (and therefore moral responsibility), not to be reduced or sacrificed, as in Hobbes, to that Leviathan—the common will. In the last analysis, one should follow one's conscience, for not to do so is to do what one thinks is evil, which is always wrong. Of course, following one's conscience will not automatically make one right, for there is also the responsibility to correctly inform one's conscience, since we should always pursue the good in the best possible way.[41] But informing one's conscience is never a matter of merely yielding to power or majority opinion. Moral responsibility lives in the free act of the individual conscience.

Nor is the command of the natural law to promote and not violate the basic goods anywhere near as restrictive as the utilitarian injunction to do the act which brings about the greatest net amount of pleasure or good, for, according to the natural law position, there is no one best act. While one is under an absolute obligation to do good and avoid evil, there are a plurality of human goods. Thus, one may follow the natural law by fostering the good of life as a nurse or doctor, or by promoting the good of knowledge as a teacher or researcher, or by participating in the good of friendship by marrying and raising a family or fostering community on its various levels, or by pursuing the other goods of play, beauty, and religion. All these goods are worthy of pursuit, nor is one essentially better than another so that it could be said to be better in some absolute way to be a doctor than an artist or *vice versa*. Since all the goods are self-evidently and irreducibly good, none takes universal precedence over any other. They are all good in themselves and hence the suitable objects of free choice.

The single absolute restriction on one's freedom of choice and action is that one must not choose directly against any basic good. While it is also true that one is obliged to pursue and promote the basic goods, and not just to avoid violating them, this positive requirement is general and not specific as to which good to promote, at what time, in what situation, to what extent, etc. One is not obliged to pursue each of the basic goods to the same degree, for such a requirement, besides being impossible to fulfill, would be unreasonable.

It would be impossible to fulfill because, in pursuing any good, one inevitably leaves others unpursued. If one reads a book, pursuing the good of knowledge, then one is not painting a picture or entertaining friends. If one marries and has a family, then one's time for religion and play will be inevitably restricted.

Such a requirement to pursue all the goods to the same degree would also be unreasonable. We all have different talents and personalities, and while it would be wrong to denigrate a basic good simply because one has no particular talent for it, there is no reason why one should not specialize in the good or goods for which one is most suited and to which one is most attracted. There is no intrinsic limit to how much each basic good ought to be pursued, beyond which one would be said to be wasting one's time. As John Finnis puts it, the basic goods are "open-ended"; that is, they are infinitely good in the sense that neither oneself nor the whole community of persons past, present, and future could ever completely attain them.[42] There is always more that is worth doing. Hence, specialization is justified. The latitude allowed in what one may do is very broad, opening the way to creative, morally good activity.

Conflict among Basic Goods

If the specific restriction of the moral life is the absolute command never to intentionally and directly act against any of the basic human goods, the question arises: What is one to do if the basic goods conflict? What if one has to choose between them? I have saved this question until now for a couple of reasons. First of all, when defining moral principles, one should not base one's principles on the few possible exceptions to the rule. For one thing, cases where one might be forced to sacrifice one basic good for another are going to be exceedingly rare. For another, such cases would tend to be very complicated factually as well as morally, and hence mistakes about the facts of the situation could be the cause of a mistaken judgment as well as conflicts among ethical principles. Secondly, this is a difficult question whose answer requires some familiarity with the natural law principles we have discussed in the preceding pages. Still, it is important to address such an objection, for it presents a strong challenge to the claim of natural law ethics to offer certain and reliable principles on which to act.

To begin with, we should ask whether or not there are cases in which one would be forced to choose. Literally speaking, one cannot be forced to choose since choosing involves freedom and being forced denies it. However, there might be cases where not to choose would be immoral, so that one could be said to be "forced" by moral obligation.

Equality of Basic Goods Before considering a couple of such possible cases where one or another basic good might take preference, it would be well to get the full flavor of the argument for their fundamental equality. John Finnis says that the equality of the basic goods can be understood in three ways.[43] First of all, they are all self-evidently good. Upon reflection, one knows that they are good; one does not need someone else to prove their goodness. Secondly, no one of the basic goods is merely an aspect or a derivative of another good. While there is some overlapping (e.g., beauty and play, knowledge and religion), no basic good is entirely reducible to any other or even to all the others. Finally, each of the basic goods can be argued to be the most important. For example, one can argue that life is most important because without it none of the other basic goods could be pursued. But then one could argue, with Socrates, that life without knowledge is not worth living. Friendship is both good in itself and in many cases a prerequisite for the other goods since these other goods are common goods which grow in community. And because God is the first principle of all things true, good, and beautiful, ordering one's life in proper relation to God (religion) can be argued to be the most important good. That each good can reasonably be argued to be the most important indicates that none actually is the most important.

Basis for Choosing   However, while none of the basic goods is reducible to another or the others, it might be that a basic good involves the others in some way which would justify preferring it if one were morally obliged to choose. Taking as our point of reference Finnis's seven basic goods (life, knowledge, friendship, aesthetic experience, play, practical reasonableness, and religion), there seem to be three such goods—life, practical reasonableness, and religion.

Consider practical reasonableness first. This good involves the ordering of the basic goods in proper relation within oneself, and the honoring of this ordering in one's choices and actions; that is, it involves by its very essence the other goods. Since to participate in this good is to treat all goods in a reasonable way through honoring and not violating them, it is clear that there can be no conflict between this good and any other.

Of possible conflicts, that between life and the other goods is most likely to arise. This is because life can be seen as either the most important or the least important of the goods. As has already been said, life can be considered most important in the sense that, without it, one cannot participate in any good at all. It is thus a prerequisite, or necessary cause, of all morally responsible activity. However, looked at in another way, it could be said to be the least important of the goods. One could say that what makes life valuable is the fact that it allows one to participate in the other goods. Understood in this way, the other goods are the ends and life the means. As the end is always more important than the means, all the other basic goods can be understood to be more important than life.

Finally, religion occupies a special position vis-à-vis the other basic goods. While religion is like the other goods in being a final cause of life, its object (God, creator and sustainer of the universe) is also the efficient cause of every good. In a sense, the basic goods are derivative—derived from God. If a conflict were to occur between the good of religion (rendering to God proper thanks and respect) and any other good, it might be argued that one should always choose God. This relationship between religion and the other goods we shall examine in Chapter Eight. Here let us look at a couple of cases involving conflicts between the good of life and other goods and how they might be resolved by the principles of natural law.

Natural Law and Conflicting Goods

That it might be permissible in some cases to act directly against one of the basic goods for the sake of life, but not vice versa, seems pretty clear. For example, it would be permissible to burn up beautiful antique furniture or an important scientific manuscript in order to keep oneself or another alive (if no other option were available), but it would not be permissible to kill a human being who prevented one from appreciating a beautiful painting or in order to gain knowledge that could not be obtained in any other way. The reason for this nonreciprocal relation is that human life involves implicitly all the basic goods (for they are human goods). To burn a beautiful work of art or a great book of philosophy in order to save a human life is permissible because the same act that destroys beauty or knowledge also preserves it (in the human life that is saved). Every human being is an ethical world, a microcosm of human goods. This is what makes murder and suicide so wrong: not only is the basic good of life destroyed, but all the basic goods in the particular ethical world that is this human person are violated. However, the contrary relation (killing the person for the sake of another basic good—beauty or knowledge) cannot be justified in any similar way. While I have argued that actions against basic goods for the sake of life could be justified, let me add that essential rider: one should use the least force necessary. Thus, if there is another way to preserve life, it should be taken; if less beautiful artifacts or less important books are available, one should sacrifice these lesser instances of the goods in question rather than the greater. In other words, one should never directly intend the violation of these basic goods.

This nonreciprocal relation does not, however, imply that life is absolutely better than the other goods. If it were, it would never be permissible to risk one's life for anything but another's life. Yet we do not think that those (like Socrates and the martyrs) who have risked their lives rather than deny the truth are immoral for doing so. As a case in point, consider the following example. One has learned from reliable sources that an enemy is intent on taking over one's country and brainwashing the people so that they will not think that knowledge, family, and religion are important (things one knows are good).[44] The only way to stop the enemy from accomplishing its plan is to risk one's life. In such a case, it is certainly permissible to do so. It would even seem to be required were the threat to someone for whom one had the first responsibility—i.e., one's children or oneself. We have an obligation to remain in a state where pursuing good is possible. (Thus, one is required to refrain from getting addicted to drugs.) To allow, in the name of protecting biological life, oneself or one's family to be permanently denied the freedom and rationality required for morally responsible action would be wrong.

Complicated situations where more than one basic good are directly involved require many particular judgments to sort out the proper choice and course of action. It might be that in some cases either course of action would be permissible (e.g., perhaps in conflicts between the goods of beauty and knowledge) or neither (e.g., in a conflict where the choice was between two innocent lives). However, what could never be the case is that a course of action could be justified without recourse to practical reason with its knowledge of basic goods as first principles of obligation. Nor would it ever be permissible to sacrifice a basic good for another except as the very last resort—an indication that the intended object of the act is clearly the preservation or promotion of a basic good and not the violation of a basic good.

The natural law tradition allows both for the possibility of freedom and for a wider scope of free activity than the other moral theories we have examined. While ethical theories which take pleasure and pain as first principles actually imply determinism, natural law ethics, by placing reason at the center of ethics, makes room for freedom. Even when ethical theories of pleasure and pain inconsistently assume the freedom to choose the means to some end, the end is either dictated by desire (whether benevolent or selfish) or by some unknowable best overall consequence. In neither case is the choice really one's own to make. By recognizing that there are many equally basic human goods, each worthy of pursuit for its own sake, natural law ethics ensures a wide scope of free choice, granting to the individual the honor of being a unique creative center of meaningful activity.

7

Retrospective and Reevaluation

Having discovered that justification or condemnation of any moral claim is to be found in the principles of practical reason known as the natural law, let us turn and retrace our steps, applying these principles in a review and reevaluation of the moral systems which have been found wanting. Inadequate as utilitarianism, social contract theory, emotivism, and relativism are, it would be surprising if they had absolutely no connection with moral obligation. After all, the philosophers espousing such theories have all had access (as rational beings) to the very same moral principles as any philosopher of the natural law tradition; and they have been motivated, at least in part, by a desire to provide a better foundation for ethics than what they inherited. While it is clear that none of these theories can provide, on its own terms, any foundation for real responsibility, each is founded on a moral insight worthy of recognition and preservation. However, these insights can only be justified within the tradition we have called natural law.

UTILITARIAN THEORY

Consider, in the first place, the utilitarian theory of ethics. Insofar as this theory claims that we ought to consider consequences in our decision-making processes, it is surely correct. For example, if one were confronted with two ways of accomplishing some objective (say building a bridge or combatting some disease), one of which had a high risk of leading to the deaths of innocent people, there would certainly be an obligation to take the safer alternative. Again, if one were planning a national health care system and came up with two projected plans providing equal coverage but at different costs, one would surely be obliged to choose the cheaper plan since more funds would then be available for health care or to promote other of the basic goods. However, the basis for the obligation in each of these examples is not to be found purely and simply in an analysis of consequences, for a statistical balance of facts does not validly imply any obligation. The underlying moral principle in each of these examples is not the summation of projected pleasurable and painful consequences but rather the precept that one should promote and not violate the basic good of life.

Since one is obliged to pursue what is good and avoid what is evil, one should promote good and avoid evil consequences insofar as they can be foreseen, that is, insofar as they fall within the realm of intention. Consideration of consequences may be of central importance when deciding on the best way to accomplish some good end. While in our examples, the good end has been life, one could apply the same argument to cases which involve other basic goods. For example, choosing the best way to teach some piece of knowledge would depend in part on how well the students learn from various approaches. Again, one consideration in developing an acceptable law enforcement policy would be how well different policies would promote and protect community life.

However, the ideal of promoting consequences is a secondary precept based on prior foundations of ethical obligation found in natural law. One must not let the requirement to consider consequences override its own foundation in the requirement to respect every basic good. For example, because it is always wrong to choose directly against any basic good, the intentional killing of one innocent hostage to save the lives of ten other innocent hostages could never be morally justified—contrary to the utilitarian argument that, since more lives would be saved by killing one innocent person, such an act would be permissible and even required. Thus, too, one must not lie in order to get one's idea across more effectively; and it would be wrong to institute an antireligious policy in order to promote social cohesion and security through uniformity.

Greatest Net Sum of Good

Up to now, we have considered utilitarianism in various forms which developed out of Bentham's attempt to provide a scientific account of how to maximize pleasure and minimize pain. This theory, we found, founders on the impossibility of deriving obligation from biological and psychological facts about what promotes pleasure and avoids pain. However, there is a species of utilitarianism which would agree with the natural law tradition that there are goods irreducible to pleasure and which would argue that one must do the act which brings about the greatest net sum these basic goods. G. E. Moore, for example, holds that human beings have a direct intuition into such goods as friendship and beauty.

No one, probably, who has asked himself the question, has ever doubted that personal affection and the appreciation of what is beautiful in Art or Nature, are good in themselves; nor, if we consider strictly what things are worth having *purely for their own sakes*, does it appear probable that any one will think that anything else has *nearly* so great a value as the things which are included under these two heads.[1]

However, if one attempts to apply the utilitarian criterion of maximizing consequences beyond the realm of one basic good (life, or knowledge, or community life) to the whole of our intentional life with its range of basic goods, one must fail to come to any justifiable conclusion, for such a thing literally *cannot* be done. The reason for this is that the basic goods are incommensurable; that is, there is no common denominator by which the goods could be measured so that overall utility could be tallied. Just as there is no common denominator which can enable one to sum up the many dimensions of quantity (such as number, volume, length, and weight), so it is impossible to sum up the many dimensions of human good (such as life, knowledge, friendship, and beauty). These goods are distinct dimensions of human well-being.

> In short, no determinate meaning can be found for the term "good" that would allow any commensurating and calculus of good to be made in order to settle those basic questions of practical reason which we call "moral" questions. Hence, . . . the consequentialist methodological injunction to maximize net good is senseless, in the way that it is senseless to try to sum up the quantity of the size of this page, the quantity of the number six, and the quantity of the mass of this book.[2]

Ultimate Good

Bentham and his disciples had, of course, an answer to this problem of incommensurable goods; they simply said that there is, in fact, only one basic good—pleasure. Thus, all one needs to do is to find out how much pleasure (and what kinds, for Mill) an action brings in order to know whether or not one should follow through on it. Although we have discussed the drawbacks of classical utilitarian theory already, let us reconsider the plausibility of the claim that pleasure is the ultimate end we seek. For even after having discussed the natural law theory of the basic human goods, one may still be tempted to say that really, in the final analysis, we only want to participate in these goods for the pleasure they bring.

The point that pleasure is not the *only* thing desirable as an end (that the meaning of "good" is not reducible to pleasure) seems quite obvious. The desires for truth or virtues such as courage, justice, and friendship, for example, are not reducible to the desire for pleasure. But perhaps pleasure is the only thing desirable as an end *in itself*. Perhaps the only reason human beings desire knowledge or friendship is for the pleasure each brings. This was Mill's position: There is only one ultimate good, and that is pleasure. Knowledge and virtue are originally and ultimately desired for the pleasure which results from them.

On this question of the ultimate human good, it is helpful to compare Mill and Aristotle. Both Mill and Aristotle say that the ultimate end every human being seeks is happiness, and both include in the idea of happiness pleasure and goods such as knowledge and friendship. However, there is a world of difference between what each finally means by happiness. For Mill happiness is ultimately a life of bodily and psychic pleasure, free of pain. Knowledge and virtue are not naturally desired for their own sakes but because they lead to pleasure. Ultimately, they are merely means to the end of pleasure.[3] Aristotle, on the other hand, holds that the essence of happiness is found in activities of reason, such as knowledge and virtue. Pleasure is a "consequent end," something indeed desired for its own sake but always dependent on another activity.[4] Since every activity of the human being is an activity of the whole human being (body and soul), even the most intellectual of our activities, if performed well, brings with it an appropriate pleasure. But the pleasure is not what is sought in these activities.

Aristotle shows in a couple of ways that pleasure cannot be what we intend when we seek knowledge or virtue.[5] In the first place, pursuing the good of knowledge or virtue is not always pleasant, and yet one thinks that such activities are worth pursuing. In fact, the activities when performed at their highest levels disregard pleasure. They must do so or fail to be the activities in question. Consider pursuing knowledge: the quickest way to cease to pursue the good of knowledge is to focus on and aim at the pleasure it brings. If one is conducting a scientific experiment, for example, the most certain path to destroying its integrity is to let one's desire for pleasure (the pleasure of having the experiment be successful in verifying one's hypothesis, or the pleasure of being famous for making an important contribution to one's field) affect one's judgment. Or consider the good of what Aristotle calls the friendship of virtue—i.e., friendship for the sake of the other. The quickest way to lose such a friendship is to care about the friend only insofar as he or she brings one pleasure. If it is hard to see this point about another person's response, one need only reverse the relation and ask how long one would cherish a friend after discovering that the friend cared for oneself only as an object of pleasure.

In the second place, not only does one lose the activity in question if one aims for the pleasure it brings, but one also loses the pleasure itself. Since every activity has its own appropriate pleasure, the only way to experience the pleasure of knowledge or virtue is to engage in the activity of knowledge or virtue. Thus, logically implied by the fact that one wants to experience the pleasure of knowledge or friendship is the fact that one understands knowledge and friendship as distinct from pleasure and from each other.

Thus, pleasure is simply not the only thing desirable as an end in itself. In fact, pleasure as an object of choice has no meaning in and of itself. It is meaningful only as defined by the activity which it accompanies.[6] The kinds of activities which one recognizes as good in themselves are those which participate in the basic goods; and these goods, as incommensurable, cannot be tabulated by any kind of utilitarian calculus.

Moral Obligation

Even if the summing up of basic goods were possible (which it is not) the fact of the sum would not itself provide obligation. Only if there is a first principle of practical reason such as "do good and avoid evil" could the factual premises about the balance of goods and evils lead to a conclusion of obligation. Thus the utilitarian method, even if it makes use of the basic goods, fails to provide a reasonable answer to the question of what ought and ought not to be done.

Still, while utilitarian theory fails on a number of accounts to provide an adequate foundation for moral obligation, there is an element of truth in the idea that one ought to care about the consequences of one's acts. The element, however, is grounded in the natural law theory of ethical obligation and cannot be derived from the principles of utilitarianism itself (whether based on pleasure and pain alone or on a range of basic goods).

SOCIAL CONTRACT THEORY

Like utilitarianism, egoism and the social contract theory have a certain moral plausibility. The social contract theory seems to provide for a measure of stability and cooperation within society. Since stability and cooperation are certainly good, the social contract theorist who intends these ends is acting in a good, and hence morally justifiable, way. However, the goodness arises not from self-interest, but from the obligation to promote the basic goods for all people. This obligation is a requirement of natural law, not of egoism.

Orderly social life is good for both the individual and the community. Contrary to Hobbes' position, which holds that human beings naturally hate each other and would prefer pleasure in isolation to any kind of social interaction, the natural law tradition holds that society is natural, that it is good for the individual to live with others. In fact, the individual can only be perfected within society. A consideration of some of the basic goods makes this evident. The goods of life, knowledge, and beauty are all enhanced for the individual by interaction with others. These common goods grow in community. Nor is orderly social life (a species of friendship) good only because it allows for the promotion of the basic goods mentioned. On reflection, it is evident that friendship is good in itself, standing in need of no further justification. Thus, it is certainly true that the ideals of social stability and cooperation, which might be said to lie behind the social contract theory, are good, but they do not follow from the first principle of self-interest.

EGOISM

Even the more radical principle of egoism—that one should care for oneself first—has some plausibility. There is indeed a special obligation to care for oneself which, understood properly, is more binding than the obligation to help others. This is not to say that one is, in fact, of more intrinsic value than others, nor would this condone actions which unjustly favor oneself. The reason one has a special obligation to care for oneself is that the only direct contribution one can make to the moral goodness of the world is to make oneself and one's actions good. It is this insight which prompts Thomas Aquinas to say that suicide is a worse sin than murder.[7] Any intentional action against the good of innocent life is intrinsically wrong. Therefore, all intentional taking of innocent life—one's own or another's—is absolutely prohibited. What makes suicide worse is that one is intentionally attacking the very heart of morality in taking one's life. It is by being human that one knows what is right and what is wrong. One's conscience, properly informed, is the seat of morality. To kill oneself is thus to destroy morality at its very foundation—one's own self as rational and free. It is to remove completely one's only direct avenue (one's own actions) to promoting good.

Egoism, then, is not wholly without moral plausibility. But the moral plausibility does not come from itself, especially as interpreted by its adherents, for human nature understood as able to react to pleasure and pain and instinctively programmed to pursue safety is not the seat of morality. In fact, if this were all there is to being human, there would be no moral obligation at all. The plausibility of egoism, such as it is, comes not from itself but from the principles of the natural law tradition.

EMOTIVISM

Emotivism, too, has a moral element which recommends it as worthy of choice. To have benevolent feelings (passions, emotions) toward mankind is certainly a good thing. Conversely, to have no feelings of affection for others (or worse, that one should hate others) is an appalling state of affairs. To be human is to have feelings, and to be fully human is to have feelings which have been humanized, not brutalized. But notice what has been introduced here—an element of judgment which transcends the realm of the feelings themselves. That we have passions is a simple fact of our being animals. It is, in itself, neither good nor bad in an ethical sense. This is clear from the fact that we do not count other animals who are capable of displaying behavior akin to hatred, affection, and anger as morally obliged. That we should have "humanized" passions indicates that there is something about being human which transcends the other beasts. It is our ability to distinguish good from evil that sets us apart from the other animals, and this ability (not the emotions themselves) is the seat of morality.

Thus, while human beings should have benevolent feelings and should "feel good" about each other, there simply is no way to find any meaning for such terms as "benevolent" and "good" within the feelings themselves. It is only feelings as guided by reason which can be said to be good. This is really the ancient theory of the virtues. Moral character is a kind of second nature, born of nurturing such virtues as courage, temperance, and kindness through imitation and practice. But as Cicero pointed out, these virtues are incompatible with a simple following of feelings prompted by pleasure and pain. The virtues require the discernment of practical reason. The stabilization of one's emotions to feel good about acts of justice and kindness and feel outrage at acts of injustice and cruelty requires the intervention of a guide which knows justice and kindness to be better than injustice and cruelty, and this guide is practical reason, not another passion.

RELATIVISM

Even relativism—that most outspoken critic of the natural law's insistence on absolute moral norms—carries with it a grain of moral truth. Did it not, it seems hard to believe that it could gain so much credence in the world today. The plausibility of relativism rests on two insights.

First, relativism points to the importance of the situation in making concrete ethical decisions. This is certainly correct. There is nothing wrong with throwing stones—unless there are people in the line of fire. There is nothing wrong with shouting—unless one is in a library or attending a performance of classical music. But notice, if relativism were absolutely correct in its denial of objective moral norms, there could be no distinction between situations that do and do not excuse; one could not say that it is wrong to stone people or shout during musical performances since every thrown stone or strained vocal chord is a unique and unrepeatable event. So while circumstances must be taken into account in ethical decisions, the very ability to distinguish between the permissible and impermissible cases based on differences of situation implies the understanding of universal moral norms. These norms are obviously not found in relativism; they are found in the principles of practical reason.

Secondly, as we mentioned in our opening chapter, tolerance is a real moral requirement. Moral absolutism can be, and often has been, used as an excuse for prejudice against people or for the glorification of a particular and arbitrary point of view. Insofar as relativism (in the name of tolerance) points this out and seeks to combat it, it is surely standing up for something good. But insofar as it is standing up for something good, it is not relativism, for relativism is the theory that good and evil are meaningless terms. What is morally plausible in relativism (i.e., tolerance) is just a requirement of the natural law—that every human life is intrinsically valuable and should be respected and promoted. This is a command of reason, understood to be universally binding.

While tolerance is a real obligation, embracing it does not mean judging all choices as equally acceptable. Most obviously, being tolerant does not mean that one should accept intolerant choices. Nor does it mean that one should countenance willful murder, betrayal, lying, or wanton destruction of beauty. One of the supports for tolerance is that we think people should be free to choose. However, the idea that an act is justified because it is freely done could only make sense where all options are good. Since some choices are not good, the mere fact that a choice is freely made cannot possibly justify that choice. An evil choice is not the least bit better for being freely made (in fact, this makes it worse).

The idea that it is good to choose evil is obviously a contradiction, and the idea that it is good to leave others free to choose evil (a mistaken view of tolerance) also makes no sense, except under the assumption that the only way to be free to choose good is also to be free to choose evil. But this assumption is simply false; the exercise of free choice does not require that we ever choose evil. Since human good is irreducibly plural, there are ample opportunities to choose freely among really good options—a life devoted to medicine, or family, or knowledge, or art, or religion, for example, or the multitude of particular choices which participate in these goods. The exercise of free choice does not logically entail ever making an evil choice.

It makes no sense to say that people have a right to be allowed to choose evil, for all rights and obligations are founded on the basic command "do good and avoid evil." Freedom of choice is not a transcendent good prior to the other basic goods of life, knowledge, friendship, etc. It can only be good to choose if there are good things to be chosen and if, in fact, the good things are chosen. Thus, the basic goods are logically prior (in the realm of final causality or purpose) to freedom of choice. All this analytical explanation only says something obvious; since not all free choices choose what is good, not all free choices should be accepted. Relativism, which amounts to saying that all free choices are equally acceptable, is clearly unacceptable. The real requirement of tolerance, which often lies behind the moral plausibility of relativism, finds its justification only in the universal dictates of natural law.

NATURAL LAW AND PLURALISM

Having retraced the steps of our quest for moral foundations, it should be admitted that there is some plausibility to all the systems of morality we have examined, even the one (relativism) which rejects the very idea of any moral norms. However, the plausibility cannot be derived from the principles of these theories—not from utilitarianism, nor egoism, nor emotivism, nor relativism. If these systems are consistent with their own principles, they all must fail to justify their own moral integrity. Only in natural law, which is grounded on the human being's ability to know and choose what is good, can the foundations for the moral plausibility of the very systems which seek to replace or destroy it be found.

There are some who, while agreeing that all these ethical theories hold some moral truth, would deny that there is one normative theory, such as natural law, from which this truth originates. In the final analysis, these philosophers would say that one must apply the ethical principle which the situation calls for. Since no one theory is sufficient to solve every ethical problem, sometimes it is best to invoke a utilitarian principle, sometimes one based on egoism, sometimes a theory of moral absolutes, sometimes relativism.

Ethical Pluralism

This position may, in general, be called ethical pluralism, although it appears under many names. Epicurus could, perhaps, be called an ethical pluralist. Recall how his theory involves principles of emotivism, egoism, and utilitarianism. The position of Brandt in his book *A Theory of the Good and the Right*, which he calls "a pluralistic welfare-maximizing moral system,"[8] incorporates the principles of egoism, act utilitarianism, and utilitarian generalization.

Ethical pluralism has arisen in modern times in response to criticisms (some of which we have brought up) leveled against the various theories.

One way to deal with these criticisms is to trade them off against each other. Since feelings are not always correct, since egoism cannot account for our sense that we ought to care for others, since consequences cannot always be known and involve too much particularity, we must be flexible enough to invoke the theory appropriate to the particular situation. Thus, Amelie Rorty suggests that moral pluralism is a kind of "checks and balances" system. "In principle, the very plurality of moral perspectives would provide some check on the territorial ambitions of any one of them. . . . The more fragmented and cross-categorized the varieties of moral pluralism, the greater the safety."[9]

Pragmatism

The theory known as pragmatism, which developed among American philosophers in this century, involves such a flexible ethical perspective. In any given situation, one should do what is expedient. This may mean doing what feels right, or doing what is in one's best interests, or that which brings the best results. As William James wrote in his work *Pragmatism*, "'The true,' to put it very briefly, is only the expedient in the way of our thinking, just as 'the right' is only the expedient in the way of our behaving."[10] One should not be too concerned about following any exacting scientific method; rather, one should do what any commonsensical person would do.[11]

Joseph Fletcher's situation ethics owes a lot to pragmatism, as he himself professes.[12] Fletcher, however, admits three other presuppositions of this theory: relativism, positivism, and personalism. Unlike the pragmatists, he even admits principles of natural law. These principles, however, do not have any absolute value. "It is necessary to insist that situation ethics is willing to make full and respectful use of principles, to be treated as maxims but not as laws or precepts. We might call it 'principled relativism'."[13] All ethical choices depend on the situation and what love calls for in the situation.

Fallibilistic Ethical Pluralism

On the contemporary scene, Lawrence Hinman, after distinguishing the theories we have discussed in this work, argues for what he calls "fallibilistic ethical pluralism," which is a kind of middle ground between relativism and absolutism.[14] What is more, Hinman's pluralism is what he calls a "robust pluralism"; competing theories do not just seem to have disagreements which can ultimately be overcome but really are different and irreconcilable. "This text approaches moral theory within the context of robust pluralism. It assumes that there are many standards of value, and that these are not necessarily consistent with one another."[15] Compatibility is not a requirement for a such a moral theory. On the contrary, Hinman sees disagreement and diversity of moral opinion as something positive.[16] In "Varieties of Pluralism," Amelie Rorty makes this same point: "The plurality of practical moral systems can not only constrain but also enhance one another, set phrases and phases for further development. Multiplicity is in itself valuable, not only for the liberal reason that debate is necessary for the discovery of truth, but because a multiplicity of modes of life expressed in habits and practices are necessary for any one of them to be sound life."[17]

Ethical Obligation

While pluralism is similar in some ways to what I have proposed in this chapter, it is different in two major respects. First of all, it implies that each theory, on its own terms, succeeds in providing ethical obligation. Against this, I have argued that none of the theories which take modern science as a model either as to content (assuming a materialism which implies pleasure and pain as first principles) or as to method (restricting reason to the operations of description and prediction) can justify its moral conclusions. Only if "good" has some meaning beyond just the inevitable drives which mechanically determine our actions can there be justification for any theory of morality or indeed for criticism of any theory of morality. And only if reason is also prescriptive (i.e., if there are first principles of practical reason) can there be grounds for justifying or condemning any particular choice or action at all.

Secondly, if we are to accept the principle that sometimes one theory should be invoked and sometimes another, we still have the question of what principle is to guide us in deciding which theory to invoke. If it is the situation, then we are back to relativism; if it is one's feelings, then we are back to either Hume's emotivism where benevolence reigns or to Hobbes' self-interest; if it is consequences, then we are back to the pure tabulation of facts which can imply no obligation. None of these theories can give a reasoned account of one's choice, for none of these theories recognizes that reason is at the heart of moral obligation.

Guiding Principles

Fletcher and Hinman do have answers to this question of what principles should guide us in our decision making; for Fletcher it is love, for Hinman, character. But neither of these ultimately succeeds in providing foundations which can justify moral action.

Fletcher says that the only absolute obligation is to love, and he understands this love to be primarily Christian love. To the objection that Christian love is not admitted by everyone and therefore needs to be shown to be axiomatic for believers and unbelievers alike, Fletcher responds by saying that believing in love as a first principle is no more absurd than any other moral judgment—not that Christian love is not absurd, but that *all* moral principles are absurd. "Any moral or value judgment in ethics, like the theologian's faith proposition, is a *decision*—not a conclusion. . . . Value choices are made and normative standards embraced in a fashion every bit as arbitrary and absurd as the leap of faith."[18] What Fletcher is following here is the logic of Hume's insight that there is no deriving values from facts, no prescriptive statements from descriptive; and like Hume, Fletcher denies that reason is practical as well as theoretical. If reason does not justify our actions, then what does? If it is some irrational, "absurd," impulse, then we are thrown back into the problems of emotivism, and by that route to radical, subjective relativism.

As for Hinman, he claims that the guide is character. He is not arguing for virtue ethics alone, for it is but one of the many theories that contribute to the richness of our moral lives. However, it is character which must settle the question of which theory to invoke when theories provide contrary opinions on a given point. "Without good character, we often only will be able to apply moral principles in a mechanical manner, largely insensitive to the nuances of the situation. . . . The wise person is the individual who is able to know when the concerns of one tradition take precedence over the concerns of the other traditions."[19] While this guide seems better than emotions, since character means some stable disposition toward acting in a consistent manner, to make character the ultimate criterion for distinguishing right from wrong has two problems. In the first place, there is the question of what kind of character is a good guide. Obviously a consistently bad character would not be a good guide. If we can distinguish between a good and a bad character, what do we use for criteria? Secondly, one can ask the same question of Hinman as we did of the adherents of virtue ethics: How is it that character is formed? If it is just a matter of tradition, as it is in the thought of Alasdair MacIntyre,[20] then we are back to cultural relativism, which ultimately denies the existence of any absolute moral norms. If, on the other hand, one wants to argue (as Aristotle does in his famous definition[21]) that virtue stabilized in character is ultimately a matter of reason, then we are back to some analysis of how reason can guide our choices—that is, to the kinds of foundations we find in natural law ethics.[22]

Choice of Principles

While I would agree with pluralism that features of all the ethical theories we have discussed come into play in moral decision-making, the choice of which one to invoke must be made by practical reason if it is to be justified. And if by practical reason, then there must be some first, self-evident principles of practical reason. These principles are those irreducible elements of human flourishing (those things we know, upon reflection, to be good) and that most fundamental obligation to do what we know to be good. As I said at the outset of the last chapter, these are not at all esoteric, and they were undoubtedly the motivations (or at least part of them) of the philosophers who argued for the different theories we have discussed. But it is also undoubtedly true that such principles are not the irrational or absurd leaps of which Fletcher speaks. While neither a first principle of reason nor an impulse can be deductively proven, they do not have the same status in our rational lives; the former are inescapable in one's reasoning while the latter are beside the point, irrelevant. Although first principles cannot be deductively proven, their reasonableness can be proven indirectly by showing that their denial leads to absurdity. Impulses, on the other hand, are nonrational and therefore cannot be justified directly or indirectly.

Human good is, indeed, irreducibly plural, but it is reason which tells us this, not a conglomeration of reason, environment, and passion. The latter two, while certainly influencing our behavior, do not tell us anything about what is worthwhile or what ought to be done; they move us subconsciously. Our free choices, upon which all responsibility rests, issue from reason, from our ability to know the difference between good and evil.

HISTORICISM

Besides the pluralist claim that there are many different foundations for moral judgment, there is a current view which proposes that there are no rational foundations at all, that all concepts are conditioned by language, which is itself conditioned by historical context. This position holds that there are no ahistorical truths which could serve as certain foundations for ethical judgments (or for any judgments). Nor, since all choices are situationally conditioned, is there a transcendent human freedom which could provide the basis for autonomous choice and the ultimate responsibility this entails. Aware of the historical narrative which provides meaning to all propositions, one enters the conversation with others and takes from that conversation what works—what is good for the individual and for the community.

Thus the new historicism is also a new pragmatism. For, after denying any absolute status to moral principles and freedom, one must still act and have a guide for action. That guide, as in science, is the utility of the theory, how useful it is in predicting outcomes and in getting us where we want to go.[23]

Jeffrey Stout defends this position in his book *The Flight from Authority*. In his preface, Stout acknowledges the influence of Alasdair MacIntyre and Richard Rorty, whom we discussed in Chapter One.[24] While such a theory might seem to imply relativism, Stout firmly denies that historicism's rejection of foundationalism implies conceptual relativism. For this reason I take up this theory here, rather than in the chapter on relativism. Since Stout claims that his book is more historical than philosophical,[25] a brief account of how he places foundationalism in its historical context is in order.

Historical Background

Stout sees the quest for moral foundations as an Enlightenment phenomenon issuing from epistemological questions of certainty. The fathers of this movement were Descartes and Kant, but emotivism, social contract theory, and utilitarianism are also foundationalist theories. Stout holds that the thinkers of the Enlightenment were searching for a moral point of view which would be autonomous and eternal.[26] This was true both for the descriptivist theories, which tried to draw connections between facts and values whether the facts be natural (as in some versions of natural law, though not the version for which I have argued) or theological (as in divine command theories), and for the prescriptivist theories, which tried to show how universal obligation is self-evident, whether on the basis of some kind of emotivism (like Hume's) or rational universalizability (under which would fall Kant, the social contract position, and utilitarianism).[27] Stout accuses all of these positions of being reductivist, of considering only one or some of the uses of language, in contrast to the approach taken in "holism," which maintains that language cannot be divided up into different kinds of propositions, that all statements are defined within the overall context of language and culture. "Holism, as I shall use the term, consists simply in the view that language cannot be divided up in the way envisioned by proponents of the distinctions between the analytic and the synthetic, theory and observation, or fact and value. Holists typically hold that once one has said all there is to say about how an expression is used, there is nothing remaining to be said about its 'meaning.'"[28]

Stout claims that there is no need for foundations (whether descriptive or prescriptive), for language carries with it its meaning in terms of narrative context. Historicism, Stout argues, is the natural successor to analytic philosophy. The move is from linguistic analysis of moral terms to a general understanding of the relation between language and culture and of how moral meanings come to be in history. "It matters relatively little how we decide to explicate the term 'morality.' What matters more is the quality of the story we tell with the words we choose. . . . If such expressions eventually get in our way, we are free to use our explications as rules for elimination, clearing the channels for better conversation."[29] Thus "quality stories" and "better conversation" are the criteria by which we are to judge the usefulness of our moral terms.

Now in favor of such a position are its focus on community, both as an ideal of human activity and in its role in forming character, and its concern for understanding context and history. Community is a key moral ideal in the natural law tradition, and understanding the theoretical components of any act (whether these components be historical, or sociological, or anthropological) is essential to understanding one's responsibility in any given situation.

Need for Moral Foundations

While not disagreeing about the appropriateness of studying these aspects of morality, I must take issue with Stout's claims that there is no need for moral foundations and that the denial of moral foundations does not lead to relativism. Consider the following passage in which Stout sums up his position.

> The upshot of our genealogy of morals is not that moral skepticism is, even for the time being, justified. Moral knowledge has not lost a foundation. It does not, in any event, need a foundation. We know a great deal indeed about the rightness and wrongness of acts, the values worth pursuing in life, and the virtues worth instilling in our children. We know, for example, that genocide is wrong, that racial supremacy is not a goal to be encouraged, and that Hitler is not a man to be held up as a model for imitation. These are extremely important things to know.[30]

They certainly are important things to know. The question is: How can we be sure that genocide is wrong, that racial supremacy is not to be encouraged, that Hitler should not be imitated? If there are no moral foundations, how do we justify our position? And why do we think that those who practice genocide or worship racial supremacy ought to know better? After all, according to Stout's position, no part of an ethical background "should be deemed, a priori, immune from revision or rejection."[31] Why then, might we not legitimately revise or reject our views on genocide or Hitler? To point to historical narrative is not much help, for genocide has been part of western history (sadly), and at present—history in the making—there are disturbing trends in the direction of genocide (Rwanda and Bosnia) and racial supremacy (Germany and the United States). Shall we say to those heading in these directions that they are unaware of the narrative that informs their culture? Evidently they are (at least of some of the narrative), but can we expect them to change because we point this out to them? Finally, is theirs a position with which we should enter into conversation? Should we give their position the dignity of being a factor in a compromise reached through negotiations? Stout apparently thinks not; but why not, if no choices can be characterized as absolutely wrong?

Cultural Background

Stout's answer is that, although any part of the cultural background can be called into question, "the entire background cannot succumb to doubt in an instant."[32] This is probably true as a matter of fact,[33] just as it is true that people's moral sphere of reference is informed by their culture as they grow up in that culture. However, this says nothing about whether or not and to what extent it is permissible to reject one's background. One does not need to call all things into question to be able do any action one chooses. Since, according to Stout, no moral norm is immune from revision or rejection, there is no basis for saying that anyone ought not to do what he or she desires, even to the point of genocide or worshipping Hitler.

It should be said that the cultural tradition which Stout says is ours resembles what I have called the natural law tradition which stems from Aristotle and Aquinas. He and I agree that this is a good background and that there is much to be learned from the tradition. However, he argues that embracing an ethical position such as Aquinas' is not a live option (to use James' term[34]). "Thomistic ethics is not a real option for us today. History *has* undermined our ability to settle moral disagreements by appealing to the *telos* of a determinate human nature or the commands of an omniscient and benevolent God."[35] Again we have an appeal to historical fact as making it impossible for us to accept a theory from the past. But how can we know that we cannot accept it unless we understand it?

Besides, Stout's understanding of Aquinas's ethics as derived either from natural facts (human nature) or theological facts (revelation) is simply mistaken. Aquinas is very explicit about distinguishing the principles of practical reason from those of theoretical reason and arguing that the former as well as the latter are naturally and immediately known.[36] As Finnis says in his book *Moral Absolutes*, it is not a question of deducing moral absolutes from human nature. Rather our understanding of moral absolutes reveals to us more about human nature. "A moral absolute such as that excluding adultery is indeed to be understood as a requirement of human reason and nature. But it is not deduced by us from a prior knowledge of human nature. Rather, it discloses to us a form of human fulfillment and thus an aspect of human nature."[37] Genocide is wrong because the arbitrary and irrational violation of the good of human life is always and everywhere wrong, not because our culture at this time happens to think it wrong. It was wrong in Nazi Germany under Hitler; it is wrong in Rwanda and in Bosnia; and it will be wrong at any future time and place.

Historicism and Relativism

Stout's reason for saying that his historicist perspective does not lead to conceptual relativism is that it has not been proven that rational agreement about morality is impossible. He offers no refutation of relativism, except to point out that moral disagreements, however serious, may still be worked out by rational means. What these rational means might be, he does not say. "We have yet to find good reasons for concluding that some disagreements are in principle incapable of rational resolution."[38] This, it seems to me, is an extremely weak attempt at stemming the tide of relativism. It is like saying that, although we have no good arguments for moral objectivity, neither has relativism any definitive arguments against moral objectivity. Thus, we are left with a draw. And if a draw, then why place one's bets on rational argument convincing anyone to do or not to do anything? This certainly seems to leave one without any good grounds for rejecting relativism.

Meanwhile, Stout proposes that, while moral disagreements continue, we must keep the lines of communication open, keep the conversation alive. Again, I have no objection to this point; communication is obviously essential to the building of a moral community. However, unless there are principles by which each member of the conversation can understand what is at stake in moral conversation, the conversation is to no purpose. If one did not think that others could understand some moral position, one would never attempt to convince them of it. Stout's optimism is encouraging but seems ill-founded. "If we focus on historically situated people and their attempts to solve problems, instead of conceptual schemes in static opposition, we should be able to see that impasses can and do get resolved—given enough time, luck, and moral ingenuity."[39] But why trust time and luck to bring us answers when reason cannot do it? And can we (should we) wait for time and luck to convince the advocates of genocide? Certainly, attempting to understand the culture and historical background of the individual people with whom we morally disagree is important. By so doing, we might be able to recognize and rectify injustices that have prompted other injustices. For example, treating people fairly economically and politically might prevent an outbreak of violent killing. But the requirement to treat people justly is an absolute or exceptionless requirement of the natural law, not just a matter of historical narrative.

Good Will and the Role of Reason

Stout ends his book with the following inspiring lines. "The real hope for rational discourse lies in the will to create communities and institutions in which the virtues of good people and good communities can flourish. Philosophy is no substitute for that, but its value can be measured by the contribution it makes."[40] With such a statement the natural law tradition is in full agreement. Good will is prerequisite for the achievement of communities in which individuals flourish; without it, no amount of talk about moral absolutes will avail. However, as Stout also recognizes, reason has a role to play in directing the will. Where Stout differs from the natural law tradition is in his view of reason's role in bringing about this moral community. Stout's historical pragmatism leads him away from the affirmation of moral absolutes: the value of ideas is to be found in their usefulness in creating communities of good people. The problem with such a position lies in the vagueness of the pragmatic understanding of the term "good." In pragmatism, useful and good are basically synonymous terms which are defined by context. This means that the good person and the good community are to be reached without knowing what they mean since their meaning is evolving according to what is useful, and every possible moral definition is subject to revision and rejection. How is it possible to work for a good community unless we have some fairly clear understanding of what "good" means? Awareness of the narrative which has led to the present will not in itself direct us, for how is one to know which elements of our past should be kept and which rejected? The past of every culture includes such horrors as slavery and genocide; how do we know that these are to be rejected? We all want a good community, but unless "good" has some constant and universal meaning, such are we find in the natural law tradition of basic goods and virtues, we cannot expect to escape relativism in our communities and in our own thinking.

CONCLUSIONS

Our retrospective and reevaluation have revealed that every moral theory that we have discussed is at least partly right, or at least begins with some correct moral insight (as relativism begins with the insight that tolerance is good). This, as I said at the beginning of this chapter, is not surprising, for every thinker who cares enough to proclaim some theory of morality is motivated by some understanding of the good (even if that understanding is narrow or incomplete). The natural law position for which I have been arguing seeks to provide the broadest and most complete account of what is fundamental to human well-being. Any such attempt is, quite obviously, an attempt by reason, for to ask and to formulate what elements should be included, which should not, which modified, and which complemented by others are clearly acts of reason. And it is not just reason as tabulating facts and establishing patterns of cause and effect and understanding means-to-ends relationships; it is also, and primarily, reason understanding what is good and directing the will to pursue that good. This is practical reason as understood by the natural law tradition. It is the coherent and consistent application of self-evident principles of morality (that one ought to do good, and what the basic forms of good are) to the multifarious nature of human experience.

8

Ethics and Religion Revisited

Our retrospective would be incomplete without another look at the relation between ethics and religion. It is a fact that people have associated ethics and religion since earliest recorded time, and there seems to be good reason for this association since religions have, traditionally, had something to say about moral responsibility. However, the conclusion that many people (believers as well as unbelievers) have drawn—that moral responsibility is derived from religion and stands or falls with it—is not the proper understanding of the relation between religion and ethics. While it is true that they are related, the relation is of quite another kind.

ETHICS DERIVED FROM RELIGION

Before presenting this other relation between ethics and religion, let us review the terms of the more common perspective, reconsidering its implications and its ultimate plausibility. This perspective holds that ethics is derived from religion. Whether this position is held in order to strengthen moral absolutes (as is the case with many believers) or to discredit them (as was the case with Epicurus, Lucretius, and Hume), the position is incoherent.

Consider the case where moral support is sought in such a connection between ethics and religion. While intending to support traditional morality with its absolutes, this position actually ends up destroying it. It is simply a fact that there are many different religions. According to this position, it follows that there are many different ethics. For those who think of religion as a personal relationship with the divine, there are as many ethics as there are religious people. And for the atheist, apparently there is no ethics at all. Thus, the assumption that ethics is derived from religion leads directly to moral relativism. Since moral relativism is clearly untenable (killing five-year-old children is always and everywhere wrong), the assumption that ethics is derived from religion must be false. The absurdity of the conclusion indicates the absurdity of the premise.

Consider the other case, where the derivation of ethics from religion is thought to warrant the rejection of moral absolutes. Oddly enough, this position is also self-refuting, showing the absurdity of the assumption that ethics is based on religion. Recall the main lines of this position as presented by Epicurus and reiterated by Lucretius and Hume. It begins with the assumption that there really are no moral absolutes, only the arbitrary commands of the religious myths. Religion has decreed that obeying or disobeying these moral norms will merit eternal reward or punishment in the afterlife; the absoluteness of the punishment is tied to the absoluteness of the moral norms that have been broken. The attack on this religious doctrine comes *via* the moral judgment that the divine commands (that Iphegenia should be sacrificed or more generally that human beings should be oppressed by fear of eternal punishment) are arbitrary and in fact immoral. Here is the self-refutation. If one is able to judge that the commands of the gods and hence of religion are immoral, it can only be because one possesses a criterion for judging moral worth which is independent of divine and religious decree. Hence, for all those who so eloquently rail against the immorality of the divinity or of religious believers, it is clear that the very strength of their case rests on the universal judgment that the immoral activities in question are absolutely wrong and therefore ought not to be done. This is a judgment of practical reason based on a requirement of natural law. The very criticism of absolutist religious morality finds its only possible justification in the absolute moral requirement that one ought not to do what one knows to be evil (in this case, demand human sacrifice and oppress others). Thus, the argument is incoherent in using an absolute standard of morality to argue against the existence of such absolute standards.

The assumption that ethics depends on religion turns out to be absurd on either ground. Our ability to make judgments about right and wrong has nothing to do with religion, neither its embrace nor its rejection. As Kai Nielsen writes in his book *Ethics Without God*: "God or no God, the torturing of innocents is evil; God or no God, wife beating or child molesting is vile. More generally, even if we can make nothing of the concept of God, we can readily come to appreciate, if we would but reflect and take the matter to heart, that, if anything is evil, inflicting or tolerating unnecessary and pointless suffering is evil, especially when something can be done about it."[1] The question of God's existence is irrelevant to moral principles. We have access to such principles naturally, through reason.

RELIGION AS AN ETHICAL OBLIGATION

However, the idea that there is a relation between ethics and religion is not altogether false. There is indeed a relation, but it goes in the opposite direction. While it is *not* true that ethics is based on religion, religion *is* an ethical requirement. Such a radical reversal of the commonly understood relation between ethics and religion demands some explanation. A clarification of what is meant by "religion" would be a start. Religion, here, does not mean any particular set of beliefs or practices based on a tradition or divine revelation. One is not morally required to join any particular religious group. Rather, religion refers to the proper ordering of the human being to the source of existence, intelligence, and freedom. Ultimately, this would seem to involve some form of communal worship, for there is good reason to believe (as we shall see presently) that every person's existence, intellect, and freedom come from the same source. It would be appropriate, as well as a promotion of the good of friendship, for the community to place itself in proper relation to the origin of all things.

Religious Obligation

The basis for religious obligation is the general moral principle that good should be acknowledged and appreciated wherever it is found; one is really required to give thanks to the source of the good things one receives. This is part of the basis for the virtue of friendship and is the core of the obligation to honor one's father and mother.[2] This requirement is especially pertinent when the party in question is the source of everything.

The respect, honor, and thanks owed to God can be most easily grasped though the analogy with what is owed to one's parents. Since the parental gift of life is prerequisite to any other good, everything one has is due, in a way, to one's parents. Without this gift, one could not participate in any human goods. If one owes such a debt to one's parents, how much more does one owe to the source of all reality, whom people have traditionally called "God." In the way that duty to parents arises from their position as source of one's life, duty to God arises from his position as source of all existence. As Aristotle said, "The friendship of children towards parents, and of men towards gods, is one towards something good and superior; for parents have done the greatest of goods, since they are the causes of the existence and nurture of their children and then of their education."[3] Aristotle goes on to add that, although we can never sufficiently repay such gifts, we must do what we can.

Existence of God

While it may be true that we would owe thanks, respect, and honor to a being from whom we have received all good things, the existence of such a being is not obvious the way the existence of one's parents is. In order for such an obligation to be real, there must really be a creator. Since science cannot prove the existence of any such immaterial being, it might be thought that the assent to the existence of God, and hence to the obligation we owe God, is merely a matter of faith. If so, we are back at square one, with ethics dependent on faith. Thus, for there to be a natural obligation of religion, there must be reason to think that God exists.[4]

Since this is not a book about metaphysics or philosophy of God, the brief excursion into such realms which we are about to take demands some justification. Indeed, it may seem more than just inappropriate to deal with theoretical points in a book on ethics; it may seem that such a move violates the principle that from facts alone no obligation can be drawn. If the claim being made here were that the simple knowledge that God exists implies that one should worship God, then the argument would be invalid. But the premise that God exists does not stand alone. It is joined in the argument by the strictly moral premise that one should be grateful to anyone from whom one has received good. It is not true that a theoretical premise has no place in a moral argument, just that there must also be a practical premise, a premise of value and obligation.

As a matter of fact, *all* specific moral obligations involve a theoretical component. The prohibition against murdering John involves at least two premises, one practical and the other theoretical. The practical premise is that one should never intentionally take human life. The theoretical premise is that John is a human being. Were John the name for the mouse who is wreaking havoc on the kitchen supplies, the prohibition would not be of the same absolute character. Just as it is essential to the moral prohibition against murdering John that John is a human being and not a mouse, so it is essential to the moral argument for religion that God exists and that our existence and everything we have comes from God.

Proof from Moral Obligation   This said, let us consider a proof of God's existence based on moral obligation.[5] While there are many other arguments for the existence of God, I choose this one because it has for its foundation moral responsibility, the subject of this book. Most briefly, the argument looks like this: If any ethical judgment is certain (e.g., it is wrong to kill five-year-old children), then there is a creator. Let us spell out the connecting links between premise and conclusion. Our ability to make the ethical judgment that killing small children is always and everywhere wrong indicates that we transcend materiality, for matter is never always and everywhere but peculiar to a specific time and place. There is something about being human (it has been traditionally called the rational soul) that is not material, that is not, therefore, reducible to the material universe and its laws of matter and energy.

Since knowing is not merely a material process, it cannot be sufficiently explained by science (i.e., by hypothesis and sense verification). Material factors are indeed necessary causes of our knowing; we could not know without a body, brain, nervous system, chemical secretions, atoms in motion, and the four forces of physics. However, they are not sufficient causes since they fail to explain the object known, which is something other than the brain—the wrongness of murder, in our case, but equally the objects of mathematics and science. Since the object known is not a material thing, knowing cannot be fully explained through normal scientific channels such as evolution, chemical analysis, or the matter/energy matrix of physics.

But this immaterial component of knowing is not self-explanatory. Nor is it self-evident why there are many intellects. It is clear that one did not create one self, nor did one of us create the others. Thomas Aquinas presents a beautifully simple metaphysical principle for understanding the implications of any multiplicity: for any two things, either one is the cause of the other, or they are both caused by a third.[6] Except for one of these explanations, there is no accounting for what is obvious, that there are two distinct things. But when the things in question are immaterial (such as human intellects), the cause required to explain their existence cannot be one of the forces of matter and energy described by physics. The cause must be a metaphysical one (literally, "beyond nature").

If human minds cannot be explained by material evolution, yet they clearly exist (one cannot even deny this without using the mind), then there must be an immaterial cause of the existence of human minds, a cause which is not within the material universe. It must itself be intelligent, for one cannot get more from less. And it must be a cause which can bring something into being out of nothing (for no matter is involved); that is, it must be an infinite power. Thus, the answer to the question of why human minds exist is that there is an intelligent, creating cause of these minds.[7] This cause has traditionally been named "God."

One could, as some philosophers have done, respond that things like the universe and rational minds just are, that there is no need for any ultimate explanation.[8] But this is a renunciation of the pursuit of truth and the good of knowledge. Such a refusal to seek a complete explanation is in conflict with both the scientific enterprise itself and the fundamental human requirement to seek the truth. So long as there is a question based on obvious evidence, there is need for an answer. Since the existence of intellectuality is not self-explanatory and cannot be explained by the material workings of the universe, yet is as obvious as any meaningful word, it stands in need of an explanation. Whether or not one wishes to call such an infinite creating power "God" is beside the point. What is certain is that we owe our existence to this power.

Combining this theoretical premise that there is a creator on whom we depend and from whom all good things come with the practical premise that good is to be appreciated wherever it is found, the conclusion follows that one is obliged to give thanks, respect, and honor to the creator.[9]

Natural Law Tradition

Articulation of this requirement of religion can be found repeatedly in the natural law tradition. We have already mentioned Aristotle and his point about our obligation to the gods from whom we have received such great benefits. Cicero also holds that our most important duty is to the gods. "Social duties can be divided into grades so that the priority of any given duty is apparent. The order would be as follows: first our duty to the immortal gods, secondly to our country, thirdly to our parents, and lastly to the rest of society in due order."[10] Thomas Aquinas, when discussing the ten commandments, claims that they are all commands of the natural law.[11] Even the first three commandments, requiring one to honor God above all else, to refrain from taking God's name in vain, and to worship, are commands of natural reason, not merely the religious duties of those to whom revelation has been given. By not honoring God, one would be failing to fulfill one's natural moral responsibilities. The contemporary natural law theorist John Finnis counts religion, understood as the right relation to the source of all being and freedom, among his basic goods which we are obligated to honor, promote, and not violate.[12]

Natural Virtue

Besides being a requirement of the natural law, religion is also a natural virtue. Thus, just as we said in Chapter Six that the virtues are dispositions of character from which actions in accordance with the natural law readily issue, so one needs to develop through practice a state of character which readily gives to God due honor, respect, and thanks. As Aquinas says, religion is a moral virtue, part of natural human perfection. "Religion is neither a theological nor an intellectual virtue, but a moral virtue, since it is a part of justice. And its measure is taken not from the passions, but according to a certain appropriateness of the actions which are given to God."[13]

MORAL IMPORTANCE OF RELIGION

Not only is religion a requirement of natural morality, it is arguably the most important. For one thing, being grateful to God stands as our first positive obligation. As Cicero said, the first of our duties to others is to God. This debt is a real obligation by which one is bound prior to any other. For another, the unflagging effort to fulfill this obligation puts one in good shape in general for virtuous living. Such a debt to God can never be entirely repaid, no matter how much one may do. It is a constant reminder of one's responsibility to do more and more good. Humble in the knowledge that there is yet much to do before one even begins to accomplish what should be done, one is eager to do good for others wherever one can, even beyond what is strictly due them. Thus, not only is acknowledging this debt to God the first of one's moral obligations, the effort to do "what one can" (as Aristotle said) leads to the conscious choice to do more than what justice requires. As Josef Pieper puts it: "The just man, who has a more keenly felt experience of these first inadequacies the more fully he realizes that his very being is a gift, and that he is heavily indebted before God and man, is also the man willing to give where there is no strict obligation. He will be willing to give another man something no one can compel him to give."[14] Indeed, one's very existence as a moral agent is a gift from God. Every free and responsible act is a reminder of the great gift we have received from God, and of the thanks, honor, and respect we owe in return.

However, to say that one's obligation to God transcends any other is not at all to say that, so long as one is serving God, one is automatically justified in one's action. This, unfortunately, has been one attitude toward the importance of religion, and many atrocities have been committed in the name of religion and God. The absurdity of such an attitude is evident from a reflection on what we know about God and moral obligation. God is creator of everything we possess, including our reason. But it is this very reason, given us by God, which is the source of ethical obligation, not only of our obligation to serve God, but also to serve our fellow human beings, and especially to refrain from harming them in any way. It would make no sense at all to say that one serves God by turning one's back on the natural light he has given us. Since this light tells us that we should not directly violate any of the basic goods, it would be wrong to lie, rape, and murder in the name of religion and God. Nor is there an absolute distinction in favor of religion over the other basic goods. Each is self-evidently good, and, as Finnis says, one can serve God by participating in the other basic goods;[15] to appreciate God's gifts is to appreciate God.

9

Epilogue:
To Care or Not to Care

Our revisitation and reevaluation are now complete. With our discussion of the relation between ethics and religion, we have come full circle in our quest for the foundations of moral responsibility. We have found religion to be a basic good and an ethical requirement, not the origin of arbitrary moral norms.

The argument that, since ethical obligation is merely a matter of religion (assumption) and there are many different religions (fact), there are no absolute moral obligations has been shown to be false. First of all, it is absurd to hold that murder and rape are wrong only if they violate one's religious convictions. Secondly, the very rejection of the idea of moral absolutes on the grounds that they are products of religion (or some other particular group) is incoherent For in saying that people should not be subject to the morality of a particular religion (or culture, or historical era, or economic status, or gender, etc.), one appeals to the obligation to be fair and tolerant, which obligation one obviously does not consider to be derived from the particular religion (or other particular group) in question. Thus, cultural relativism in its many forms fails to justify its rejection of moral absolutes.

Subjective relativism, as a preferred moral position, is contradictory, for it cannot be in any way better to embrace a theory which denies that the term better has any meaning. The other main reasons for professing relativism not as a preferred theory, but as an unavoidable fact—the inability of science to verify moral norms and the supposed incompatibility of the democratic ideals of freedom and tolerance with such an ethics—have also been shown to be unwarranted. Again, this is not to say that the ideals of science or democracy are unwarranted, only that they provide no warrant for rejecting moral absolutes.

While scientific method with its rigorous demand for sense verification is good in its own sphere, it cannot claim to be the only way to truth. If it does, then it denies itself, for the idea that scientific method alone should prevail is not itself susceptible to sense verification. It is true that if the assumption of materialism is accepted, it logically follows that there can be no moral norms; but it also logically follows that there can be no true or false judgments at all, not even, of course, the judgment that all that is real is material nor any other judgment of science. Every act of understanding or judgment transcends, in its essential universality of meaning, the spatial and temporal particularity of material interactions.

Thus, those theories of ethics which assume that only scientific method is valid (emotivism, egoism, and utilitarianism) cannot refute the claims of the natural law tradition that there are moral absolutes. Nor, in addition, can they justify any obligation on their terms, for from theoretical premises which describe how things are, no practical conclusion about how things ought to be can logically be drawn.

Democracy, as an ideal of political organization designed to invite universal participation in communal life and to avoid the excesses of idiosyncratic personalities, is also a great good. However, the democratic ideal of one vote per person applied to other arenas of human life can be disastrous. This is the case in matters of truth and aesthetics; majority opinion does not always tell us what is really true about reality or what is really beautiful. And it is especially true in ethics, for here there is the particularly great danger of our "voting" in a convenient and pleasant morality (at least for the majority) rather than a right one. Implied by such a democratic morality of majority rule is the rather frightening prospect of actions becoming better simply because more people do them; so, for example, material gratification, self-aggrandizement, and indifference to others become better and better as our families and communities disintegrate. The very ideal of tolerance, with its push toward the acceptance of all points of view, is itself threatened by a purely democratic approach to ethics; for if the majority favor the persecution, enslavement, or extermination of a minority, on what democratic grounds can one object? The true virtue of tolerance and the ideal of political democracy are not derived from majority opinion, but from the moral absolute that every human being should be respected.

Not only is natural law ethics with its focus on reason and moral absolutes not in conflict with the democratic ideal (the ideal itself is not voted in); it is no rival to freedom of choice. In fact, freedom of choice is only possible if there are goods which we apprehend by reason and not just patterns of behavior directed by environment and passion.

In short, we have found that moral responsibility is precisely the same for the believer and the atheist, for the scientist and guardian of freedom— for everyone. The knowledge of what should and should not be done and the ability to choose are intrinsic to every human being insofar as that person can exercise reason and the freedom of choice which comes with reason. Of course, expertise in matters of fact is an important ingredient in making correct moral decisions in specific situations, and such expertise comes to moral decision-making with study and experience. Here one's background and upbringing can make a great deal of difference. But the foundations of moral responsibility—the basic directive that good should be done and evil avoided and the range of basic human goods which give to this directive its content—these are self-evident to everyone who can exercise reason.

About the basic foundations of moral responsibility there need be no uncertainty nor confusion nor disagreement. In fact, unless there are first principles to which everyone must agree (or cease to be a creature of reason), there cannot even be grounds for disagreement about which choices are right and which wrong. That there are various cultures or that there are various religions or that human beings are unique individuals—none of these facts undermines the foundations for moral responsibility, for the foundations lie in the natural human ability to know and choose what is good. To the question "Who's to say what is right and wrong?" the answer is the informed conscience of the individual, the individual who listens to the demands of practical reason and who carefully puts them into practice.

Of course, one *can* refuse to listen, and one *can* refuse to care; the natural law is not determinism. It is quite possible to ignore the dictates of practical reason. There is no want of distractions to keep us from ourselves and other people. It is easy to find things to do besides thinking about what would be the best. Pascal comments on this human penchant for distractions in his *Pensées*.

> *Diversion.* If man were happy, the less he were diverted the happier he would be, like the saints and God. Yes: but is a man not happy who can find delight in diversion?
>
> No: because it comes from somewhere else, from outside; so he is dependent, and always liable to be disturbed by a thousand and one accidents, which inevitably cause distress. [1]

In the best natural law tradition, Pascal equates happiness with moral goodness and moral goodness with thinking. It is because we refuse to think that we are engulfed in such moral malaise. "Thus all our dignity consists in thought. It is on thought that we must depend for our recovery, not on space and time, which we could never fill. Let us strive to think well; that is the basic principle of morality." [2] But thinking is not something that happens to us like being entertained; it is something we must do.

Not only is it quite easy to ignore the demands of natural law which can be found in conscience; even if one knows all about them, one can still choose not to follow them. For it is one thing to know what should be done, and quite another to do it. Sometimes doing the right thing is easy, but more often it requires attention and effort. Much of our selfishness is due to laziness. We all know that the common goods—knowledge, friendship, beauty, etc.—grow by being shared, but sharing requires planning and reaching out of ourselves to others. Such actions are not automatic; they must be initiated against the inertia of passivity. Some of our selfishness is due to fear—of failure, of being rejected, of being left alone and ignored. And all too often, it is due to spite; that is, we sometimes seem to do evil just for the sake of being bad. Augustine's analysis of why he stole peaches in the *Confessions* is a haunting reminder of this feature of our moral difficulties.

> Let that heart now tell You what it sought when I was thus evil for no object, having no cause for wrongdoing save my wrongness. The malice of the act was base and I loved it—that is to say I loved my own undoing, I loved the evil in me—not the thing for which I did the evil, simply the evil: my soul was depraved, and hurled itself down from security in You into utter destruction, seeking no profit from wickedness but only to be wicked.[3]

Whether this spite is aimed at God, or as others, or at ourselves, it effectively blocks our participating in the basic goods and our promoting these goods for others. Indeed, indulgence in the so-called seven deadly sins—pride, envy, anger, sloth, avarice, gluttony, and lust—diverts us from the reflection necessary to apprehend what is good and blunts the courage we need to act on the good we know.[4] We cripple ourselves and isolate ourselves from each other, from the communion in which we flourish.

As the natural moral law is not a physical law which cannot be broken, nor a political law which carries an obvious and immediate penalty if broken, it neither determines us nor coerces us by threats of punishment. Nor does the argument from ultimate divine punishment force us to be good; since divine punishment is not obvious or immediate, the effectiveness of the argument depends on one buying into the notion of good and evil and affirming that good choices ought, ultimately, to be rewarded and evil choices punished. One can simply refuse to entertain such a notion. If one does, there is nothing anyone else can do to make one take moral obligation seriously. In short, one cannot be forced to be good. Equally, one cannot be forced to be evil. If we choose to be good, we can be good. If we choose to be evil, we can be evil.

Here we come to the ultimate act of freedom—to care or not to care. One must choose whether to listen or not to listen to the voice of reason and the call to do good. One must choose whether to take up or not to take up the arduous task of making oneself and the world better. And if one chooses to listen and to care, one must keep on choosing this way, for not to choose is to drift back into diversions and self-imposed exile from community. No amount of knowledge about the principles of natural law—of Kant's categorical imperative, the basic goods, the virtues—can replace this simple act of will. The quest still beckons. Shall we go?

Notes

NOTES FOR CHAPTER 1

1. Amos 1 & 2.

2. Romans 2:14–15, Revised Standard Version.

3. For documentation on this point, see Germain Grisez, *The Way of the Lord Jesus*, Volume One: *Christian Moral Principles* (Chicago: Franciscan Herald Press, 1983), Ch. 3, Qu. A & B, Ch. 7, Qu. A & B.

4. Tertullian, *Prescription Against Heretics*, Ch. VII (dates: c. 160–c. 240).

5. This was the school of the Ash'arites founded by Al Ash'ari (dates: 873–935).

6. William of Ockham, *On the Four Books of the Sentences* II, 19, O; see also III, 12, AAA; (dates: d. ca. 1350).

7. See David Hume, *Dialogues Concerning Natural Religion*, Part X (New York: Hafner Press, 1951) pp. 61–70.

8. Ruth Benedict, "Anthropology and the Abnormal," in *The Journal of General Psychology* 10 (1934): 59–82, reprinted in *An Anthropologist at Work*, ed. *Margaret Mead* (Boston: Houghton Mifflin, 1959), p. 276. For a defense of moral relativism based on disagreement, see J. L. Mackie, *Ethics: Inventing Right and Wrong* (New York: Penguin Books, 1976).

9. Edward Westermarck, *Ethical Relativity* (London: Routledge and Kegan Paul, 1932), p. 197.

10. G. W. F. Hegel, *Philosophy of Right*, Preface, tr. T. M. Knox in *Hegel's Philosophy of Right* (Oxford: Clarendon Press, 1952), p. 11.

11. See *Friedrich Nietzsche, Beyond Good and Evil*, tr. Walter Kaufmann (New York: Random House, 1966).

12. "Hence debate between fundamentally opposed standpoints does occur; but it is inevitably inconclusive. Each warring position characteristically appears irrefutable to its own adherents; indeed in its own terms and by its own standards of argument it *is* in practice irrefutable. But each warring position equally seems to its opponents to be insufficiently warranted by rational argument." Alasdair MacIntyre, *Three Rival Versions of Moral Inquiry: Encyclopaedia, Genealogy, and Tradition* (Notre Dame, Ind.: University of Notre Dame Press, 1990), p. 7.

---

13. Richard Rorty, *Philosophy and the Mirror of Nature* (Princeton: Princeton University Press, 1979), p. 10.

14. Rorty, *Philosophy and the Mirror of Nature*, p. 367.

15. Karl Marx and Friedrich Engels, *The Communist Manifesto*, ed. Samuel H. Beer (New York: Appleton-Century-Crofts, 1955), p. 27.

16. Carol Gilligan, *In A Different Voice: Psychological Theory and Women's Development* (Cambridge: Harvard University Press, 1982), p. 22.

17. Aristotle, *Nichomachean Ethics* I, 2.

18. The idea of power as a principle of morality and political rule will be discussed further in Chapter Three.

19. Francis Bacon, *The New Organon: or True Directions Concerning the Interpretation of Nature*, Author's Preface.

20. By material I mean measurable by scientific method, ultimately by some material means verified by sense experience. Thus, under material I include such things as light, gravity, and electromagnetism, which, while not material in the obvious way that a stone or a tree is, are measurable by material means.

21. David Hume, *Dialogues*, Part II, p. 22.

22. The earliest philosophers were from Greece and lived in the century or so before Socrates who died in 399 B.C.—hence the name pre-Socratics. For the basics on the pre-Socratics, see Reginald Allen, ed., *Greek Philosophy: Thales to Aristotle* (New York: Free Press, 1966).

23. Related by Aristotle in *On the Soul* I, 5 (411a8).

24. For Epicurus's philosophical position, see his "Letter to Herodotus," "Letter to Pythocles," "Letter to Menoeceus," and *Principle Doctrines* in *Greek and Roman Philosophy after Aristotle*, ed. Jason L. Saunders (New York: Free Press, 1966); for Lucretius's exposition of the same theory, see *The Way Things Are: The De Rerum Natura of Titius Lucretius Carus*, tr. Rolphe Humphries (Bloomington, Ind.: Indiana University Press, 1969).

25. Lucretius, *The Way Things Are*, Book I.

26. Francis Bacon, *The New Organon*, Aphorism LXXXIX.

27. David Hume, *Dialogues*, Part X.

28. David Hume, *An Enquiry Concerning Human Understanding*, Section XI: "Of a Particular Providence and of a Future State."

29. Michel de Montaigne, *Essais*, Book I, Chapter 50: "On Democritus and Heraclitus," tr. J. M. Cohen (London/New York: Penguin Books, 1988), pp. 132–33.

30. See Friedrich Nietzsche's *Beyond Good and Evil*, Part Two: "The Free Spirit," and Jean-Paul Sartre's "Existentialism is a Humanism," tr. Philip Mairet in *The Existentialist Tradition*, ed. Nino Langiulli (New York: Anchor Books, 1971).

31. I have discussed this elsewhere, in *The Romance of Reason: An Adventure in the Thought of Thomas Aquinas* (Petersham, MA: Saint Bede's Publications, 1993).

32. For more on this distinction, see Germain Grisez and Russell Shaw, *Beyond the New Morality: The Responsibilities of Freedom* (Notre Dame: University of Notre Dame Press, 1980), Chapter 1.

33. This theory of the social contract will be discussed further in Chapter Three.

34. Much research is being done on the presence of reason and freedom in animals. If it is true that animals are more like us than we had thought (and there is some evidence that this is so, especially among the higher mammals), then the conclusion is that animals also have responsibilities, not that we, as animals, have none. With reason and freedom comes responsibility.

35. Epicurus, "Letter to Menoeceus," p. 51.

36. Epicurus, *Principal Doctrines*, 31 & 33, p. 56.

37. Epicurus, *Principal Doctrines*, 34 & 38, pp. 56–57.

NOTES FOR CHAPTER 2

1. Dates: 1711–1776.

2. David Hume, *An Enquiry Concerning Human Understanding*, Section IV, Part I.

3. David Hume, *A Treatise of Human Nature*, Book III, Part I, Section I, ed. L. A. Selby-Bigge, 2nd edition, revised by P. H. Nidditch (Oxford: Clarendon Press, 1978), pp. 468–69.

4. David Hume, *An Enquiry Concerning The Principles of Morals*, Section IX, Part I, in *Enquiries*, ed. L. A. Selby-Bigge (Oxford: Clarendon Press, 1975), p. 271.

5. Hume, *Treatise*, Book III, Part I, Section I, p. 469.

6. Hume, *Treatise*, Book II, Part III, Section III, p. 416.

7. Hume, *Treatise*, Book II, Part III, Section III, p. 416.

8. There was a philosophical school of common sense whose leader Thomas Reid (dates: 1710–1796) made some of the same criticisms of Hume as I am making. In his *An Enquiry into the Human Mind*, Reid argued against Hume's material reductionism which leads to skepticism. Reid held that we have intuitive knowledge of the principles of morality (see his essay "On Morals"). My use of "commonsensical" here does not refer in any specific way to the thought of Reid, but refers simply to our pre-analytical understanding of morality.

9. Hume, *Treatise*, Book II, Part III, Section III, p. 414.

10. Hume, *Treatise*, Book II, Part III, Section III, p. 415.

11. A. J. Ayer, *Language, Truth, and Logic* (New York: Dover Publications, 1952), p. 31.

12. Ayer, *Language*, p. 31.

13. Ayer, *Language*, pp. 108–09.

14. Westermarck, *Ethical Relativity*, p. 216.

NOTES FOR CHAPTER 3

1. Plato, *The Republic*, Book II, 358e–359b, tr. G. M. A. Grube (Indianapolis: Hackett, 1974), p. 31.

2. Thomas Hobbes, *Leviathan*, Part I, Ch. 1, ed. C. B. MacPherson (London/New York: Penguin Books, 1985).

3. Hobbes actually worked with Bacon directly for a time as his secretary. See *Aubrey's Brief Lives*, ed. O. L. Dick (London: Secker and Warburg, 1950), pp. 149–50.

4. *New Organon*, Aphorism LI.

5. Thomas Hobbes, *Leviathan*, Part IV, Ch. 44, p. 629.

6. A brief chronological note is in order here. Hobbes (1588–1679) actually preceded Hume (1711–1776) by more than a century. He appears in this work after Hume for systematic reasons.

7. Hobbes, *Leviathan*, Part I, Ch. 13, p. 185.

8. Hobbes, *Leviathan*, Part I, Ch. 13, p. 188.

9. Hobbes, *Leviathan*, Part I, Ch. 13, p. 186.

10. Hobbes, *Leviathan*, Part I, Ch. 14, p. 189.

11. Hobbes, *Leviathan*, Part I, Ch. 14, p. 190.

12. Hobbes, *Leviathan*, Part I, Ch. 14, p. 190.

13. Hobbes, *Leviathan*, Part I, Ch. 5, pp. 110–14.

14. Hobbes, *Leviathan*, Part I, Ch. 14, p. 190.

15. Hobbes, *Leviathan*, Part I, Ch. 15, p. 201.

16. Hobbes, *Leviathan*, Part I, Ch. 15, pp. 204–05.

17. John Locke, *Second Treatise of Government*, II, 9, ed. C. B. MacPherson (Indianapolis: Hackett, 1980), p. 9; (dates: 1632–1704).

18. Hamilton, Madison, Jay, *The Federalist Papers*, No. 51, ed. Garry Wills (New York: Bantam Books, 1982), p. 265.

19. In his *A Theory of Justice* (Cambridge, Mass.: Belknap Press, 1971), Rawls says that he is part of the social contract tradition stemming from Locke, Rousseau, and Kant (p. 11). While no one would, I think, deny that Locke and Rousseau are social contract theorists (although there are additional principles at work in Locke), to call Kant a social contract theorist is to misunderstand Kant's ethics, or at least to consider only Kant's first version of the categorical imperative where elements of self-interest remain. This point will become clearer when we discuss Kant in Chapter Five.

20. Rawls, *Theory*, p. 11.

21. Rawls, *Theory*, p. 14.

22. Rawls, *Theory*, p. 12.

23. Rawls, *Theory*, p. 12.

24. Rawls, *Theory*, p. 60.

25. Rawls, *Theory*, p. 83; on this affirmative action principle, see also Ch. 14: "Fair Equality and Pure Procedural Justice."

26. Rawls, *Theory*, p. 12.

27. While Locke had our equality as creatures before God to explain why we should be concerned for others, this option is not open to Rawls. And in fact, without a good deal of metaphysics (which Locke's empiricism does not allow), such a position as Locke's could not be a matter of natural reason, and hence is subject to all the criticisms against deriving morality from religion. Rawls, too, has no room for metaphysics in his empirical method. Thus, given that he does not bring in religion, nor allow reason to be practical in the sense of knowing what is good in itself, his only option in explaining how one is motivated to consider others equally with oneself is some kind of passion.

NOTES FOR CHAPTER 4

1. Jeremy Bentham, *The Principles of Morals and Legislation*, (New York: Hafner Press, 1948), Ch. I, p. 2 (dates: 1748–1832).

2. Bentham, *Principles*, Ch. II, p. 9.

3. Bentham, *Principles*, Ch. I, p. 2.

4. Bentham, *Principles*, Ch. IV, p. 29.

5. Bentham, *Principles*, Ch. IV.

6. Bentham, *Principles*, Ch. IV, p. 31.

7. Admittedly, these are extreme examples, and the utilitarian might respond by saying that one is not required to consider all consequences, but only those which are most foreseeable. But how and where is one to draw the line? One is supposed to include "propinquity" and "certainty" in one's calculus of the consequent pleasure and pains of one's act. Thus, although consequences which occur further in the future than others might count less on that score, if their intensity and duration were severe enough (as in the examples), they might indeed overshadow those consequences nearest in time and more certain.

8. J. S. Mill, *Utilitarianism*, Ch. 2, ed. Oskar Piest (Indianapolis, Ind./New York: Bobbs-Merrill, 1957), p. 10 (dates: 1806–1873).

9. Mill, *Utilitarianism*, Ch. 2, p. 11.

10. Mill, *Utilitarianism*, Ch. 4, pp. 44–45.

11. Bentham, *Principles*, Ch. I, p. 3.

12. Henry Sidgwick, *The Methods of Ethics*, 7th ed., (Chicago: University of Chicago Press, 1907), p. 508 (dates: 1838–1900).

13. Mill, *Utilitarianism*, Ch. 2, p. 22.

14. See Richard Brandt, *Ethical Theory* (Englewood Cliffs, N.J.: Prentice-Hall, 1959) Chapter 15, in which he introduces the distinction between "act-utilitarianism" and "rule-utilitarianism." Marcus G. Singer, in *Generalization in Ethics* (London: Eyre and Spottiswoode, 1963), makes the same distinction, calling the two kinds of utilitarianism "Direct Utilitarianism" and "Indirect Utilitarianism," respectively (p. 203).

15. This analysis follows Brandt's somewhat later discussion of rule utilitarianism in "Toward a Credible Form of Utilitarianism," in *Morality and the Language of*

Conduct, ed. Hector-Neri Castañeda and George Nakhnikian (Detroit: Wayne State University Press, 1963), pp. 107–43 (particularly, pp. 109–10).

16. Brandt, "Toward a Credible Form of Utilitarianism," p. 124.

17. Richard B. Brandt, *A Theory of the Good and the Right* (Oxford: Clarendon Press, 1979), pp. 234–45.

18. Brandt, *Theory,* p. 304.

19. Brandt, *Theory,* title of Chapter XV, p. 286.

20. As a theory of judgment about an action already done, utilitarianism fares somewhat better, for then the judgment can be based on an analysis of actual consequences. And indeed, Bentham's desire to find a scientific theory of punishment was the driving force behind the development of his ethics. While more plausible in this capacity, utilitarianism still faces a rather large problem: why should someone be punished for failing to perform a calculation which, since there is no present sense data, cannot be performed by the supposedly only legitimate method? For other objections to the utilitarian theory of punishment, see C. S. Lewis, "The Humanitarian Theory of Punishment," in *God in the Dock: Essays on Theology and Ethics,* ed. Walter Hooper (Grand Rapids, Mich.: William B. Erdmans, 1970), pp. 287–300.

21. Bentham, *Principles,* Ch. I, pp. 1–2.

22. There are utilitarians who argue that the "good" that utilitarianism is to maximize and the "bad" it is to minimize are not reducible to pleasure and pain. Thus, Peter Singer, in his book *Practical Ethics* (Cambridge: Cambridge University Press, 1979), holds that "best consequences" should be understood as "what, on balance, furthers the interests of those affected" (pp. 12–13). Even more removed from pleasure and pain are the intrinsic goods (beauty and friendship) and evils (those things which violate these intrinsic goods) known by intuition, which G. E. Moore discusses in his *Principia Ethica* (Cambridge: Cambridge University Press, 1965), Chapter VI: "The Ideal." While these elements—beauty and friendship—are not material, the decision-making process is still the theoretical method of tabulating consequences which, as a description of a state of affairs, does not and cannot legitimately imply obligation. Moore's position will be discussed further in Chapter Seven.

NOTES FOR CHAPTER 5

1. See Immanuel Kant, *Grounding for the Metaphysics of Morals,* tr. James W. Ellington in *Kant's Ethical Philosophy* (Indianapolis: Hackett, 1983), First Section (dates: 1724–1804).

2. Kant, *Grounding,* First Section, p. 7.

3. While Kant's point is clear—that isolated virtues can be misused—he misunderstands the position of the ancients, whose moral theory centered on the virtues. Plato, Aristotle, Cicero, and their disciples argue consistently that virtue is a whole, that a virtue in isolation from other virtues is not really a virtue at all. Virtue ethics will be discussed more fully in Chapter Six.

4. Kant, *Grounding,* First Section, fn. 14, p. 14.

5. Kant, *Grounding*, Second Section, p. 25.

6. This is not to say that fulfilling the requirements of an art course is really more important than appreciating the beauty of the art itself, only that the agent could care more about the grade and graduation than about the beauty of the paintings, in which case seeing the art exhibit is intended by the agent as a means to a further end.

7. This meaning of happiness must be distinguished from the natural law tradition of Aristotle, Cicero, and Aquinas, who mean by happiness the fulfillment of human beings as rational animals. For them the prime ingredient in happiness is the participation, through reason, in what is true and good.

8. Kant, *Grounding*, Second Section, p. 26.

9. Kant, *Grounding*, Second Section, pp. 41–42.

10. Kant, *Grounding*, Second Section, p. 30.

11. Disciples of Kant fall into two main camps: those who focus on the first version of the categorical imperative as the locus of moral obligation and those who focus on the second. That is, despite Kant's insistence that the two versions are to be read as analyses of the one principle of duty, his disciples often separate the two. Thus R. M. Hare is an example of a follower of the first version. In his book *Freedom and Reason* (Oxford: Oxford University Press, 1963), Hare develops a theory of ethics based on two principles: "prescriptivity" and "universalizability" (Part I: "Describing and Prescribing"). The first refers to the notion of obligation contained in the idea of duty; the second refers to the universal character of obligation. As proposing fundamentally the same theory as Kant sets out in his first version, Hare's theory is subject to the same criticisms which can be brought against Kant's first version.

12. Kant, *Grounding*, Second Section, p. 32.

13. Kant, *Grounding*, Second Section, p. 31.

14. Here are the grounds for the connection which some people (such as Rawls) make between social contract ethics and Kant. While this connection is plausible if one only considers Kant's first version of the categorical imperative, it is incompatible with what he says about duty and respect in general and also with the fullness of the categorical imperative which is not in one version but in all three.

15. Kant, *Grounding*, Second Section, p. 35.

16. Kant, *Grounding*, Second Section, p. 36. I mentioned earlier that disciples of Kant tend to follow either the first or the second version of the categorical imperative. Alan Donagan is an example of those who follow Kant's second version. (Actually, any follower of the second version is a follower of the first version, as well, for all obligation implies universality.) In his book *The Theory of Morality* (Chicago/London: University of Chicago Press, 1977), Donagan reformulates Kant's second version of the categorical imperative as follows: "It is impermissible not to respect every human being, oneself or any other, as a rational creature" (p. 66), declaring this to be the fundamental principle of morality.

17. Kant, *Grounding*, Second Section, p. 36.

18. Kant, *Grounding*, Second Section, p. 41.

19. Kant, *Grounding*, Second Section, p. 38.
20. Kant, *Grounding*, Third Section, pp. 52–53.
21. Kant, *Grounding*, Third Section, p. 50.
22. René Descartes, *Meditations on First Philosophy*, Meditation One, tr. Donald A. Cress, 2nd ed., (Indianapolis: Hackett, 1983), p. 16.
23. Kant, *Grounding*, Second Section, p. 36.

NOTES FOR CHAPTER 6

1. Later in this chapter, in order to discuss some of the debates among those who agree that ethics is grounded in practical reason, we shall distinguish duty ethics (Kant), natural law ethics (Cicero and Aquinas), and virtue ethics (Aristotle). However, the moral position for which I am arguing, and which I am calling the natural law tradition, includes all three of these positions. C. S. Lewis, in his book *The Abolition of Man* (New York: Macmillan, 1955), presents a helpful list of equivalent terms for the natural law tradition which we shall be discussing. "This thing which I have called for convenience the *Tao*, and which others may call Natural Law or Traditional Morality of the First Principles of Practical Reason or the First Platitudes, is not one among a series of possible systems of value. It is the sole source of all value judgements" (p. 56).

2. Hume explicitly objects to deducing obligation from facts, which is why he reverts to emotivism. However, even he makes this illegitimate deduction from time to time, either explicitly—"Reason is and ought only to be the slave of the passions" (*Treatise*, Book II, Part III, Section III, p. 414)—or implicitly in his rhetoric favoring benevolence.

3. See Lewis, *Abolition*, Appendix.

4. Westermarck, *Ethical Relativity*, p. 197.

5. Thomas Aquinas, *Summa theologiae* (hereafter *ST*) I–II, 94, 2 (dates: 1225–74); see Aristotle, *Topics* VI, 6, and *Nichomachean Ethics* VI, 3–5 (dates: 384–322 B.C.).

6. See *Physics* II, 3–7.

7. This claim is subject to a good deal of debate. In holding this position, I am in agreement with a number of interpreters of Aquinas and the natural law tradition, including Germain Grisez, John Finnis, and Joseph Boyle. See Germain Grisez, *The Way of the Lord Jesus: Christian Moral Principles* (Chicago: Franciscan Herald Press, 1983) and John Finnis, *Natural Law and Natural Rights* (Oxford: Clarendon Press, 1980). See also the joint article by Grisez, Finnis, and Boyle, "Practical Principles, Moral Truth, and Ultimate Ends" in *American Journal of Jurisprudence* 32 (1987): 99–151. There are, however, other interpreters of Aquinas and the natural law tradition who think that ethics must be grounded in metaphysics, for example, Henry B. Veatch in his *For an Ontology of Morals* (Evanston: Northwestern University Press, 1971), Ralph McInerny in his *Ethica Thomistica: The Moral Philosophy of Thomas Aquinas* (Washington, D.C.: Catholic University of America Press, 1982), Russell Hittinger in his book *A Critique of the New Natural Law Theory* (Notre Dame, Ind.: Uni-

versity of Notre Dame Press, 1987), and Jean Porter in *The Recovery of Virtue: The Relevance of Aquinas for Christian Ethics* (Louisville, Ky.: Westminster/John Knox Press, 1990). In the passage we are discussing here (*ST* I–II, 94, 2), it seems clear that Aquinas is granting practical reason its own first principles which are parallel to, but not derived from, the principles of theoretical reason.

8. Aquinas, *ST* I–II, 94, 2: Cicero, *On Moral Obligation*, Book I, Ch. 4; John Finnis, *Natural Law*, Part Two, Ch. III and IV.

9. There are many other formulations besides these. Even proponents of such a view present different lists at different times. Consider the list presented in the joint article by Grisez, Finnis, and Boyle "Practical Principles, Moral Truth, and Ultimate Ends." In this article they distinguish between substantive goods—life, esthetic experience, excellence in work or play—and reflexive goods which are forms of harmony—harmony among people, among one's inner judgments and choices, between these judgments and choices and one's actions, and harmony with some "more-than-human source of meaning and value" (pp. 107–08). These differences in formulation do not show that relativism is the case, only that what the lists are about is not particular words but the sum total of intelligible good and that this good can be formulated in different ways.

10. Bruno Schüller, *Wholly Human*, tr. Peter Heinegg (Washington, D.C.: Georgetown University Press, 1986), p. 164.

11. Again, my position is rather like that of Grisez and Finnis. Schüller, however, allows consequences to play a greater role in decision-making, arguing for a position known as proportionalism, which holds that doing evil can sometimes be justified by a good end. This, however, is not to say that only consequences matter, as some utilitarians would say. Schüller distinguishes between moral evil and nonmoral evil in his discussion of the permissibility of taking an evil means to a good end: "(1) the causing of a moral evil, by its very nature, cannot be justified by anything in the world; (2) the causing of a non-moral evil is justified as long as it has either an appropriately important non-moral good or the preservation of moral goodness as its end" (Schüller, *Wholly Human*, p. 165). Aquinas does use the word "proportionate" in his discussion of killing in self-defense (II–II, 64, 7), but the proportionality is between the force used and what is needed to accomplish the end, not a kind of balancing of good and bad consequences. In addition, Finnis argues in *Moral Absolutes: Tradition, Revision, and Truth* (Washington, D.C.: Catholic University of America Press, 1991) that Schüller's absolute prohibition of doing moral evil is incompatible with his proportionalism: "A proportionalist, even one who like Schüller holds that moral wrong is the worst type of evil, has no coherent ground for denying the maxim, Better one murder than two murders. Better to participate in ten murders than make a choice which one knows will directly result in a hundred murders" (p. 49). Thus, Finnis agrees with Schüller that one must never do moral evil, but suggests that proportional analysis and its resulting choice ignore this prohibition.

12. *ST* I–II, 94, 4.

13. See Aquinas's treatment of killing in self-defense, *ST* II–II, 64, 7. That Aquinas allows for capital punishment has often been raised as an exception to this absolute prohibition against intentional killing. There are two things that can be said in reply here. First of all, the act of the state can be seen as an act of self-defense—a defense of the common good. Not to punish a murderer is not to defend the public good. Secondly, the principle that the least force necessary should be used must be upheld. If there is a better way to defend the public good from murderers than capital punishment, one which succeeds yet does not take a life, then that way should be followed. Thus, the issue of capital punishment can be addressed within the context of Aquinas' treatment of killing in self-defense.

14. *ST* I–II, 18, 5, ad 3; see also 1, 3, ad 3 and *De Malo*, 2, 4. John Finnis makes this essential distinction in *Moral Absolutes*, pp. 37–40.

15. While one could argue that the good of knowledge is also being violated, the essence of the violation concerns the good of orderly social life (friendship), for in lying one is not disregarding truth so much as refusing to share the truth with another.

16. Some (e.g., Veatch, McInerny, Hittinger, and Porter) argue that the idea of duty lacks sufficient grounds. They think that the theoretical (metaphysical, ontological) aspects of natural law—knowledge of human nature and the fact that human nature is created by God for happiness—are necessary in order to know what we should do. See, for example, the point of view of Henry Veatch and Joseph Rautenberg in their article "Does the Grisez-Finnis-Boyle Moral Philosophy Rest on a Mistake?" *Review of Metaphysics* 44 (June, 1991): 807–30. "Aquinas and Aristotle would contend that ethical knowledge is unquestionably based on a knowledge of nature, and more specifically on an understanding of human nature, for a human being is an integral part of nature, and possibly of supernature as well" (p. 818). Others (Grisez, Finnis, and Boyle) argue that such a grounding of obligation on physical and metaphysical principles falters on Hume's insight that one cannot derive obligation from fact. This is the position for which I have been arguing.

17. Among the interpreters of Thomas Aquinas, whose ethics has been characterized as both natural law and virtue ethics, some argue for the primacy of duty or obligation. Among these are Germain Grisez and John Finnis, whom we have already discussed in terms of the basic goods. Also in this group is Alan Donagan who, in "Teleology and Consistency in Theories of Natural Law," in *The Georgetown Symposium on Ethics*, ed. Rocco Porreco (Lanham, Md.: University Press of America, 1984), writes: "if we scrutinize the structure of St. Thomas's theory of natural law, we shall find that the teleology underlying it is not a Christianized version of eudaimonism, but an anticipation of the very same teleology Kant was to arrive at a little more than five hundred years later" (p. 93). On the other side, supporting the primacy of virtue ethics is Ralph McInerny who, in his *Ethica Thomistica* writes: "The doctrine of the virtues is thus the centerpiece of Thomas's view of the moral life. It is not just knowledge of virtue we seek, but the acquisition of virtue, and virtues are acquired, not by the study of moral philosophy, but by repeated acts of a given kind" (p. 102). See also Jean Porter in her *The Recovery of Virtue*. Concluding this work, she writes: "Ultimately,

Aquinas' theory of morality is significant today because it is successful on Aquinas' own terms. That is, he offers an account of the moral life which integrates the central concepts of his metaphysics into a unified account of human goodness and the virtues" (p. 179). John Keenan, S.J. in *Goodness and Rightness in Thomas Aquinas's Summa Theologiae* (Washington, D.C.: Georgetown University Press, 1992) finds both goodness (virtue of a person) and rightness (the moral quality of acts) to be major themes in Aquinas but not always adequately distinguished (Introduction, x). "Goodness, then, is descriptive of the first and most formal movement in a person. Unlike earlier approaches, goodness is not a judgment consequent to action, but a judgment antecedent to action. Rightness, on the other hand, concerns whether one's life and actions attain what is necessary for the protection and promotion of values. As attaining pertains to rightness, striving pertains to goodness" (p. 15). That goodness and rightness are not clearly specified by Aquinas helps account for some of this disagreement. On the other hand, it may also be (and this is my position) that the two are irreducible elements in what I am calling natural law ethics.

18. Bruno Schüller argues for a similar position in *Wholly Human*. He thinks that, far too often, philosophers and theologians get tangled up in defending competing positions which are distinguished more by name than by content. "The value ethics of a thinker like N. Hartmann and Stoic ethics are just as much virtue ethics as is that of Aristotle. Depending upon what we understand the 'natural law' to be, all the names in the list [adherents to Aristotelian virtue ethics, Stoic natural law ethics, Kantian duty ethics, utilitarian ethics, and value ethics] qualify in one way or another as natural law ethicians" (fn. 8, p. 216).

19. *Newman's University Sermons*, eds. D. M. Mackinnon and D. Holmes (London, 1970), 200 (sermon X, n. 45), quoted in Schüller, *Wholly Human*, p. 11. Even the morally sound features of the theories we have found wanting are to be found in this generalized notion of the natural law, as we shall argue in the next chapter.

20. Plato, *The Crito*, 46b, tr. G. M. A. Grube, in *The Trial and Death of Socrates* (Indianapolis: Hackett, 1975), p. 46 (dates: 428–348 B.C.).

21. Plato, *Crito*, p. 49.

22. Aristotle, *Nicomachean Ethics* IX, 8.

23. Aristotle is not saying that the rational soul is the self, but that it is the specific difference which distinguishes human beings from animals and which makes self-awareness possible.

24. See Plato, *Gorgias*, 507b–c; Aristotle, *Nicomachean Ethics* VI, 13 (1144b18–1145a12); Cicero, *On Moral Obligation*, Book I, Ch. 19.

25. Aristotle, *Nichomachean Ethics* VIII, 3.

26. Aristotle, *Nichomachean Ethics* II, 6 (1106b36–1107a2), tr. Hippocrates G. Apostle (Grinnell, Iowa: The Peripatetic Press, 1984), pp. 28–29.

27. See Finnis in *Natural Law*, pp. 101–02.

28. Aristotle, *Nichomachean Ethics* VI, 13 (114461–18).

29. Aristotle, *Nichomachean Ethics* II, 6 (1107a9–18), p. 29.

30. First, note that out of ten books in his *Nichomachean Ethics*, Aristotle devotes two (Books VIII and IX) to the good of friendship. Note also that Aristotle's final word on human happiness in Book X, 7, is that it is contemplation (knowledge of the truth). On the good of life, see *Nichomachean Ethics* IX, 4 (1166a9–23) and IX, 9 (1170a19–b8); on procreation and family see VIII, 12 (1162a14–32); on obligations to parents and elders see VIII, 12 (1162a4–9) and IX, 2 (1165a21–30); on religion, see VIII, 12 (1162a4–9) and VIII, 14 (1163b13–30).

31. Aristotle, *Nichomachean Ethics* VIII, 15 (1163a23), p. 159.

32. Cicero, *On Moral Obligation*, Book I, Ch. 2, tr. John Higginbotham (Berkeley/Los Angeles: University of California Press, 1967), p. 40 (dates: 106–43 B.C.).

33. Cicero, *On Moral Obligation*, Book I, Ch. 2, p. 41.

34. Cicero, *On Moral Obligation*, Book I, Ch. 2, p. 41.

35. Cicero, *On Moral Obligation*, Book I, Ch. 4, p. 44.

36. Consider the formulation of natural law morality presented by Diogenes Laertes: "Again, living virtuously is equivalent to living in accordance with experience of the actual course of nature, as Chrysippus says in the first book of his treatise *On Ends*; for our individual natures are parts of the nature of the whole universe. And this is why the end may be defined as life in accordance with nature, or, in other words, in accordance with our own human nature as well as that of the universe, a life in which we refrain from every action forbidden by the law common to all things. . ." (SVF III, 4, tr. R. D. Hicks in *Greek and Roman Philosophy after Aristotle*, p. 112). This formulation seems to tie moral law into the physical laws of human nature and the universe. Such a move would be in violation of Hume's insight that obligation cannot be derived from facts alone.

37. See Cicero, *On Moral Obligation*, Book I, Ch. 4, and Aquinas, *ST* I–II, 94, 2, ad 2 & 3, and 94, 4, ad 3.

38. Cicero, *On Moral Obligation*, Ch. 4 & 5.

39. One might argue that, for all practical purposes, being virtuous is enough: one need not know why what one does is right. But Aristotle says that to act without knowledge is not to be virtuous in the full sense (*Nichomachean Ethics* VI, 13).

40. Fr. Keenan argues that the virtues are not alternative moral guides which make us good in some way other than by our following reason's dictates; rather, the virtues dispose us to follow reason in our choices and actions. "No longer can we presume (if we follow Thomas) that somehow the virtues make us good, loving, or holy people. Rather they make us rightly ordered, so that we may reason and act well in the practical order" (*Goodness and Rightness*, p. 109).

41. On following one's conscience, see Thomas Aquinas, *ST* I–II, 19, 5 & 6.

42. Finnis, *Natural Law*, p. 96.

43. Finnis, *Natural Law*, p. 92.

44. This is not so farfetched: these very goods were objects of attack from the Marxist ideology of the former Soviet Union.

NOTES FOR CHAPTER 7

1. G. E. Moore, *Principia Ethica*, pp. 188–89. Although Moore disagrees with classical utilitarianism about pleasure being the only good, he agrees with the principle that consequences are the final word on the moral quality of any act. "What I wish first to point out is that 'right' does and can mean nothing but 'cause of a good result,' and is thus identical with 'useful': whence it follows that the end always justifies the means, and that no action which is not justified by its results can be right" (*Principia*, p. 147). While the nature of the goods differs from classical utilitarianism (friendship and beauty as opposed to pleasure), still the method is the same. The ideal of scientific method with its hypothesis (estimation of what act will bring about the greatest good for the greatest number) and verification (measuring the results of the act) has not changed.

2. Finnis, *Natural Law*, p. 115.

3. Mill does say in one place that virtue is desired as an end as well as a means, but when pointing out why people desire virtue as an end, he returns to pleasure as the ultimate explanation. "Those who desire virtue for its own sake desire it either because the consciousness of it is a pleasure, or because the consciousness of being without it is a pain, or for both reasons united. . ." (J. S. Mill, *Utilitarianism*, Ch. IV, p. 48).

4. "But pleasure perfects the activity not as a disposition which resides in the agent but as an end which supervenes like the bloom of manhood to those in their prime of life" (Aristotle, *Nicomachean Ethics*, X, 4 [1174b33], p. 187).

5. Aristotle, *Nichomachean Ethics* X, 2.

6. Aristotle, *Nichomachean Ethics* X, 5.

7. *ST* II–II, 64, 5, ad 3; II–II, 26, 4.

8. Brandt, *Theory*, from Title of Ch. XV, p. 286.

9. Amelie Rorty, "Varieties of Pluralism in a Polyphonic Society" in *Review of Metaphysics* 44 (Sept. 1990): 3–20, at 17.

10. William James, *Pragmatism* (London/New York: Longmans, Green and Co., 1907), p. 222. The other chief exponents of classical American pragmatism were Charles Peirce and John Dewey.

11. In his essay "The Will to Believe," X, in *The Will to Believe and Other Essays in Popular Philosophy* (New York: Dover Publications, 1956) James writes: "We ought, on the contrary, delicately and profoundly to respect one another's mental freedom: then only shall we bring about the intellectual republic; then only shall we have that spirit of inner tolerance without which all our outer tolerance is soulless, and which is empiricism's glory; then only shall we live and let live, in speculative as well as in practical things" (p. 30).

12. Joseph Fletcher, *Situation Ethics* (Philadelphia: The Westminster Press, 1966), pp. 40–43.

13. Fletcher, *Situation Ethics*, p. 31.

14. Lawrence M. Hinman, *Ethics: A Pluralistic Approach to Moral Theory* (New York: Harcourt Brace, 1994), p. 48.

15. Hinman, *Ethics*, p. 68.

16. "It [fallibilistic ethical pluralism] offers a way of appreciating such diversity and disagreement as sources of richness in our moral lives and it suggests ways in which we can live together in the face of such disagreements." Hinman, *Ethics*, p. 48.

17. Rorty, "Varieties of Pluralism," p. 18.

18. Fletcher, *Situation Ethics*, pp. 47–48.

19. Hinman, *Ethics*, p. 315.

20. See Alasdair MacIntyre, *After Virtue: A Study in Moral Theory* (Notre Dame, Ind.: University of Notre Dame Press, 1981).

21. "[Ethical] virtue, then, is a habit, disposed toward action by deliberate choice, being at the mean relative to us, and defined by reason and as a prudent man would define it" (Aristotle, *Nicomachean Ethics* II, 6 [1106b36], pp. 28–29).

22. Other contemporary pluralists offer different guides. For example, John Kekes in *The Morality of Pluralism* (Princeton, N.J.: Princeton University Press, 1993) argues that the guide that limits certain behaviors is the effects on human beings. "Possibilities are seen as being good or evil depending on the effects their realization has or would have on us, human beings" (p. 15). Thus, his pluralism turns out to be a kind of rule-utilitarianism similar to Brandt's. Robert Kane in *Through the Moral Maze: Searching for Absolute Values in a Pluralistic World* (New York: Paragon House, 1994) argues for an openness to all positions based on what he calls the "Ends *Principle*: Treat every person in every situation as an end and never as a means (to your or someone else's ends)" (p. 21). While we are awaiting the revealing of absolute standards for morality which we do not yet possess, this principle is nonnegotiable. But on emotivist, egoistic, or utilitarian grounds such a principle would be negotiable; hence, Kane's view reverts to Kant's formalism, which is a species of moral absolutism.

23. Note the similarity to Hume's second operation of reason—dealing with such relations as cause and effect and means to ends.

24. Jeffrey Stout, *The Flight from Authority: Religion, Morality, and the Quest for Autonomy* (Notre Dame, Ind./London: University of Notre Dame Press, 1981), Preface, p. xi.

25. "If we ever achieve a general theory of justification that is worth having, it will probably be a sociological theory of the kind that emerges from extensive historical and anthropological research" (Stout, *Flight from Authority*, p. 194).

26. Stout holds that both Kant and Rawls are attempting to define this moral point of view, and he basically equates their moral principles (Stout, *Flight from Authority*, pp. 232 ff.). Here I think Stout is mistaken, for only if one considers merely the universalizability criterion of Kant's first version of the categorical imperative, where we noted that self-interest plays a part, could one consider Rawls and Kant as having the same moral foundations.

27. Stout, *Flight from Authority*, p. 197–200. "The prescriptivist theory of universalizability, ideal-observer theories, and utilitarian appeals to sympathy that would

count each rational agent (oneself or another) as one in the calculation of utility can all be read as attempts to explicate or model the kind of abstraction involved" (p. 232).

28. Stout, *Flight from Authority*, p. 19. Note the pragmatic emphasis on use here.

29. Stout, *Flight from Authority*, p. 229.

30. Stout, *Flight from Authority*, pp. 253–54.

31. Stout, *Flight from Authority*, p. 260.

32. Stout, *Flight from Authority*, p. 260.

33. It is, in fact, impossible to violate all moral norms (whether historically described or absolutely required) at once, for such a violation would require multiple acts.

34. See William James, "The Will to Believe," I, pp. 2–3.

35. Stout, *Flight from Authority*, p. 252.

36. *ST* I–II, 94, 2.

37. Finnis, *Moral Absolutes*, p. 29.

38. Stout, *Flight from Authority*, p. 270.

39. Stout, *Flight from Authority*, p. 271.

40. Stout, *Flight from Authority*, p. 272.

NOTES FOR CHAPTER 8

1. Kai Nielsen, *Ethics Without God* (Buffalo, N.Y.: Prometheus Books, 1990), p. 10.

2. See Aristotle, *Nicomachean Ethics* IX, 2.

3. Aristotle, *Nichomachean Ethics* VIII, 12, (1162a4–8), tr. Apostle, p. 156.

4. Kai Nielsen denies that there is a natural obligation to God, for he does not think that there are any good answers to the Enlightenment (Hume *et alia*) rejection of immaterial realities (*Ethics Without God*, p. 39). If we cannot know by natural reason that God exists, we cannot have a natural obligation to God. So while Nielsen and I agree that ethics is not based on religion, we disagree about whether or not reason can know anything about God, even that God exists. In general, Nielsen's ethical position is a kind of social contract theory like Rawls' in which morality is a matter of agreement within the group (pp. 193–206). "There can be true or false moral claims, an intersubjective validity to moral claims, and a rationale to a morality rooted in an underlying function of morality that in turn determines what it is to take the moral point of view. People have objective interests and moral needs" (p. 205). Nielsen rejects natural law morality (pp. 25–47) and the idea that there are any moral absolutes which might serve as foundations to justify moral action (pp. 128–60). "The natural moral law stands as a consoling fable that tries to give *a type* of objectivity to morality that it does not and cannot possess. . . . We must be on guard against the irrational heart of rationalism and not set out on the quest for certainty" (p. 47). Nielsen's position is much like Jeffrey Stout's; and, as in Stout's case, it is hard to see how

Nielsen can claim that certain acts are clearly wrong if he denies moral absolutes and reason's ability to know with certainty.

5. The general structure for this proof I owe to C. S. Lewis. It appears in Chapter V of his book *Miracles* (New York: Macmillan, 1947).

6. Thomas Aquinas, *Summa contra gentiles* II, 15, [2]. This principle, when applied to any two things, leads ultimately to a first cause of everything.

7. This argument need not imply that the real human being is the mind, as Plato and Descartes thought. In fact, Thomas Aquinas would deny that this is the case. However, it remains that intellect is not reducible to matter, and therefore its existence cannot be adequately accounted for by any scientific (material) explanation.

8. In the Third Programme debate between Bertrand Russell and Father Frederick C. Copleston (British Broadcasting Corporation, 1948), Russell responds to Copleston's question about the origin of the universe by stating: "I should say that the universe is just there, and that's all." Reprinted in Louis P. Pojman, ed., *Philosophy of Religion* (Belmont Ca.: Wadsworth, 1987), p. 10.

9. One might object that not all things we receive are good (e.g., sickness or persecution) and that, if God is the source of everything, then he is also the source of the bad things we receive. This is the so-called problem of evil. The intricacies of sorting out this problem are more appropriate to a work of natural theology than ethics. (I discuss the issue in *The Romance of Reason*, Chapter Five.) However, we need not solve this problem in order to recognize our obligation to God. The very same reasons Aristotle says we are obligated to our parents make us obliged to God. Like our parents, God is the cause of our existence, our nurture, and our education, only in a more profound sense. While parents are the cause of one's material existence by providing the genetic material which directs one's growth, God is the cause of everything, of all material reality and of the unique intellect that makes one an individual. Parents nurture their children, but it is God who keeps all things in existence—food, parents, etc.—and is thus a deeper cause of one's nurturing. And not only does God provide things and teachers as a means for one's education; he also gives one the intellect that makes all learning possible. Here is the crux of the insight—not so much what God has done for one in the past, but one's dependence on God now, when one is able to think about what is good and will to be happy. Essential to human well-being is reasoned choice (the choice to promote good and avoid evil); without it we cannot be happy. When one realizes that one's fulfillment as a human being depends on making good choices, one is grateful for being able to make such choices. But since we did not give ourselves rationality or freedom, nor have we received them from material nature, our gratefulness must be directed toward another source, one which transcends ourselves and the material world. Such a source, as beyond our experience, is indeed mysterious—as is a proper understanding of what we mean when we use the word "God." Whether or not one chooses to call this source God is beside the point: what is certain is that we owe a debt of thanks for our ability to think and choose, and we owe it to a being who transcends ourselves and the world in which we live.

10. Cicero, *On Moral Duties*, Book I, Ch. 45, p. 96.

11. *ST* I–II, 100, 1.

12. Finnis, *Natural Law*, pp. 89–90.

13. *ST* II–II, 81, 5, ad 3 (my translation).

14. Josef Pieper, *The Four Cardinal Virtues* (New York: Harcourt, Brace & World, Inc., 1965), p. 111.

15. Finnis, *Natural Law*, p. 113.

NOTES FOR CHAPTER 9

1. Pascal, *Pensées*, 132, tr. A. J. Krailsheimer (New York: Penguin Books, 1966), p. 66.

2. Pascal, *Pensées*, 200, p. 95.

3. Augustine, *Confessions* II, 4, tr. Frank J. Sheed (Indianapolis/Cambridge: Hackett, 1993), p. 27.

4. See Henry Fairlie, *The Seven Deadly Sins Today* (Notre Dame Ind.: University of Notre Dame Press, 1979).

Index

absolute moral norms, 11–12, 20–21,
110–11; conflicts among, 111–14; and
freedom, 11, 18–20, 110; and science,
11–18; and relativism, 20–21;
required for freedom of choice, 21.
adultery, 99
altruistic sentiment, 32
Anaximenes, 14
anthropology, 128, 160 n.25; and cultural
relativism, 4–5; and natural law, 88
Aristotle, 37, 101; on basic goods, 105,
158 n.30; on distinction between
theoretical and practical reason, 92;
his definition of moral virtue,
160 n.21; his doctrine of the four
causes, 93; on friendship, 104; on
God, 94; on happiness, 153 n.7; on
importance of good upbringing; on
intention, 104–6; and Kant, 85; on
moral absolutes, 105; and natural law
ethics, 89, 130, 157 n.18; on obligation to parents and God, 136, 139,
162 n.9; on pleasure, 159 n.4; on practical reason, 94; on self-interest, 103;
and traditional moral norms, 24; on
virtue, 98, 104–6
atomism, 14–17; and its anti-religious
foundations, 15–16; and its disregard
for justice, 16–18; and immortality,
15–16
Augustine of Hippo, St., on choosing
evil, 145
autonomy, 80–82
Ayer, A. J., 31–33

Bacon, Francis: on absolutist ethics, 17;
on the limits of reason, 93–94; on
metaphysics, 17; on religion, 17, 24;
and scientific method, 12, 37; and
Hobbes, 150 n.3
basic good(s), 96, 110–14; and Aristotle,
105, 158 n.30; and Cicero, 96, 106;
and Finnis, 96; their fundamental
equality, 111; as good in themselves,
96; and Grisez/Finnis/Boyle, 155 n.9;
as incommensurable, 117, 119; and
G. E. Moore, 116–117; as open-
ended, 110; as self-evident, 96, 144;
and Thomas Aquinas, 96; and virtue,
108
Benedict, Ruth, 4
benevolence, 27, 33, 35, 38; and direct
inclination, 70; and duty, 69; and
Hume, 59–60, 66; and Mill, 59–60;
and Rawls, 48, 61. *See also* moral
sense and benevolent impulse
benevolent impulse, 26–27, 30, 32; and
Hume, 35; and Rawls, 47; rejected by
Hobbes, 38. *See also* moral sense and
benevolence
Bentham, Jeremy, 50–66, 116–17;
and determinism, 81, 84; and happiness, 74, 91; and heteronomous
causality, 82; and hypothetical imperative, 75; and limits of reason, 92; and
materialism, 81; on scientific method,
87; and his theory of punishment,
152 n.20
Berkeley, George, and empiricism, 24

biology: and moral action, 64; and scientific method, 67

Boyle, Joseph: on basic goods, 155 n.9; and natural law tradition, 154 n.7; on theoretical foundations for morality, 156 n.16

Brandt, Richard, 60–62, 151 n.14, 151–52 n.15; and pluralism, 123, 160 n.22

capital punishment, 156 n.13

cardinal virtues, 102–8; in Hobbes' state of nature, 38

character: as second nature, 121; in Hinman, 126

Cicero, 101, 106–8; on basic goods, 96, 106–7; on duty, 106; on happiness, 153 n.7; and Kant, 85; on obligation to gods, 139–40; and natural law, 106–108; on natural law and natural inclinations, 107; on virtue, 106–8; on virtues and feelings, 107

common good: and Bentham, 51, 55; and Mill, 58. *See also* community

commonwealth, 111

community: and Bentham, 51; and Brandt, 60; good of, 119–20, 132; and Mill, 58. *See also* common good

conscience, 2; at center of ethics, 109, 120; informed, 144; and Thomas Aquinas, 158 n.41

consequences, 21–22, 159 n.1; and Bentham, 50–56, 66; and Brandt, 60–63; and duty, 69, 71, 75; and Mill, 59; and natural law, 116; and proportionalism, 155 n.11

Copleston, Frederick C., 162 n.8

culture, and moral action, 130

Darwin, Charles, 6

democracy, and moral absolutes, 142–43

Democritus, 14, 17

deontological ethics, 101, 107. *See also* Kantian ethics

Descartes, René, 84; and the Enlightenment, 128; on human nature, 162 n.7

descriptivist theories, 128

determinism, 84; and Hobbes, 41; and Hume, 28–29; and materialism, 74, 81; and pleasure/pain theories, 65–66, 69, 72, 108, 114; and utilitarianism, 64

Diogenes Laertes, 158 n.36

direct inclination, 70–71, 73, 81; as subjective and particular, 70

distractions, 144

diversion, 144, 146

divine command theory, 3

Donagan, Alan, 153 n.16; on primacy of duty over virtue in ethics of Thomas Aquinas, 156 n.17

duty, 21, 69–72, 74, 96, 101; and autonomy, 80; content of, 78; form of, 77; imperfect, 75–77; and natural law, 156 n.17; perfect, 75–77; as objective and universal, 70

duty ethics, 101, 154 n.1; and virtue ethics, 104

economics, and cultural relativism, 6

egoism, 21–22, 35–49; and Brandt, 123; and determinism, 64, 109; and duty, 69; and moral absolutes, 143; and natural law, 119–20; and relativism, 85; and responsibility, 88

emotion(s): benevolent, 120; and Hobbes and Hume, 62; as origin of morality, 26, 32–34; as particular, 49. *See also* feeling(s) and passion(s)

emotivism, 21–22, 23–34; and determinism, 64, 109; as foundationalist theory, 128; and materialism, 65; and moral absolutes, 143; and natural law, 120–21; and relativism, 42, 85; and responsibility, 88

Empedocles, 14

empiricism, 24, 31, 43; and materialism, 24

empirical method, 151 n.27

end, 73; given by passion, 75; given by reason, 75; justifies the means, 159 n.1

end in itself: human being as, 78–80, 97; basic good as, 97–98; pleasure as, 117–19

Engels, Friedrich, 6

Enlightenment, 128, 161 n.4

environment, and moral action, 7, 64–65

Epicurus, 14–17, 21–22, 72; and anti-religious attitude, 14–18, 24, 134–35; and disregard for justice, 16–18; and egoism, 21–22; and emotivism, 21–23; on happiness, 91; and Hume, 23–24; and Mill, 56; against moral absolutes, 134–35; and pluralism, 123; and therapeutic foundations of philosophy, 14

experience, as origin of all our ideas, 69. *See also* empiricism

feeling(s): benevolent, 120; as origin of morality, 21–22, 23, 25–27. *See also* emotion(s) and passion(s)

feminism, 8

Finnis, John: on adultery, 156 n.14; on basic goods, 96, 110–12, 155 n.9; on the incommensurability of the basic goods, 117; on moral principles as not derived, 130–31; and the natural law tradition, 154 n.7; on primacy of duty over virtue in the ethics of Thomas Aquinas, 156 n.17; on proportionalism, 155 n.11; on religion and the other basic goods, 141; on the theoretical foundations of morality, 156 n.16

first principle of practical reason, 95; self-evidence of, 144

first principles: and the impossibility of proving them directly, 127; the nature of, 127

Fletcher, Joseph, 124–27; on love as a moral principle, 125–26

formalism, 21, 68–86

foundationalism, 128–129

freedom: and animals, 149 n.34; and cultural relativism, 8–9; desire for, 18; and divine providence 18; as ideal of democracy, 142; moral, 18–20; and natural inclinations, 107; and natural law, 108–11, 114; practical proof of, 81, 83–84; presupposed to obligation, 68–69; and relativism, 19–21; social/political, 18–19; theoretical proof of, 81–83; to care or not to care, 145–46; as transcending material world, 162 n.9. *See also* freedom of choice

freedom of choice, 18–20, 74; essential to human nature, 143; and happiness, 162 n.9; illusion of, 64; not a basic good, 122–23; and practical reason, 30; and responsibility, 127

friendship, in Aristotle, 104

Galileo, and Hobbes, 37

gender, and cultural relativism, 6–8

Gilligan, Carol, 7

God: as creator, 136–39; existence of, 137–39; obligation to, 136, 139–40, 162 n.9

good in itself: each basic good as, 97–98; good will as, 71; humanity as, 78, 97; pleasure as, 117–19

good(s): common, 103; instrumental, 96; lesser, 96; material, 103; more fundamental than right(s), 100; reflexive and substantive, 155 n.9. *See also* basic good(s) good will, 71, 132

Grisez, Germain, 147 n.3, 149 n.32, 155 n.11; on basic goods, 155 n.9; and natural law tradition, 154 n.7; on primacy of duty over virtue in the ethics of Thomas Aquinas, 156 n.17; on theoretical foundations of morality, 156 n.16

happiness: as activity of wisdom and virtue, 91, 118–19; and Aquinas, 153 n.7; and Aristotle, 118, 152 n.7; and Bentham, 52, 72; and Brandt, 60; and Cicero, 153 n.7; and Hobbes, 74; and Hume, 74; and Kant, 90–92; as metaphysical principle, 91; and Mill, 56, 58–59, 118; and natural law tradition, 90–92; as pleasure, 117–19; as psychological principle, 91; and reasoned choice, 162 n.9; as tranquillity, 91; and virtue ethics, 104

Hare, R. M., 153 n.11

Hartmann, Nicolai, 157 n.18

hedonistic calculus, 52; and Mill, 56–58; and science, 63

Hegel, G. W. F., 5–6

Heraclitus, 14

heteronomy, 81–82

hierarchy of pleasures, 57

Hinman, Lawrence M., 124–126; on character as guiding principle, 125–26; on fallibilistic ethical pluralism, 160 n.16

historicism, 6, 127–32; and rejection of foundationalism, 128; and language, 128–29; and narrative context, 127–29; as new pragmatism, 128; and relativism, 5–6, 128, 131

Hittinger, Russell, 154–55 n.7; on theoretical foundations for morality, 156 n.16

Hobbes, Thomas, 37–48; and antipathy, 50, 52; and Bacon, 150 n.3; and Bentham, 52; on community, 119; and denial of benevolent impulse, 26; and determinism, 81; and Galileo, 37; and emotions, 62; and first version of the categorical imperative, 77; on happiness, 74, 91; and heteronomous causality, 82; and hypothetical imperative, 73, 75; and Kant, 69; on limits of reason, 92–94; and materialism, 81; and natural law ethics, 89–90; on natural laws, 107; and the obligation to follow majority opinion, 109; on physical laws, 107; and Plato on self-interest, 102–3; and psychology, 62; against religion, 24; and scientific method, 87

holism, 128

Hume, David, 23–34; and benevolence, 35, 48, 59–60; and Bentham, 52; and determinism, 81; and direct inclination, 73, 80; on emotions, 62; on fallacy of deriving obligation from fact, 27–28, 107, 156 n.16, 158 n.36; on happiness, 74, 91; and heteronomous causality, 82; and hypothetical imperative, 75; and Kant, 68–70, 81–82; and the leap of faith, 126; on limits of reason, 24–26, 92–94; and materialism, 81–82; on the nature of thought, 13; and practical reason, 94; and psychology, 63; against religion and moral absolutes, 17, 134–35; and rejection of immaterial realities, 161 n.4; and responsibility, 82; on secondary role of reason, 29–31, 52, 160 n.23; and science, 37, 47; and scientific method, 12, 87; and sympathy, 50, 59–60; and the violation of his own "no-ought-from-is" thesis, 154 n.2

immortality of the soul, 15–16

imperative(s), 73–81; apodyctic, 74; assertorial, 73, 77, 80; categorical 73–81; first version of categorical, 75; hypothetical 73–75; hypothetical imperative and happiness, 90; second version of categorical, 78; third version of categorical, 80

impulses, 127

intention(s), 98–100, 102; and Aristotle, 104–6; and Kant, 70–71, 75; and Bentham, 54; and Mill, 57; irrelevance of, 54. *See also* motive(s)

James, William, 124, 130, 159n.11

Jefferson, Thomas, 43

justice: as absolute requirement, 132; as will of the sovereign, 42, 46; Rawls' principles of, 44–48

Kane, Robert, 160n.22

Kant, Immanuel, 68–86; and the Enlightenment, 128; on happiness, 74; and Hobbes, 69, 73, 77; and Hume, 68–70, 81–82; on the importance of the individual, 109; and moral absolutes, 160n.22; and natural law, 87, 89, 96–97, 100–107; and the rejection of virtue ethics, 104; and social contract theory, 150n.19

Kantian ethics, on the derivation of the precepts of the natural law from inclinations, 107. *See also* deontological ethics

Keenan, John, 157n.17; on virtues and reason, 158n.40

Keekes, John, 160n.22

killing in self-defense, 98–99, 155n.11, 156n.13

knowing: material aspects of, 138; as irreducible to material causes, 138–39

language and philosophical meaning, 128

law: in Hobbes, 39–40, 45, 89; in Kant, 72, 75; moral and physical, 158n.36; in natural law tradition 89–90; of noncontradiction, 13, 95; physical law and determinism, 74; self-given, 92

Lewis, C. S., 152n.20, 154n.1, 162n.5

liberty: principle of equal, 45–46, 48; as servant of justice, 43

life, and the other basic goods, 112–14

linguistic analysis, 129

Locke, John, 43; empiricism of, 24, 43; and equality, 151n.27

Lucretius, 14–17; and anti-religious attitude, 14, 24; and disregard for justice, 16–18; and Hume, 24; and Mill, 56; on religion and moral absolutes, 72, 134–35; and therapeutic foundation of philosophy, 14

MacIntyre, Alasdair, on historicism, 6, 128, 147n.12

Mackie, J. L., 147n.8

Madison, James, 43

Marx, Karl, 6

materialism, 12–15, 148n.20; and determinism, 74, 81; of emotivism, social contract ethics, and utilitarianism, 65; and ethics, 13–17; and Hobbes, 41; and religion, 13–17; self-refuting, 13, 20; and the truncation of reason, 93–94; unjustifiable, 67

matters of fact, 24–25, 31, 33

McInerny, Ralph, 154n.7; on the primacy of virtue in the ethics of

McInerny, Ralph (*continued*)
Thomas Aquinas, 156 n.17; on the
theoretical foundations for morality,
156 n.16
means-to-end, 73
mechanism: and happiness, 91; and Hobbes, 38, 89–91
metaphysics, 93–94
Mill, John Stuart, 56–60; and Aristotle,
118; on happiness, 118; and Hume,
59–60; on virtue as end and means,
159 n.3
Montaigne, Michel de, 17
Moore, G. E., 116–17; and basic goods,
152 n.22; on utilitarian method,
159 n.1
moral absolutes, 134–35, 142–43; in Aristotle, 105; justification of, 42; and
pragmatism, 132; rejection of, 161 n.4
moral absolutism, danger of, 122
moral conversation, 131
moral luck, 131–32
moral norms: as arbitrary and absurd,
126; as revisable, 130
moral objectivity, 131
moral precepts, 96; absolute character of,
98, 100
moral sense, 23, 33; rejected by Hobbes,
38. *See also* benevolence and benevolent impulse
moral virtue, Aristotle's definition of,
104, 160 n.21
motive(s): and Bentham, 53–54; immeasurable character of, 53–54; and
Kant, 70; and utilitarianism, 63. *See
also* intention(s)

natural law, 21, 87–114, 135, 154 n.1,
157 n.18; generalized notion of, 100–
2, 157 n.19; in Hobbes and natural
law tradition, 89; and moral absolutes, 143; not a physical nor political
law, 145; rejection of, 161 n.4; supported by Scripture, 2; taught by
Roman Catholic Church, 2; and Ten
Commandments, 139
nature, in Hobbes and natural law tradition, 90
Nielsen, Kai, 135; and the denial of obligation to God, 161 n.4; and the rejection of moral absolutes, 161 n.4; and
the rejection of natural law ethics,
161 n.4; and social contract theory,
161 n.4
Nietzsche, Friedrich, 6, 18, 72

obligation, 84–85, 142; and autonomy,
80; as basis for proving existence of
God, 137–39; to care for oneself, 120;
and Cicero, 106; and freedom, 68,
109–10; to God and parents, 161 n.9;
implied by all moral theories, 115;
involves theoretical reason, 92; and
Kant, 68–72; and natural law, 87–88,
156 n.17; not derivable from facts
alone, 27–28, 42, 47, 49, 55, 59, 61,
67–68, 77, 79, 88, 94, 107, 143,
156 n.16, 158 n.36; not justified by
emotivism, egoism, or utilitarianism,
65; and pleasure/pain theories, 65–
67; and pluralism, 125; and refutation
of materialism, 67; to repay good
received, 136–39; and utilitarianism,
119. *See also* responsibility
original position, 45, 47

Pascal, Blaise, 144
passion(s): benevolent, 47, 120; and reasoned choice, 94; and determinism,
28–29; as origin of morality, 26–27,
28–34, 35, 38, 44, 47, 151 n.27;
humanized, 121; and hypothetical

imperative, 73–75; of self-interest, 44. *See also* emotion(s) and feeling(s)

personalism, and Fletcher, 124

physics: and Hobbes, 66, 89; and scientific method, 67

Pieper, Josef, 140

Plato, 101–104; on human nature, 162 n.7; on importance of good upbringing, 7; and natural law ethics, 89; on self-interest, 102–3; and the social contract theory, 36; and traditional moral norms. 24; on virtue, 101–4

pleasure: and activity, 159 n.4; as end in itself, 117–19

pleasure and pain: as absolute masters, 65; and Bentham, 51–54; and Cicero, 106; of consequences, 66; and determinism, 65, 69, 72, 114; and duty, 70; and freedom of choice, 64, 114; and Mill, 56–58; as first principles of morality, 22; and Hobbes, 36, 39, 41; and Hume, 30; and obligation, 49; qualitative analysis of, 56–58; quantitative analysis of, 52–54, 57; and Rawls, 44; and responsibility, 65–67; and scientific method, 62, 66

pluralism, 123–127, 160 n.22; and Brandt; fallibilistic ethical, 124–26, 160 n.16; and natural law, 123, 125

Porter, Jean, 155 n.7; on primacy of virtue in the ethics of Thomas Aquinas, 156–57 n.17; on the theoretical grounds for morality, 156 n.16

positivism, and Fletcher, 124

power: coercive, 40; as first principle of ethics, 38, 42; in relation to law and justice, 40; sovereign, 40, 42, 46

practical reason, 66, 94, 133, 135; and Aristotle, 92–95; and Brandt, 61; and Bentham, 50; and conscience, 144; denial of, 27, 44, 47, 50, 61, 66, 68; first principle of, 95, 155 n.7; as foun-

dation of moral obligation, 68; and freedom, 83–85; and happiness, 91; and Hume; illusion of, 48; and Kant, 72; limited notion of, 94; object of, 94; and pleasure/pain theories, 66; and Rawls, 44, 47; and responsibility, 88; and theoretical reason, 77–78, 92–95, 155 n.7; and Thomas Aquinas, 92–95

practical reasonableness, and the other basic goods, 112

pragmatism, 124; and identity of good and useful, 132

prescriptivity, 153 n.11

prescriptivist theories, 128, 160 n.27

pre-Socratic philosophers, 14, 148 n.22

principle of utility: and Bentham, 51, 64; and Mill, 56. *See also* utilitarianism

problem of evil, 3, 162 n.9

proportionate, and the intention to use least force necessary, 155 n.11

proportionalism, 155 n.11

psychology: and cultural relativism, 7–8; and Hume and Hobbes, 63, 66–77

rationality: in natural law tradition, 90; as transcending matter, 137–39, 162 n.9

Rautenberg, Joseph, 156 n.16

Rawls, John, 43–48, 150 n.19, 161 n.4; and benevolence, 61; and empirical method, 151 n.27; and Kant, 153 n.14

reason: as essential to human nature, 143; secondary role of, 29, 38–40, 44, 52, 60–61, 74, 160 n.23; as slave of the passions, 31; as technique for fulfilling self-interest, 38; as tool of the passions, 64; as unable to know right from wrong, 38. *See also* practical reason and theoretical reason

reductionism, and Hobbes, 66

Reformation, and anti-Aristotelianism, 37

Reid, Thomas, 149 n.8

relations of ideas, 24–25, 31, 33

relativism, 1–22, 42; cultural, 1, 4–5, 20–21, 42, 142; and determinism, 65–66, 109; and emotivism, 33; and Fletcher, 124, 126; and freedom of choice, 19–21; historical, 5–7; and Hobbes, 42; and Hume, 28–29; and Kant, 85; moral/ethical, 1, 10–11; and natural law, 121–23; and pleasure/pain theories, 65–66; principled, 124; and religion 1–3, 134; as self-refuting, 10–11, 88; subjective, 1, 9–10, 20–21, 33, 75, 126, 142; theoretical, 10; as unjustifiable, 10–11

religion: argument against, 3; and ethics, 2–3, 134–41; fundamentalist, 3; as a moral requirement, 135–39; as a natural moral virtue, 139–40; as the origin of ethics, 2, 134–35; and other basic goods, 112, 141

respect, 71–72, 78

responsibility, 21–22; and conscience, 109; and emotivism, 33–34; and Hobbes, 41–42; and Kant, 69–70, 80; and natural law, 87–88; and Rawls, 44, 49; possible foundations for, 21; renunciation of, 17–18; universality not a sufficient ground for, 77. *See also* obligation

rights, dependent on goods, 100

Rorty, Amelie, on pluralism, 124–25

Rorty, Richard, on historicism, 6, 128

Rousseau, Jean Jacques, 154 n.19

Russell, Bertrand, 162 n.8

Sartre, Jean-Paul, 18

school of common sense, 149 n.8

Schüller, Bruno, 98, 155 n.1; on natural law ethics, 157 n.18

science, 11–18, 20–21; as unable to verify moral norms, 142

scientific method, 12–13, 20–21, 67, 68; and Ayer, 31; and Brandt, 61; and Bentham, 50, 54; and consequences, 63; and the denial of practical reason, 88; and Hobbes, 37; and Hume, 24; and the limitation of reason, 65, 93; and obligation, 59; and the rejection of formal and final causes, 93; and Moore, 159 n.1; not itself verifiable, 12; not the only way to truth, 142; and Rawls, 47

self-interest: and Aristotle, 103; and duty, 69–72; and first version of categorical imperative, 77–78; and Hobbes, 38–39, 41–42, 59, 66, 102–3; and hypothetical imperative, 73; and Kant, 69–72; 73, 77–78, 81; and natural law, 120; and Plato, 102–3; as principle of morality, 21–22, 35–49; and Rawls, 44–48

selfishness: and fear, 145; and spite, 145

sense of justice, 47

seven deadly sins, 145

Shaw, Russell, 149. 32

Sidgwick, Henry, 56

Singer, Marcus, 151 n.14

Singer, Peter, 152 n.22

situation, and its importance in moral argument, 98–99, 121

situation ethics, 124

skepticism, 68; not implied by historicism, 129

Skinner, B. F., 84

social contract theory, 35–49; as foundationalist theory, 128; and Kant, 153 n.14; and materialism, 65; and natural law, 119–120; and Nielsen, 161 n.4; and the obligation to follow majority opinion, 109

sociology, 129, 160 n.25

Socrates, 36, 89, 102, 113

state of nature: and Hobbes, 38–39, 76; and Locke, 43

statistics: and Bentham, 66; and scientific method, 67

Stoics: and natural law, 107, 157 n.18, 158 n.36; and virtues, 98

Stout, Jeffrey, 128–30, 160 n.25, 161 n.4; on Kant and Rawls, 160 n.26; on prescriptivism and utilitarianism, 160–61 n.27

sympathy and antipathy, 50, 59

telling an untruth, 99–100

Tertullian, 3

Thales, 14

theoretical reason, 66; arbitrary limitation of, 92–93; and happiness, 91; object of, 92; as part of every moral argument, 92, 137; and practical reason, 77–78, 92–95, 155 n.7; and science, 88

Thomas Aquinas: on act and intention, 99; on basic goods, 96; on capital punishment, 156 n.13; on conscience, 158 n.41; on the distinction between theoretical and practical reason, 92, 94–95; on first principles, 155 n.7; on happiness, 153 n.7; on human nature, 162 n.7; and his interpreters, 154 n.7, 156–57 n.17; and Kant, 85; metaphysical principle of, 138; on natural law and natural inclination, 107; and natural law tradition, 100–1, 130; on practical reason 94–95; and proportionalism, 155 n.11; and Reformation thinkers, 37; on religion as a natural virtue, 139–40; on self-evidence of practical principles, 130; on the Ten Commandments and natural law, 139; on suicide, 120

tolerance, 11, 122–23; as ideal of democracy, 142–43

tranquillity: and Epicurus, 56, 91; and happiness, 91; and Lucretius, 56; as ultimate goal in life, 56

universality: required for obligation 68–69, 75; necessary but not sufficient condition for obligation, 77–78

universalizability, 153 n.11

upbringing, as influence on morality, 7

utilitarian calculus, 119

utilitarian generalization, 123

utilitarianism, 21–22, 50–67, 155 n.11; act, 60, 123; and determinism, 64–66, 109; as foundationalist theory, 128, 160–61 n.27; and materialism, 65–67; and moral absolutes, 143; and natural law, 115–19; and pragmatism, 132; and relativism, 65–66, 85; and responsibility, 65–67, 88; rule, 60, 151 n.14

value ethics, and natural law, 157 n.18

Veatch, Henry B., on theoretical foundations of morality, 154 n.7, 156 n.16

veil of ignorance, 45–46, 48

virtue(s): and basic good(s), 108; cardinal, 38, 102–7; and character, 121; and Kant, 71, 152 n.3

virtue ethics, 101–108, 154 n.1; and Aristotle, 101, 103–6, 154 n.1; and Cicero, 101, 106–8; and Kant, 103–106; and natural law, 100–1, 156–57 n.17, 157 n.18; and Plato, 101–4; and Thomas Aquinas, 100–2

Westermarck, Edward, 4–5; 32–34; as anthropologist, 4, 32; as emotivist, 32–34, 49; and relativism, 4–5, 32–34

William of Ockham, 3